Hotel
Facility Planning

TARUN BANSAL
Faculty Coordinator
Institute of Hotel Management, Catering, and Nutrition
Lucknow

OXFORD
UNIVERSITY PRESS

OXFORD
UNIVERSITY PRESS

YMCA Library Building, Jai Singh Road, New Delhi 110001

Oxford University Press is a department of the University of Oxford.
It furthers the University's objective of excellence in research, scholarship,
and education by publishing worldwide in

Oxford   New York
Auckland   Cape Town   Dar es Salaam   Hong Kong   Karachi
Kuala Lumpur   Madrid   Melbourne   Mexico City   Nairobi
New Delhi   Shanghai   Taipei   Toronto

With offices in
Argentina   Austria   Brazil   Chile   Czech Republic   France   Greece
Guatemala   Hungary   Italy   Japan   Poland   Portugal   Singapore
South Korea   Switzerland   Thailand   Turkey   Ukraine   Vietnam

Oxford is a registered trade mark of Oxford University Press
in the UK and in certain other countries.

Published in India
by Oxford University Press

© Oxford University Press 2010

ISBN-13: 978-0-19-806463-3
ISBN-10: 0-19-806463-2

Typeset in Baskerville
by Rectographics, Delhi 110096
Printed in India by Repro India Limited, Haryana

Dedicated to

Students of Hotel Management

Preface

'I am a child who is trying to collect pebbles from the seashore of life.' This quote was penned down in my housekeeping file by my teacher Mrs Veena Sinha in 1984. I was not aware then that these words would become the guiding principle of my life and neither that the pebbles, in the form of notes, which I began to collect from that very year, would prove to be valuable inputs for my *Hotel Facility Planning* book.

Hotel facility planning involves planning and managing various facilities such as hotel building, restaurants, bars, kitchen, and other ancillary departments of the hotel and food service industry. As this subject is gaining greater importance with the globalization of the hotel industry, it is necessary for a hospitality graduate to be equipped with the fundamental knowledge and practices of facility planning. A production and operations manager in a hotel, for instance, needs to decide where to locate a new facility or how to redesign an existing one to address various markets while minimizing the overall cost of operations.

ABOUT THE BOOK

The inspiration to develop this book on hotel facility planning was due to the dearth of textbooks available on the subject as per the syllabi requirements of various state technical education boards, state technical universities, and National Council for Hotel Management.

The book has been designed keeping in view the works of eminent facility planners and practitioners, who have critically explored the process and products of the hotel industry. The contents of the book, however, are based on my own teaching experience and discussions with my colleagues and students.

The book attempts to provide an insight into the significance and various aspects of facility planning, and help students of hospitality education to take up the subject confidently by making its learning an enjoyable experience. It would also help educators and academicians who have to design study plans and innovatively train their students towards becoming facility planners. The book is designed to cater to the requirements of the four/three years B.H.M programme of hotel management of various technical universities, three years B.Sc. programme of hospitality and hotel administration, postgraduate courses in accommodation operations and food production, National Council for Hotel Management, three years diploma course in hotel management and for students pursuing their masters and bachelors in home science.

PEDAGOGICAL FEATURES

The book introduces various topics of the subject sequentially from the point of view of professionals and entrepreneurs in the hotel and restaurant business.

Each chapter starts with a brief introduction to the topic, deals with the theories and concepts, followed by established thumb rules and useful tips in planning and designing the layouts of various facilities. The chapters include a large number of tables, charts, flow diagrams, and pictures for explaining the key concepts. While the thumb rules are aimed at helping students grasp the topic easily, end-chapter practical assignments and concept review questions are aimed at putting the learning into practice.

The highlight of the book is the inclusion of separate chapters devoted to the emerging trends of energy conservation in facility planning and incorporation of design features for the physically challenged. It also contains a separate chapter on the technical aspects of facility planning and designing of renowned properties. Model test papers are provided at the end of the book for self-evaluation.

The approach of the book is simple, direct, and precise to ensure that the students from diverse backgrounds, enrolled in any hotel management programme, are able to grasp the concepts easily.

Coverage and Structure

Divided into ten chapters, the book discusses all the aspects of facility planning such as hotel project, kitchen, restaurant and bar, kitchen stewarding and planning for special guests, and also case studies and model question papers.

Chapter 1 presents an introduction to hotel classification. It includes topics such as classification norms for the hotel industry in India, comparison between facilities and services provided by star category hotels, guidelines for approval of hotel projects at planning stage, rules and regulations for hotel classification, assessment sheet for classification criteria—evaluation sheet, new trends in the accommodation industry from the point of view of an entrepreneur and students of hotel management.

Chapter 2 discusses hotel design and its thumb rules for space allocation. It covers physical layouts, hotel design consideration, development of feasibility report, flow diagram for designing a hotel, and car parking.

Chapter 3 addresses the issue of facility planning with focus on restaurant design. It includes topics such as steps involved in planning a restaurant, space allocation, restaurant staffing and equipment, bar design, and restaurant safety. The chapter also offers a list of props used in theme based restaurants.

Chapter 4 is on kitchen design and deals with planning considerations of commercial and institutional kitchens, commercial kitchen configurations, space and work area requirement, work and method study and role of the chef in the planning and designing of a kitchen.

Chapter 5 presents the key topic in the area of kitchen management, i.e., formulation of specifications for heavy-duty kitchen equipment. It also covers important areas such as care and maintenance, developing kitchen safety programme and modes of ventilation, etc.

Chapter 6, which deals with planning for stores, cellars, and kitchen stewarding includes topics such as importance of store and ancillary areas, their physical layout, space requirement, structural features and equipment required. Work flow diagrams and recommended temperatures for storage of various commodities are also included.

Chapter 7 expatiates project management and its role in the functional areas of hotel management, basic rules and procedures for network analysis, limitations of CPM and PERT, and their comparative study. Practical analytical problems are also discussed in detail for better understanding of the topic.

Chapter 8 is devoted to energy and environment conservation in hotel facility planning. It covers sections on major resources of energy and its conservation, development of energy conservation programme, energy audit, benchmarks for energy conservation and best practices adopted by Indian hospitality industry for energy conservation.

Chapter 9 introduces the readers to the needs of the physically challenged guests and the kind of disabled-friendly features to be incorporated in various facilities for them. Government guidelines for planning facilities for the physically challenged are also included in the chapter.

Chapter 10 describes some renowned hospitality and restaurant properties, with an explanation of their planning, designing, and other aspects. These provide valuable examples of putting theory to test in real life. While the first section of the chapter focuses on some hotel properties, the second section describes the design of some famous eating joints in the world.

ACKNOWLEDGEMENTS

I am grateful to the following people for their invaluable help and motivation in making this book a reality. I must begin by thanking the editorial team of Oxford University Press for their dedication and constant support.

I owe special thanks to Mr A.K. Singh, Principal, Institute of Hotel Management (IHM), Lucknow, Mr R.K. Saxena, Principal, IHM Mumbai, Mrs Suman Singh, Ex-Principal, IHM, Lucknow for always showing me the right direction. I am also indebted to Mr A.P. Rastogi, Director, J.P. Institute of Hotel Management, Mr N.L. Rastogi, H.O.D., IHM Lucknow, for introducing me to this wonderful world of hospitality education and facility planning. Their influence on me as teachers cannot be expressed in words.

I also sincerely thank my teacher and mentor Mr Arun Nagarkar, Engineer O.N. Khatri, Prof. A.K. Mitra, Director, Babu Banarsi Das National Institute of Technology and Management (BBDNITM), Lucknow, Prof. Arun Mittal, Institute of Engineering and Technology (IET), Lucknow, Engineer Anil Agrawal, Chairman, HR Group of Institutions, Ghaziabad, Mr Yoginder Mohan, Chairman, and Mr Sharad Rajan, Executive Director, IHM Meerut, Mr Uday Singh, SAMS Varanasi, Mr Messey, Ex-Project Manager, Taj Group of Hotels, Architect Arun Gupta, Mrs Manju Bose, Librarian, IHM, Lucknow for helping me in every possible way.

The book has become a reality because of the profound love and continuous encouragement of my family: My mother Smt. Vimla Bansal, my late father Sri Umesh Chandra Bansal, my uncle Mr Naresh Agrawal, my aunt Mrs Meena Agrawal, my mother-in-law Smt. Saroj Gupta, my wife Aruna Bansal, our sons Shubham and Harsh, my brother Adarash, my brother-in-law Prof. Narendra Garg, and my sister Mrs Neeru Garg.

I am also grateful to all my loving colleagues and students of hospitality education at IHM Lucknow: Mrs Arunima, Executive Housekeeper, Chef Manoj Kumar, Chef Arun Mathur, Ms Pallavi Sharma, Mr Tarun Seth, Mr Vivek Sharma, Mr Javed, Mr Gaurav Vishal, Mr Vikram Singh, Mr Pradeep Kumar, Mr Ritesh Negi, Mr Ravi for being by my side whenever I needed them.

I humbly acknowledge that it is not an easy task to cover all the practices of facility planning in a small book. Yet, I have tried to cover the basics of facility planning to the best of my knowledge. Comments or suggestions for improvement of the book are welcome. Students should feel free to clarify their doubts by writing to me: tarun_bansal_1965@rediffmail.com.

Tarun Bansal

Contents

CHAPTER 1

Hotel Classification and Guidelines

Chapter Outline:

The following topics are covered in this chapter
- Types of hotels
- Classification norms
- Comparative study of architectural features, facilities, and services provided in star category, heritage and apartment hotels
- Guidelines for approval of hotels at the project planning stage
- Guidelines for classification of hotels
- Formats for approval and classification
- Quality assessment sheet
- Classification criteria evaluation sheet

Learning Objectives:

This chapter will enable you to understand
- The types of hotels
- The classification norms of hotels in India
- The classification of hotels according to their features, facilities, and services, location, tariffs, etc.
- The architectural features, facilities, and services provided in star category, heritage, and apartment hotels
- How to draft a detailed report for a hotel project approval at the planning stage, and classification after commencement of operation

INTRODUCTION

The emergence and growth of tourism in the later half of the 19th century brought with it a great improvement in accommodation facilities for the travellers. Today, hotels provide a range of specialized services such as state-of-the-art entertainment, communication and health facilities, and multiple choices in cuisines to make their clients as comfortable as possible and capture niche markets in the hospitality sector. People are thus, likely to get confused over the services offered by various hotels and the choices to make while selecting a hotel to suit their tastes and pockets. As a result, classification of hotel properties has been introduced in the industry worldwide to provide clues to travellers to select a property that meets their requirements. There was thus, pressure on the industry associations as well as governments or regulatory authorities to set some minimum standards of facilities and services on hotel properties to enable the consumers identify a property with specific amenities. This led to the introduction of the rating system for hotels.

The government or quasi-government sources, independent rating agencies, or sometimes, the hotel operators themselves do ratings of hotels in different countries. Hence, many countries have their own system of classifying hotels according to the size, facilities, architectural features, services, and consumer's perspective on accommodation properties. For example, Britain has the AA rating system (British system), while Americans follow the AAA rating system. The British system also awards Red stars for excellence. In India, hotels are classified into star categories ranging from one star to five stars deluxe. The star rating system indicates the standard and number of facilities offered by a hotel. In August 2009, the Union Ministry of Tourism laid down new norms of classification and provided very clear directives pertaining to the assessment conditions for classification of hotels, which you will learn later in this chapter.

TYPES OF HOTELS

A hotel is the most important unit of tourist accommodation. The various dictionary meanings of a hotel are: a place, which supplies board and lodging; a large city house of distinction; a place for the entertainment of travellers; and a public building.

In brief, hotels provide accommodation, refreshments, meals at different periods of time for those who stay on the premises and pay for the services provided. Today, the range of services provided by hotels and their standards are far beyond the general expectations of a tourist or resident. Each hotel has unique features associated with it. The diversity in features can be on the basis of infrastructure, facilities, and services provided by them, their location, tariffs, type of clientele, duration of stay of guests, etc. This is one of the main reasons that the hotel industry is now termed as the hospitality industry. Classifying hotels thus is no easy task. In India, the government-formulated classification is also referred to as the standard classification, under which properties are awarded star categories depending on the size and facilities offered. They may also be categorized as heritage hotels depending on the period when they were constructed, and apartment hotels. In addition, various criteria such as size, location, clientele, level of services, ownership, etc. have evolved over a period of time to enable people get an idea of what kind of services can be expected from various hotels. A detailed classification of hotels is provided in Table 1.1.

Broadly speaking hotels can be classified on the following basis:

- Standard or Government-approved Classification
- Size
- Location
- Clientele
- Duration of Guest Stay
- Level of Services (room charges, tariffs)
- Ownership

Standard or Government-approved Classification

Classification of hotels in India is done by a Central Government constituted committee called the Hotel Restaurant Approval and Classification Committee (HRACC), which inspects and assesses the hotels on the basis of facilities and services offered before awarding the grade.

According to the latest ministry guidelines, there are three categories of hotels, namely star category, heritage hotels, and apartment hotels. The Classification Committee includes chairman (HRACC), and other members chosen from the government and industry associations such as the Federation of Hotels and Restaurants of India (FRHAI), Hotel Association of India (HAI), Indian Association of Tour Operators (IATO), etc. In case of the heritage category, a representative of the Indian Heritage Hotel Association (IHHA) is included in the committee.

Star category hotels

Hotels under the star category are divided into six types according to their architectural features, facilities, and services offered. They are awarded stars

Table 1.1 Classification of Hotels

			Classification of Hotels				
Star Classification	Size	Location	Clientele	Duration of Stay	Level of Services	Ownership	Alternate Accommodation
One star	Small	Downtown	Commercial	Commercial	Up-market	Propriety	Sarai
Two star	Medium	Suburban	Transient	Resort	Mid-market	ownership	Dharamshala
Three star	Large	Airport	Suite	Semi-residential	Budget	Franchise	Dak bungalow
Four star	Very large	Resort	Residential	Residential		Management	Circuit House
Five star		Motel	B and B Hotel			contract	Lodge
Five star deluxe		Floatel	Time share			Time share	Youth hostel
Heritage			Condominium			Condominium	Yatri niwas
Heritage Classic			Casino				Forest lodge
Heritage Grand			Conference				
			Convention				
			Motel				

in the increasing order of the complexity and range of services, such that one star is at the lower end of the spectrum, while five star deluxe is at the apex. The following are the types in star category.

- One star
- Two star
- Three star
- Four star
- Five star
- Five star deluxe

Heritage hotels

Heritage hotels comprise old properties of royal and aristocratic families that are restored and renovated to recreate an old aura and enable tourists to 'see the present while meeting the past'. Most heritage hotels in the country are located in Rajasthan and Gujarat. The international equivalents of such luxuriant accommodation are seen in the chateaux of France and Germany. *Schlosse* is the term used for heritage hotels in Austria, while historic buildings converted into heritage hotels are known as *Paradors* in Spain and Portugal.

Heritage hotels cover running hotels in palaces/castles/forts/havelis/residence of any size built prior to 1950. This is the official (Ministry of Tourism) definition of a heritage hotel. There are three types of heritage hotel:

Heritage Grand   This category covers hotels in residences, *havelis*, hunting lodges, castles, or forts and palaces built prior to 1920.

Heritage Classic   This category covers hotels in residences, *havelis*, hunting lodges, castles, or forts and palaces built prior to 1935 but after 1920.

Heritage   This category covers hotels in residences, *havelis*, hunting lodges, castles, or forts and palaces built between 1935 and 1950.

Apartment hotels

This is a new category of hotels under the new norms of classification. Apartment hotels are classified according to their architectural features, facilities, and services into the following types:

- Three star
- Four star
- Five star
- Five star deluxe

Classification on the Basis of Size

Hotels are grouped into the following types on the basis of the number of guest rooms.

Small hotels In India, hotels with 25 rooms or less are classified as small hotels. However, in the developed countries hotels with 100 rooms or less fall in this category.

Medium hotels Hotels with 26 to 100 rooms are medium hotels. In the developed world, medium hotels have between 100 and 300 rooms.

Large hotels Hotels with up to 300 guest rooms, but not less than 100, are classified as large hotels, whereas hotels with 400–600 guest rooms are termed as large in the developed countries.

Very large These are hotels with more than 300 rooms. However, very large hotels of developed countries have between 600 and 1000 rooms or more.

Classification on the Basis of Location

Hotels may be situated in the city centre, suburban areas, near airports, at hill stations or beaches. They are classified into the following types on the basis of location.

Downtown hotel A downtown hotel is one which is located in the centre (commercial hub) of the city, or within a short distance from the business centre, shopping areas, theatres, etc.

Suburban hotel These hotels are set in suburban areas and offer the advantage of quieter surroundings, although they provide the same type of services as downtown hotels.

Resort hotel Hotels that are located at tourist hot-spots such as hill stations, sea beaches, and countryside are referred to as resort hotels.

Airport hotel These are hotels situated in the vicinity of airports, or other ports of entry to a city.

Motel These are hotels located primarily on highways and provide modest services to highway travellers. An added advantage is secure parking facilities for the travellers.

Floating hotels or floatels As the name suggests, these are lodging properties that float on large water bodies such as rivers, lakes, and even sea. The houseboats in Kashmir and boats of Kerala are typical examples of floatels.

Classification on the Basis of Clientele and Duration of Stay

These are hotels which are designed to target a particular group of clients such as businessmen, vacationers, families, revelers, shoppers, etc. The following types of hotels fall in this category.

Business or commercial hotel These cater to the business traveller and are mostly situated in city centres. A highpoint of such properties is modern communication facilities and secretarial services.

Transient hotel These hotels cater to the needs of people who are on the move and need a stopover en route their journey. They are situated near airports, sea ports, major railway stations, etc.

Suite hotel These hotels provide highest level of personalized services to their guests.

Residential/Apartment hotel These hotels generally provide accommodation for a longer duration. They are patronized by people who are generally on temporary official deputation to a place. The duration of stay could vary between one month and two years.

Bed and breakfast hotel A European concept, bed and breakfast hotels are lodging establishments operating from large family residences. Guests are accommodated in bedrooms while the bathrooms may be attached or on a sharing basis. Breakfast is generally served to the guests.

Casino hotel These hotels provide gambling facilities and attract people by arranging extravagant floor shows and charter flights for the guests.

Convention hotels and conference centres These are properties that cater to the needs of a conference delegation or those that assemble for international meetings and conventions.

Classification on the Basis of Level of Services or Room Charges

On the basis of services offered by hotels, they may be classified into the following types.

Upmarket/Luxury/World class hotels Attracting the affluent section of the society, hotels in the up-market category offer world class products with personalized services of the highest standard.

Mid-market or mid-range service hotels These hotels offer modest services without the frills and attention of luxury hotels, and appeal to the largest section of travellers.

Budget/Economy hotel These hotels focus on meeting the most basic needs of guests by providing clean, comfortable, and inexpensive rooms. They are also known as economy or limited service hotels. An innovation in this category is the capsule hotels that originated in Japan.

Capsule hotel is the latest innovation in the budget hotel market segment. The first of its kind opened in Osaka in 1979. Since then, they have mushroomed not only in the big cities of Japan but also in other parts of the world. The capsule hotel is structured in the shape of a box made of glass reinforced plastic or cement, open either at one side or one end. Each cubicle or capsule is equipped with a bed, colour TV, flexible lighting, safety deposit box, and a miniature table for writing. Toilets, washrooms, vending machines, and lounge area are close by on each floor of the hotel. The function of each capsule is monitored by a central computer system and security is controlled by close circuit TV cameras. They mainly cater to business travellers.

Classification on the Basis of Ownership

On the basis of ownership hotels can be of the following types.

Proprietary ownership These include hotels or lodging properties that are under the direct ownership of a person or a company. A group of hotels that are managed by one company is called a chain.

Franchise The global hospitality industry consists of many large hotel chains that operate on a franchise basis. In this kind of contract, the franchisor allows the franchisee to use the company's ideas, methods, trademarks, as well as brand logo to do business.

Management contract In this kind of arrangement, a management company which is an expert in hotel operations is employed by the owner of the hotel and becomes responsible for running the property efficiently.

Time share hotel This entails purchasing a tourist accommodation at a popular destination for a particular time slot in a year. The buyers can either avail the facility for the appointed time or rent it out to other vacationers if they are unable to avail the facility.

Condominium hotel Condominium hotels are similar to time-share hotels except that these have a single owner instead of multiple owners sharing the hotel.

ARCHITECTURAL FEATURES, FACILITIES, AND SERVICES IN STAR CATEGORY HOTELS

The star rating system indicates the number and standard of facilities offered by a hotel. A brief description of the various categories is given as follows.

One Star Hotels

These properties are generally small and independently owned with a family atmosphere. There may be a limited range of facilities, and the meals may be fairly simple. Some rooms may not have an attached bath, but the maintenance, comfort, and cleanliness levels would be of acceptable standard. There should be adequate number of lifts in the buildings with more than 2 storeys including ground floor.

General architectural features   The general construction of the building should be good, and the locality and environment (surroundings) including immediate approach should be suitable. The hotel should have at least 10 letable bedrooms with attached bathrooms. All of the bathrooms should have modern sanitation and running cold water with an adequate supply of hot water, soap, and toilet paper. At least 25 per cent of the rooms should be air-conditioned (except in hill stations where there should be heating arrangements in all the rooms). The rooms should be properly ventilated, and have clean and comfortable furniture.

Facilities   There should be a reception counter with a telephone and an additional one for the use of guests and visitors. There should be a clean and modern toilet, well-equipped dining room/restaurant serving clean wholesome food, and a well-equipped kitchen and pantry.

Services   There should be experienced, courteous, and efficient staff in smart and clean uniforms. The senior staff coming in contact with guests should possess working knowledge of English. Housekeeping at the hotel should be of a good standard. Clean and good quality linen, blankets, towels, etc. should be supplied. Similarly, crockery, cutlery, and glassware should be of good quality.

Two Star Hotels

Hotels in this category are typically small and medium-sized and offer more extensive services than one star hotels. The rooms are generally well-equipped with attached bathrooms. Reception and other hotel staff aim for a more professional presentation and offer a wider range of straightforward services like food and beverages.

General architectural features   The general construction of the building should be good, and the locality and environment including immediate approach should be suitable. The hotel should have at least 10 guest rooms with attached bathrooms with shower. All the bathrooms should have modern sanitation and running cold water with an adequate supply of hot water, soap, and toilet paper. At least 25 per cent of the rooms should be air-conditioned (except in hill stations where there should be heating arrangements in all the rooms), and all the rooms should be properly ventilated, clean, and comfortable, with necessary, basic furniture. There should also be a well-furnished lounge. There should be adequate number of lifts in the buildings with more than 2 storeys including ground floor.

Facilities   There should be a reception counter with a telephone. There should be a call bell in each room and a telephone for the use of guests and visitors. There should be a well equipped and well maintained air-conditioned dining room/restaurant serving clean wholesome food from a well-equipped in-house kitchen and pantry.

Services   There should be an experienced, courteous, and efficient staff in smart and clean uniforms. The supervisory staff coming in contact with guests should possess a working knowledge of English. There should be a provision for laundry and dry cleaning service. Housekeeping at the hotel should be of a good standard, clean and good quality linen, blankets, towels, etc. should be provided. Similarly, crockery, cutlery, and glassware should be of good quality.

Three Star Hotels

At this level hotels are generally of the size to support higher staffing levels and their range of services is significantly higher than at the lower star classifications. The reception and other public areas are spacious. All rooms would have an en suite shower, and offer a good standard of comfort and equipment such as direct-dial phone, toiletries. Besides room service, they could offer some additional facilities for business travellers.

General architectural features   The architectural features and general construction of the building should be of a very good standard, while the locality and environment as also the immediate approach should be suitable for a good hotel. There should be adequate parking facilities for cars. The hotel should have at least 10 letable bedrooms, all with attached bathrooms equipped with bathtubs and shower. All the bathrooms should have modern design and quality sanitary fittings with hot and cold running water. At least 50 per cent of the rooms should be air-conditioned (except in hill stations where there should be heating arrangements in all the rooms, dining room, restaurant, and lounge) while the furniture and furnishings such as carpets, curtains, etc., should be of a good standard and design. There should be adequate number of lifts in the buildings with more than 2 storeys including ground floor, well furnished lounge, and a separate cloak room for men and women equipped with quality fittings of good standard.

Facilities   There should be a reception and information counter attended by qualified and experienced staff, a bookstall, recognized travel counter, money changing, and safe deposit facilities on the premises. There should be a telephone in each room except in a seasonal hotel where there should be a call bell in each room and a telephone on each floor for the use of guests and visitors to the hotel. There should be a well-equipped and well-maintained air-conditioned dining room/restaurant. Where permissible by law, there should be a bar/permit room. The kitchen, pantry, and cold storage should be clean and organized for orderliness and efficiency.

Services   The hotel should offer good quality cuisine, Indian as well as continental, and the food and beverage service should be of a good standard. There should be qualified, experienced, courteous, and efficient staff in smart and clean uniforms. The supervisory staff coming in contact with guests should possess a working knowledge of English. There should be provision for laundry and dry cleaning services. Housekeeping at the hotel should be of a good standard. There should be adequate supply of clean and good quality linen, blankets, towels, etc. Each guest room should be provided with a vacuum jug/thermos flask with cold/boiled drinking water.

Four Star Hotel

There is a fair mix of luxury and décor at hotels in this category. Bedrooms are also usually more spacious than the lower star rated hotels. There is a high staff to guest ratio, with provisions of porter service, 24-hour room service, and laundry and dry cleaning services. The restaurant too demonstrates a serious approach to the cuisine.

General architectural features   The façade, architectural features, and general construction of the building should be of distinctive qualities of a luxury hotel in this category. The locality and environment as also the immediate approach should be commensurate to the standard of a luxury hotel, and there should be adequate parking facilities for guests' vehicles. The hotel should have at least 10 guest rooms, all with well appointed attached bathrooms. At least 50 per cent of guest rooms must have long bath or the most modern shower chamber, with 24 hours service of hot and cold running water.

All public and private rooms should be fully air-conditioned (except in hill stations where there should be heating arrangements) and should be well appointed with superior quality furniture and furnishings such as carpets, curtains, etc. in good taste. It would be advisable to employ the services of professionally qualified, experienced interior decorators of repute for this purpose.

There should be adequate number of lifts working round the clock in buildings with more than two storeys including ground floor. There should be a well-appointed lobby and separate well-equipped cloak rooms for men and women.

Facilities   There should be a reception, cash, and information counter attended by trained and experienced staff. There should be a book stall, recognized travel counter, money changing and safe deposit facilities, and a left luggage room. There should be a telephone in each room and a telephone on each floor for the use of hotel guests and visitors to the hotel, and a provision for a radio or relayed music in each room. There should be a well-equipped and well-maintained air-conditioned dining room/restaurant, and where permissible by law, there should be an elegant and well-equipped bar/permit room, which should be professionally designed to ensure efficiency of operations.

Services   The hotel should offer both international and Indian quality cuisine, and food and beverage services should be of the highest standard. There should be professionally qualified, experienced, courteous, efficient, and trained staff in smart and neat uniforms. The staff coming in contact with the guests should be able to understand and speak fluently in English. The supervisory and senior staff should possess a good command of English language. It is desirable for some of the staff to have knowledge of some other foreign language, and staff knowing at least one continental language to be on duty at all times. There should be 24-hour service at the reception, information, and telephone counters. There should be a provision for reliable laundry and dry cleaning service. Housekeeping at the hotel should be of the highest possible standards with plentiful supply of linen, blankets, towels, etc. in every guest room and wherever required. Similarly, the cutlery and glassware should be impeccable and the rooms should be provided with a vacuum jug/thermos flask with ice cold/boiled drinking water. There should a special restaurant/dining room with a provision of facilities for music and dancing.

Five Star Hotel

Five star hotels offer spacious and luxurious accommodation throughout the property, matching the best international standards. The interior design should impress with its quality and attention to detail, comfort, and elegance. The furnishings should be immaculate; service formal, well-supervised, and flawless in its attention to the needs of the guests without being intrusive. The restaurant should exhibit a high level of technical skill. The staff should be knowledgeable, helpful, and well versed in all aspects of customer care combining efficiency with courtesy.

General architectural features   The façade, architectural features, and general construction of the building should be of a distinctive quality of a luxury hotel of this category. The location and surroundings, including immediate approach, should be suitable for a luxury hotel of this category, and there should be adequate parking facilities for guests' vehicles. The hotel should have at least 10 guest rooms, all with well-appointed attached bathrooms with long bath or the most modern shower chamber, with 24 hour supply of hot and cold running water.

All public and private rooms should be fully air-conditioned (except in hill stations where there should be heating arrangements) and should be well-appointed with superior quality furniture and furnishings in good taste. It would be advisable to employ the services of a professionally qualified, experienced interior decorator of repute for this purpose.

There should be adequate number of efficient lifts in more than two-storey buildings including ground floor providing 24-hours service. There should be well-designed and properly equipped swimming pool (except in the hill stations). The lobby and cloak rooms should be well appointed and equipped with fittings and furniture of the highest befitting standards.

Facilities   There should be a reception, cash, and information counter attended by a qualified and experienced staff, conference facilities in the form of one or more than one conference rooms/banquet halls and private dining rooms. There should be a book stall, beauty parlor, barber shop, recognized travel counter, money changing and safe deposit facilities left luggage room, florist and a shop for toiletries and medicines within the premises. There should be a telephone in each room and one on each floor for the use of hotel guests and visitors to the hotel, and provision for a radio or relayed music in each room There should be a well-equipped, and well-maintained air-conditioned dining room/restaurant, and where permissible by law, there should be an elegant and well-equipped bar/permit room. The kitchen, pantry, and cold storage should be well-designed to ensure efficiency of operations.

Services   The hotel should offer international and Indian quality cuisine, and the food and beverage service should be of the highest standard. There should be professionally qualified, experienced, courteous, efficient, trained staff in smart and neat uniforms. The staff coming in contact with guests should be able to understand and speak English fluently. The supervisory and senior staff should possess a good knowledge of English. It would be desirable for some of the staff to have knowledge of a foreign language, and staff conversant in at least one continental language to be on duty at all times. There should be a 24-hours service at the reception, information, and telephone centres. There should also be provision for reliable laundry and dry cleaning services. Housekeeping at the hotel should be of the highest possible standard and there should be plentiful supply of linen, blankets, and towels, etc. Similarly, the cutlery and glassware should be spotlessly clean and guest rooms should be provided with a vacuum jug/thermos flask with ice cold/boiled drinking water. There should a special restaurant, dining room with provision for music and dancing.

Five Star Deluxe

This is a qualitative extension of the five star category. While quantitatively the basic features are similar to a five star category, in a five star deluxe hotel, the comparative all round standard of services and amenities is of a very superior quality.

A comparative account of various features, facilities and services that should be provided by various categories of star rated hotels in the country is given in Table 1.2.

Table 1.2   Checklist of Facilities for Classification/Reclassification of Hotels (w.e.f. August, 2009)

D – Desirable
N – Necessary

Checklist for Facilities and Services	1*	2*	3*	4*	5*/ 5* D	Yes/ No	Comments
General							
Full time operation 7 days a week in season	N	N	N	N	N		
Establishment to have all necessary trading licenses	N	N	N	N	N		Documents as detailed in General Terms and Conditions.
Establishment to have public liability insurance	D	D	D	D	D		
24 hr lifts for buildings higher than ground plus two floors	N	N	N	N	N		Mandatory for all hotels. Local laws may require a relaxation of this condition. Easy access for the differently abled guests.
Bedrooms, bathroom, public areas, and kitchen fully serviced daily	N	N	N	N	N		

(contd)

Table 1.2   *(contd)*

Checklist for Facilities and Services	1*	2*	3*	4*	5*/ 5* D	Yes/ No	Comments
All floor surfaces clean and in good repair	N	N	N	N	N		Floor may be of any type.
Guest Room							
Minimum 10 lettable rooms, all rooms with outside windows/ ventilation	N	N	N	N	N		
Minimum size of bedroom excluding bathroom in sq. ft	120	120	140	140	200		Single occupancy rooms may be 20 sq ft less. Rooms should not be less than the specified size.
Air-conditioning	25%	25%	50%	100%	100%		Air-conditioning/heating depends on climatic conditions and architecture. Room temp. should be between 20 and 28°C. For 4, 5 and 5 Star Deluxe (the percentage is of the total no. of rooms).
A clean change of bed and bath linen daily and between check-in's	N	N	N	N	N		Definitely required between each check-in. On alternate days for 1 and 2 Star hotels.
Suites				N	N		2% of room block with a minimum of 1.
Bathroom							
Number of rooms with attached bathrooms	All	All	All	All	All		It will be mandatory w.e.f. 01.09.2010 for all 1 and 2 Star category hotels to have attached bathrooms. All bathrooms to have sanitary bin with lid.
Minimum size of bathroom in square feet	30	30	36	36	45		25% of bathroom in 1 and 2 Star hotels to have western style WC. No higher ceiling/cap on the maximum size.
1 bath towel and 1 hand towel to be provided per guest	N	N	N	N	N		
Bath mat	D	D	N	N	N		

(contd)

Table 1.2   *(contd)*

Checklist for Facilities and Services	1*	2*	3*	4*	5*/ 5* D	Yes/ No	Comments
Guest toiletries to be provided—minimum 1 new soap per guest	N	N	N	N	N		Quality products depending on the star category.
A clothes-hook in each bath/shower room	N	N	N	N	N		
A sanitary bin	N	N	N	N	N		These must be covered.
Each western WC toilet to have a seat with lid and toilet paper	N	N	N	N	N		
Floors and walls to have non-porous surfaces	N	N	N	N	N		
Hot and cold running water available 24 hours	N	N	N	N	N		It will be mandatory w.e.f. 01.09. 2010 for all 1 and 2 Star category hotels to provide hot and cold running water.
Shower cabin	N	N	N	N	N		Where shower cabin is not available, a shower with shower curtain will suffice.
Bath tubs				D	D		In 4 Star and above hotels, some rooms should offer this option to guests.
Water saving taps/shower	N	N	N	N	N		
Energy saving lighting	N	N	N	N	N		
Hairdryers	D	D	D	N	N		Where not provided in bathroom, must be available on request.
Safe keeping/in room safe				N	N		1, 2, and 3 Star hotels to have facilities for safe keeping in the reception.
Minibar/Fridge				N	N		Contents must conform to local laws.
Drinking water	N	N	N	N	N		All category hotels to provide one sealed bottle of branded bottled water of minimum 500 ml. per person per day. Ultra violet treated water will not be acceptable.

(contd)

Table 1.2   *(contd)*

Checklist for Facilities and Services	1*	2*	3*	4*	5*/ 5* D	Yes/ No	Comments
Guest linen							Good quality linen to be provided.
Shelves/drawer space	N	N	N	N	N		Necessary for hotels of 1, 2, and 3 Star category to have a wardrobe.
Room and Facilities for the Differently Abled Guests							
At least one room for the differently abled guest	N	N	N	N	N		Minimum door width should be one metre to allow wheelchair access with suitable low height furniture, low peep hole, cupboard to have sliding doors with low clothes hangers, etc. Room to have audible and visible (blinking light) alarm system. All hotels should be fully compliant by 01.09.2010.
Ramps with anti-slip floors at the entrance. Minimum door width should be one metre to allow wheelchair access.	N	N	N	N	N		To be provided in all public areas. Free accessibility in all public areas and at least one restaurant in 5 Star and 5 Star Deluxe. All hotels should be fully compliant by 01.09.2010.
Bathroom	N	N	N	N	N		Minimum door width should be one metre. Bathroom to be wheelchair accessible with sliding door, suitable fixtures like low wash basin, low height toilet, grab bars, etc. No bath tub required. All hotels should be fully compliant by 01.09.2010.
Public restrooms	N	N	N	N	N		Unisex. To be wheelchair accessible with low height urinal (24″ maximum) with grab bars. Minimum door width should be one metre. To be introduced by 01.09.2010 in 1, 2, and 3 Star hotels also.

(contd)

Table 1.2 *(contd)*

Checklist for Facilities and Services	1*	2*	3*	4*	5*/ 5* D	Yes/ No	Comments
Public Areas							
Lounge or seating area in the lobby	N	N	N	N	N		Doorman on duty. Lobby shall have furniture and fittings which shall include chairs/arm chairs, sofa, tables and fresh floral display.
Reception facility	N	N	N	N	N		Manned minimum 16 hours a day. Call service 24 hrs. Local directions to hotel including city/street maps to be available.
Availability of room, F and B and other tariff	N	N	N	N	N		
Heating and cooling to be provided in public areas				N	N		Temperatures to be between 20 and 28°C.
Public rest rooms for ladies and gents with soap and clean towels, a washbasin with running hot and cold water , a mirror, a sanitary bin with lid in unisex and ladies toilet	N	N	N	N	N	N	
Food and Beverage							
1 and 2 Star category							1 and 2 Star categories should have minimum one dining room serving all meals. Room service not necessary.
3 Star category							One Multi-cuisine restaurant cum coffee shop open from 7 a.m. to 11 p.m. and 24 hr room service.
4 Star category							<u>**Grade A cities:**</u> One multi-cuisine restaurant cum coffee shop open from 7 a.m. to 11 p.m., one speciality restaurant and 24 hr room service.

(contd)

Table 1.2   *(contd)*

Checklist for Facilities and Services	1*	2*	3*	4*	5*/ 5* D	Yes/ No	Comments
5 Star category							**Grade B cities:** One multi-cuisine restaurant open from 7 a.m. to 11 p.m. and 24 hr room service.
							Grade A cities: One multi-cuisine restaurant cum 24 hr coffee shop/all day diner, one specialty restaurant and 24 hr room service.
							Grade B cities: One multi cuisine restaurant cum coffee shop open from 7 a.m. to 11 p.m., one speciality restaurant and 24 hr room service.
5 Star deluxe category							**Grade A cities:** One multi-cuisine restaurant cum 24 hr coffee shop/all day diner, one speciality restaurant and 24 hr room service.
							Grade B cities: One multi-cuisine restaurant cum coffee shop open from 7 a.m. to 11 p.m., one speciality restaurant and 24 hr room service.

Grade–A: Delhi†, Mumbai, Kolkata, Chennai, Bangalore, Pune, Hyderabad/Secunderabad.

Grade–B: Cities in the rest of the country excluding Grade 'A' cities.

Note: The Ministry of Tourism may review and revise the cities falling under the Grade 'A' and Grade 'B' from time to time.

† Delhi would include the hotels falling in Gurgaon, Faridabad, Ghaziabad, NOIDA and Greater NOIDA.

Checklist for Facilities and Services	1*	2*	3*	4*	5*/ 5* D	Yes/ No	Comments
Crockery and glassware	N	N	N	N	N		Plastic ware accepted in pool area.
Cutlery to be at least stainless steel	N	N	N	N	N		All categories should use good quality metal cutlery. Aluminum cutlery prohibited.
Bar			N	N	N		

(contd)

Table 1.2   *(contd)*

Checklist for Facilities and Services	1*	2*	3*	4*	5*/ 5* D	Yes/ No	Comments
Kitchens							
Refrigerator with deep freeze	N	N	N	N	N		Capacity based on size of F and B service.
Segregated storage of meat, fish, and vegetables	N	N	N	N	N		Meat, fish, and vegetables in separate freezers.
Colour coded synthetic chopping boards	N	N	N	N	N		Wooden chopping boards prohibited.
Tiled walls non-slip floors	N	N	N	N	N		
Head covering for production staff	N	N	N	N	N		
Daily germicidal cleaning of floors	N	N	N	N	N		
Good quality cooking vessels/utensils	N	N	N	N	N		Use of aluminum vessels prohibited except for bakery.
All food grade equipment containers	N	N	N	N	N		
Ventilation system	N	N	N	N	N		
Garbage to be segregated—wet and dry	N	N	N	N	N		To encourage recycling.
Wet garbage area to be air-conditioned			N	N	N		
Receiving areas and stores to be clean and distinct from garbage area	N	N	N	N	N		
Six monthly medical checks for production staff	N	N	N	N	N		
First-aid training for all kitchen staff	N	N	N	N	N		
Pest control	N	N	N	N	N		

(contd)

Table 1.2 *(contd)*

Checklist for Facilities and Services	1*	2*	3*	4*	5*/ 5* D	Yes/ No	Comments
Staff							
Staff uniforms for front of the house	N	N	N	N	N		Uniforms to be clean and in good condition.
English speaking front office staff	D	D	N	N	N		This may be relaxed outside the metros/sub-metros for 1 and 2 Star category hotels.
Percentage of supervisory staff	20%	20%	40%	40%	80%		Hotels of 4 Star category and above should have formally qualified Heads of Departments. The supervisory or the skilled staff may have training or skill certification as follows: Degree/diploma from central or state IHM's/FCI's or from NCHMCT affiliated IHM's or from other reputed hospitality schools.
Percentage of skilled staff	20%	20%	30%	30%	60%		The supervisory or the skilled staff may have training or skill certification as follows: i. Degree/diploma from Central or state IHM's/FCI's or from NCHMCT affiliated IHM's or from other reputed hospitality schools. ii. Skill training certificate issued under the guidelines and scheme of the Ministry of Tourism.
Staff Welfare/Facilities							
Staff rest room	D	D	N	N	N		Separate for male and female employees with bunk beds, well lighted and ventilated.
Staff locker room	D	D	N	N	N		
Toilet facilities	N	N	N	N	N		Full length mirror, hand dryer with liquid soap dispenser.

(contd)

Table 1.2   *(contd)*

Checklist for Facilities and Services	1*	2*	3*	4*	5*/ 5* D	Yes/ No	Comments
Dining area	D	D	N	N	N		
Guest Services							
Provision of wheelchair for the differently abled guest	N	N	N	N	N		Wheel chair to be available on a complimentary basis in hotels of all categories
Valet (parking) services to be available	D	D	N	N	N		
Dry-cleaning/laundry	D	D	D	D	N		In-house for 5 Star Deluxe hotels. For 5 Star category and below, maybe outsourced.
Iron and iron board				N	N		Iron and iron board to be made available on request in 1 to 4 Star category hotels on complimentary basis. For 5 and 5 Star Deluxe categories, to be available in the room.
Linen room	N	N	N	N	N		Well ventilated
Paid transportation on call	D	D	N	N	N		Guest should be able to travel from hotel.
Shoe cleaning service	D	D	D	N	N		Free facility to be provided for in-house guests.
Ice (from drinking water) on demand	D	D	N	N	N		Complimentary on request.
Acceptance of common credit cards	D	D	N	N	N		
Assistance with luggage on request	N	N	N	N	N		
A public telephone on premises. Unit charges made known	D	D	N	N	N		There should be at least one telephone no higher than 24″ from floor level in 5 and 5 Star Deluxe (to also cater to differently abled guests).
Wake-up call service on request	N	N	N	N	N		

(contd)

Table 1.2 *(contd)*

Checklist for Facilities and Services	1*	2*	3*	4*	5*/ 5* D	Yes/ No	Comments
Messages for guests to be recorded and delivered	N	N	N	N	N		A prominently displayed message board will suffice for 1 and 2 Star categories.
Name, address, and telephone numbers of doctors with front desk	N	N	N	N	N		Doctor on call in 3, 4, 5 and 5 Star Deluxe.
Stamps and mailing facilities	D	D	N	N	N		
Newspapers available	D	D	D	N	N		This may be placed in the lounge for 1, 2 and 3 Star hotels.
Access to travel desk facilities	N	N	N	N	N		This need not be on the premise for 1, 2 and 3 Star categories.
Left luggage facilities	D	D	N	N	N		This must be in a well secured room/24 hour manned area.
Provision for emergency supplies toiletries/first aid kit	D	D	N	N	N		May be chargeable.
Health/fitness facilities	D	D	D	D	N		Indian system of treatments should preferably be offered.
Beauty saloon and barber's shop			D	D	D		
Florist				D	D		
Shop/kiosk	D	D	D	N	N		5 and 5 Star Deluxe category hotels to have one utility and one souvenir shop. 4 Star to have minimum one utility shop.
Money changing facilities	D	D	D	D	D		Money changing facility to be made available.
Bookshop	D	D	D	D	N		

(contd)

Table 1.2   *(contd)*

Checklist for Facilities and Services	1*	2*	3*	4*	5*/ 5* D	Yes/ No	Comments
Safety and Security							
Metal detectors (door frame or hand held)			N	N	N		
CCTV at strategic locations	N	N	N	N	N		
X-Ray Machine					N		For 5 Star Deluxe category, it would be 'Necessary' to have an X-Ray machine at the guest entrance for screening of baggage. Manual checks may be conducted for staff and suppliers at designated entry points.
Under belly scanners to screen vehicles				N	N		
Verification	N	N	N	N	N		All hotels should conduct a verification of their staff and suppliers by the police/private security agencies.
Staff trained in fire fighting drill	N	N	N	N	N		All hotels to conduct periodic fire drills and maintain 'manuals' for disaster management, first-aid and fire safety. Quarterly drill or as per law.
Security arrangements for all hotel entrances	N	N	N	N	N		
Each bedroom door fitted with lock and key, viewport/peephole and internal securing device			N	N	N		A safety chain/wishbone latch is acceptable in place of viewport/peephole.
Smoke detectors	N	N	N	N`	N		These can be battery operated.
Fire and emergency procedure notices displayed in room behind door	N	N	N	N	N		

(contd)

Table 1.2   *(contd)*

Checklist for Facilities and Services	1*	2*	3*	4*	5*/ 5* D	Yes/ No	Comments
Fire and emergency alarms should have visual and audible signals	N	N	N	N	N		
First aid kit with over the counter medicines with front desk	N	N	N	N	N		
Communication Facilities							
A telephone for incoming and outgoing calls in the room	D	N	N	N	N		4 Star and above should have direct dialing and STD/ISD facilities. 1, 2, and 3 Star category hotels may go through a telephone exchange.
PC available for guest use with internet access	D	D	N	N	N		This can be a paid service. Upto 3 Star, PC can be in the executive offices. Internet subject to local access being available.
E-mail service	D	D	N	N	N		Subject to local internet access being available.
Fax, photocopy, and printing service	N	N	N	N	N		
In room Internet connection/dataport	D	D	D	N	N		Subject to local internet access being available. Wi-Fi wherever possible.
Business Center	D	D	D	N	N		This should be a dedicated area. (This provision maybe relaxed for resort destinations, tourist and pilgrimage centres).
Swimming Pool			D	D	N		This can be relaxed for hill destinations. Mandatory that trained Life Guard to be available. Board containing do's and don't's, no diving sign, pool depth, etc. should be displayed at a strategic location in the pool area.

(contd)

Table 1.2 *(contd)*

Checklist for Facilities and Services	1*	2*	3*	4*	5*/ 5* D	Yes/ No	Comments
Parking Facilities	D	D	N	N	N		Should be adequate in relation to the number of room and banquet/convention hall capacities. Exclusively earmarked accessible parking nearest to the entrance for differently abled guests.
Conference Facilities			D	D	N		

Note: There is no relaxation in the necessary criteria except as specified in the comment column.

Source: Union Ministry of Tourism (www.incredibleindia.com) August 2009.

ARCHITECTURAL FEATURES, FACILITIES, AND SERVICES IN HERITAGE HOTELS

The original architectural design of the properties to be considered in the category of a *heritage hotel* should be maintained. Any extensions/improvements/change must be in keeping with the existing architecture appearance. The location, including the immediate approach and surroundings, should be suitable for a hotel of this category.

General features The façade, architectural features, and general construction should have the distinctive qualities, ambience, and décor in keeping with the local traditions and there should be adequate parking facilities for guests' vehicles. All public rooms and areas, and the guest rooms should be well maintained and well equipped with quality furniture and furnishings like carpets or area rugs, fittings, etc. in keeping with the traditional life style of the place that is sought to be showcased. The guest rooms should be clean, airy, pest free, without dampness and musty odours, and or reasonably large size, with attached bathrooms with modern facilities such as flush commodes, wash basins, running hot and cold water, etc. There should be a well-appointed lobby/lounge that should be furnished lavishly and in style, while the cloak rooms for men and women should be adequately equipped with stylish fittings reminiscent of the grandeur of the bygone era.

Facilities There should be a reception and information counter attended by qualified and experienced staff. There should be money changing and safe deposit facilities on the premises. There should be a telephone in each room except in a seasonal hotel where there should be a call bell in each room and a telephone on each floor for the use of hotel guests and visitors to the hotel. There should be a well-equipped and well-maintained dining room/restaurant, and where permissible by law, there should be a bar/permit room. The kitchen and pantry should be professionally designed to ensure efficiency of operations, and should be well equipped keeping in view the life style, and commensurate with the number of guests to be served. Drinking water must be bacteria free while the kitchen must be clean, airy, well-lit and protected from pests. There must be a three-tier washing system with running hot and cold water, hygienic garbage disposal arrangements; and a pest free deep freezer and refrigerator (where the arrangement is to cook fresh food for each meal, stand by generator will not be insisted upon). The gardens/grounds must be very well maintained.

Services The hotel should offer high quality cuisine, and the food and beverage service should be of good standard. The staff should be qualified, trained, experienced, efficient, and courteous. They should be dressed in clean uniforms. The staff coming in contact with the guests should be able to understand English. Housekeeping at these hotels should be of the highest standard and there should be plentiful supply of linen, blankets, towels, etc., which should be of high quality. Each guest room should be provided with a vacuum flask with bacteria free drinking water. Arrangements for heating/cooling must be provided for in the guest rooms in cold/hot seasons. Places which have telephone lines must have at least one phone in the office with call bells in each room. Arrangement of medical assistants must be there in case of need. The staff/room ratio must be in keeping with the number of guest rooms in each property. The heritage hotels must be run on a professional basis. They must present a distinct and traditional lifestyle of the bygone era and the level of services provided in terms of accommodation and cuisine should be of high quality.

ARCHITECTURAL FEATURES, FACILITIES, AND SERVICES IN APARTMENT HOTELS

Apartment hotels are a new category added to the official list of classification of hospitality properties, which are specially targeted at guests who would be staying for long periods ranging from a couple of months to a few years. These properties are generally small, have fewer guest rooms all of which provide a high level of quality service in every aspect of the clients' needs. They have the added advantage of providing privacy without compromising on the luxury and customized services offered by large up-market hotels in that category.

The star rating for these hotels itself begins from three stars indicating the quality and high standards desired in such properties. Table 1.3 provides a summary of the general architectural features, facilities and services that are mandatory for a property to be classified and rated in the apartment hotel category.

Table 1.3   Checklist of Facilities and Services for Classification/Reclassification of Apartment Hotels
Legends: D = Desirable, **N** = Necessary, **N/A** = Not Applicable

Criteria	3* and 4*	5* and 5 * Deluxe	Comments
Lift: adequate number of efficient lifts in building of more than 2 floors	N	N	Mandatory for new hotels. Local laws may require a relaxation of this condition. Easy access for physically challenged persons.
Parking	N	N	One parking space per unit should be provided.
Guest rooms			
Minimum 10 let-able rooms all rooms with outside window/ventilation	N	N	
Minimum floor area studio including sleeping, living, bathing, cooking, and dining – sq. ft.	250	251–300	Living, dining, bedrooms, and kitchen areas are separate with doors.
Minimum floor area 1 bedroom including sleeping, living, bathing, cooking, and dining – sq. ft.	500	500–650	Living, dining, bedrooms, and kitchen areas are separate with doors.
Minimum floor area 2 bedrooms including sleeping, living, bathing, cooking, and dining – sq. ft.	760	950	Living, dining, bedrooms, and kitchen areas are separate with doors.
Minimum floor area 3 bedrooms including sleeping, living, bathing, cooking, and dining – sq. ft.	1000	1250	Separate dining table and chairs to accommodate maximum bedding.
Air-conditioning	N	N	Air-conditioning/heating depends on climatic conditions and architecture. Room temperature should be between 20 and 28°C for 4*, 5*, and 5* deluxe between 20 and 24°C. for 3 Star minimum 50 per cent of the apartments should be air-conditioned.
A 15 ampere earthed power socket	N	N	
Television	N	N	
Internet connection	D	N	For 3* and 4* Internet facility be made available in the business centre.
Telephone in the room	N	N	

(contd)

Table 1.3 *(contd)*

Criteria	3* and 4*	5* and 5 * Deluxe	Comments
Wardrobe with 12 clothes hangers per bedding	N	N	
Shelves or drawer space	N	N	
Iron and ironing board on request	N	N	
Number of bathrooms with dedicated (private) bathroom—studio	1	1	Dedicated bathrooms need not be 'attached' but must have private access.
Number of bathrooms with dedicated (private) bathroom—1 room	1	1.5	Half bath toilet and wash basin.
Number of bathrooms with dedicated (private) bathroom—2 room	2	2.5	
Number of bathrooms with dedicated (private) bathroom—3 room	2	3.5	
Minimum size of bath room in square feet	36	40	
Each western WC toilet to have a seat and lid, toilet paper	N	N	
Floors and walls to have non-porous surfaces	N	N	
Water saving taps/shower	N	N	
Kitchen/kitchenettes for studio	N	N	Screened area—2 burner stove top, no open flame, microwave oven or OTG, fridge (165 litre), utensils, crockery, cutlery, tea/coffee maker, sink, exhaust fan
Kitchen/kitchenettes for 1 bedroom and larger			Dedicated kitchen—4 burner stove top, microwave oven, fridge full size , utensils, crockery, cutlery, tea/coffee maker, sink, exhaust fan.
Washing machine/dryers	D	D	Arrangements are made available for laundry/dry cleaning services.
Public areas			
A lounge or seating in the lobby area	N	N	
Reception facility manned 24 hours	N	N	

(contd)

Table 1.3 *(contd)*

Criteria	3* and 4*	5* and 5 * Deluxe	Comments
Heating and cooling to be provided in enclosed public rooms	N	N	Temperatures to be between 20–28°C.
Dining room serving breakfast	N	N	
Garbage to be segregated—wet and dry	N	N	
Acceptance of credit cards	N	N	
Assistance with luggage on request	N	N	
A public telephone on premises. Unit charges made known	N	N	
Wake-up call service on request	N	N	
Messages for guests to be recorded and delivered	N	N	
Name, address and telephone numbers of Doctors with front desk	N	N	
Stamps and mailing facilities	N	N	
Room for left luggage facilities	N	N	
Utility shop	N	N	
Health fitness facilities		N	Necessary for 4 Star and above and desirable in 3 Star.
Safekeeping facilities available	N	N	
Smoke detectors	N	N	These can be battery operated.
Fire and emergency procedure notices displayed in room behind door	N	N	
Fire exit signs on guest floors with emergency power	N	N	
Public liability insurance	D	D	
Swimming pool		N	This can be relaxed for hill station destinations. Necessary for 4 Star and desirable for 3 Star.
Fax and photocopy service	N	N	
Indoor games activity room	N	N	
Outdoor games like tennis, badminton	D	N	

Source: www.incredibleindia.com, August 2009.

GUIDELINES FOR APPROVAL OF HOTEL PROJECTS AND FOR CLASSIFICATION OF HOTELS UNDER 1,2,3,4,5, AND 5 STAR DELUXE CATEGORY

The Hotel and Restaurant Approval and Classification Committee (HRACC) inspects and assesses the hotels based on the facilities and services offered. Project approvals are granted in all the categories at the project implementation stage. The Ministry of Tourism, which is the nodal regulatory agency for the hospitality sector, has formulated certain guidelines for approval of hotels (refer to Annexure 2 for details) at the project planning. The broad guidelines are as follows:

1. The hotel industry is entitled to various benefits including, among other things, income tax, priority consideration of its various requirements like telephone, telex, LPG, etc. by the government authorities at the municipal, state, and Union level, or a semi or quasi-government body. To be eligible for these benefits, a hotel has to be approved according to its architectural features, façade, facilities and services provided by the tourism ministry at state/Central level. Such approval is granted from the point of view of the sustainability of a hotel for foreign tourists and approved hotels are required to maintain certain minimum level of standard of service and amenities. There are six categories of approved hotels ranging from 1-star to 5-star deluxe.

2. The approval can be applied for at the project planning stage. A hotel approved at the project state is eligible for allocation of foreign exchange for the essential import of its equipment and provision. On completion and becoming operational, like other running hotels, it also gets worldwide publicity through literature published by the Department of Tourism for overseas audience. Approved hotel projects are also eligible to apply to the Industrial Finance Corporation of India and the respective state finance corporations for the grant of loan.

   The application of loan is considered by these financial corporations in the context of detailed feasibility studies, etc. However, project approval by the Department of Tourism should not in any way be construed as an assurance for the grant of any loan thereto.

3. The application for classification and approval of a hotel in the 5 star deluxe, 5 star, 4 star, and heritage categories should be submitted in the prescribed format (refer Annexures 1, 2, and 3) along with the requisite fees. It should be sent:

   To

   The Member Secretary (HRACC)/Hotel and Restaurant Division
   Department of Tourism, Government of India
   C-1, Hutments, Dalhousie Road, New Delhi-110011

In the case of hotel projects planned for the 3 star, 2 star and 1star categories, the applications along with the requisite fees are to be sent to the Regional Director, India Tourism Office at Delhi/Mumbai/Kolkata/Chennai/Guwahati. A copy of the application should be endorsed for the Director/Manager of the nearest office of the Union Ministry of Tourism, and to the Director (Tourism) of concerned state government.

4. Various documents and information to be furnished about hotel projects when applying for classification/project approval are given in detail in the application form. The basic documents required are as follows and these should be sent along with the application form.
   - Ownership Deed of the land.
   - Urban Land Ceiling Certificate, if applicable.
   - Approval of International airports Authority of India/Director General of Civil Aviation if hotel project is near an airport.
   - Name and business antecedents of the promoters.
   - Proposed ownership structure, giving full details as to whether the new undertaking will be owned by individual(s) or a firm or a company.
   - Estimated cost of the project and the manner in which it is proposed to raise the funds to meet the cost.
   - The Department has prescribed regulatory conditions to be adhered to by promoters of approved hotel projects. The promoters should furnish the acceptance of these regulatory conditions in the prescribed form.

5. In the event of the promoters making any change in the plans of the project as submitted earlier, the approval will have to be applied for afresh.

6. Officers of the Department of Tourism or any other officer deputed by the Department to inspect the site of the proposed hotel premises form time to time will be allowed free access with or without prior notice.

7. As a project which has been approved from the point of view of its suitability for foreign tourists the promoters will be eligible for grant of loan from Central/State Financial institutions and priority in the procurement of building material, telephones, and telex, etc. However, this approval should not in any way be construed as an assurance for the grant of these facilities since this would fall with in the jurisdiction of the concerned authorities.

8. The Department of Tourism approves hotels at project stage based on documentation.

9. Project approvals are valid for 5 years. Project approvals of the Government of India, Department of Tourism, cease 3 months from the date when hotel becomes operational even if all its room are not ready. The hotel must apply for classification within these three months.
10. The Government of India, Department of Tourism reserves the right to modify the guidelines/terms and conditions from time to time.
11. All documents must be valid at the time of application and a gazette officer or notary must duly certify copies furnished to the Department. Documents in local language should be accompanied by a translation in English/official language and be duly certified.
12. Incomplete applications will not be accepted.

Recommendations for New Hotel Business Entrepreneurs

- The site selected should be suitable for the construction of a hotel if intended for use by foreign tourists. While selecting the site such aspects as its accessibility from airport/railway station/shopping areas, etc. making it a convenient location, may be kept in mind in as also that its environs are not crowded noisy, unhygienic, etc.
- A land-use certificate from the concerned state/local authority certifying that it is permissible to construct a hotel on the site selected. Blueprints of the sketch plans of the project (including front and side elevation) indicating the areas, with dimensions of the rooms/bathrooms/public rooms, etc. duly signed by the architect and the promoter. The department has prescribed certain minimum areas standards for guest rooms and attached bathrooms. It should be ensured that none of the guest rooms/attached bathroom fall short of the prescribed minimum carpet area limits, which are given in Tables 1.2 and 1.3.

GUIDELINES FOR HOTEL CLASSIFICATION (HERITAGE/APARTMENT HOTELS)

Classification of newly operational hotels must be sought within 3 months of completion of approved hotel projects. Operating hotels may opt for classification at any stage. However, hotels seeking reclassification should apply for reclassification one year prior to the expiry of the current period of classification. The following are the guidelines for the HRACC regarding classification of hotels.

1. If the hotels fail to reapply one year before the expiry of the classification order, the application will be treated as a fresh classification.
2. Once a hotel applies for classification/reclassification, in the prescribed format, it should be ready at all times for inspection by the HRACC. No requests for deferment of inspection will be entertained.

3. Classification will be valid for 5 years from the date of issue of orders or in case of reclassification from the date of expiry of the last classification provided that the application has been received within the stipulated time mentioned above, along with all valid documents. Incomplete applications will not be accepted.

4. Hotels which propose to let out part of or all its rooms on time share basis are not eligible for classification.

5. Hotels applying for classification must provide the necessary documentation (refer Annexure 1).

6. The above-mentioned approvals/no objection certificates are the responsibility of the owners/promoters/concerned company as the case may be. The department's substitute for any statutory approval and the approval given is liable to be withdrawn without notice in case of any violations/misrepresentation of facts.

7. All applications for classification/reclassification must be complete in all respects—application form, application fees, prescribed clearances, NOCs certificates, etc. Incomplete application forms are liable to be rejected.

8. A hotel will qualify for classification as a heritage hotel provided a minimum of 50 per cent of its floor area was built before 1935 and no substantial changes have been made in the façade. Hotels which have been classified/reclassified under heritage categories prior to issue of these guidelines will continue under heritage categories if they were built between 1935–1950.

9. The application fees for various hotels are given in Table 1.4.

10. The composition of the classification committee for various hotel categories is as follows:

For 4 Star, 5 Star, and 5 Star Deluxe and heritage and apartment hotels   The committee is chaired by the Chairman (HRACC) or his representative, and a representative from FHRAI/HAI/IATO/IHM/ Local India tourism office/Member Secretary. In case of heritage category, a representative of IHHA will be a member of committee.

For 1 Star, 2 Star, and 3 Star   The committee would be chaired by Secretary (T) of the concerned state Govt or his representative not below the rank of a deputy secretary in the Central government. In his absence the Regional Director, India Tourism office will chair the committee, and a representative from FHRAI/HAI/IATO/IHM.

Table 1.4 Application Fees for Classification/Reclassification of Hotels

Star Category	Classification/Reclassification Fees in Rs
1 Star	6,000
2 Star	8,000
3 Star	10,000
4 Star	15,000
5 Star	20,000
5 Star Deluxe	25,000
Heritage (grand, claSSic, heritage categorieS)	15,000
3 Star apartment hotel	10,000
4 Star apartment hotel	15,000
5 Star apartment hotel	20,000
5 Star Deluxe apartment hotel	25,000

Source: www.incredibleindia.com, August 2009.

Summary of the Procedure for Approval

1. The chairman and other 3 members will constitute a quorum.
2. The recommendations will be sent to with in 3 weeks to HRACC division.
3. The minutes will be approved by the chairman.
4. In case of dissatisfaction with the decision of HRACC the hotels may appeal to Secretary (T), Government of India for review and reconsideration within 30 days of receiving the communication regarding classification/reclassification. No requests will be entertained beyond this period.
5. Hotels will be classified following a two stage procedure:

   • The presence of facilities and services will be evaluated as per HRACC guidelines (Table 1.2).
   • The quality of facilities and services will be evaluated against a mark sheet (Table 1.5).

6. The hotel is expected to maintain required standards at all times. The classification committee may inspect a hotel at any time without previous notice. The committee may request that its members be accommodated overnight to inspect the level of services.
7. Any rectification/deficiencies pointed out by the HRACC must be complied with within the stipulated time, which has been allotted in

consultation with the hotel representatives during inspection. Failure to do so will result in rejection of application.

8. The committee may assign a star category lower but not higher than that applied for.

9. The hotel management must be able to convince the committee that they are taking sufficient steps conserve energy and harvest water,

Table 1.5   Mark Sheet for Quality Star/Apartment Hotel Classification

Criteria	Max. Marks	Comments (Division of Marks)
Exterior and grounds	8	Exteriors approach 2/landscaping 2/ exterior lighting 2/parking 2
Guest room	10	Furniture 2/furnishings 2/décor 2/room facilities and amenities 2/linen 2
Bathroom	8	Facilities 2/fitting 2/linen 2/toiletries 2
Public areas	8	Furniture 2/furnishing 2/décor 2/restrooms 2
Food and beverage	8	Choice of cuisine, menu 3/décor 2/food quality 3
Kitchen	8	Equipment 3/state of repair 2/food storage 3
Cleanliness	8	Over all impression
Hygiene	8	Pot and dish washing 2/drinking water 2/staff facilities 1/pest control 2/garbage disposal 1
Safety and security	8	Fire fighting equipment 2/signage 2/awareness of procedures 2/public area and room security 2
Communications	6	Phone service 2/e-mail access 2/ Internet access 1/pc and other equipment 1
Guest services	5	Overall impression
Eco-friendly practices	5	Waste management, recycling, no plastics 1/water conservation, harvesting 1/pollution control-air, water, sound, light 2/alternative energy usage 1
Facilities for physically challenged persons	5	At list a room for physically challenged persons 1/ public toilet in lobby 1/telephone in public places 1/ramps, etc. 1/facilities for aurally or visually handicapped 1
Staff quality	5	Overall impression
Total	**100**	
Comments		
....		
....		
HRACC MEMBER		
1.2.3.4.5.6.		

Source: www.incredibleindia.com, August 2009.

garbage segregation, and disposal/recycling as per Pollution Control Board (PCB) norms and following other eco-friendly measures.

10. For any change in the star category/heritage category the promoters must apply afresh with a fresh application form and requisite fees for the category applied for.
11. Any change in plans or management of the hotel should be conveyed to the HRACC, Government of India, Department of Tourism, within 30 days otherwise the classification will stand withdrawn/terminated.
12. Applicants are requested to go through the checklist of facilities and services contained in the relevant document before applying.
13. Incomplete applications will not be considered. All cases of classification would be finalized within three months of the application being made.
14. The Government of India, Department of Tourism reserves the right to modify the guidelines/terms and conditions from time to time.

New Norms for Assessment of Star Category of Hotels

Hotels seeking classification under various official categories are evaluated by the members of the HRACC, which inspect the premises and make their assessment in accordance with the enclosed check list. Marks are given separately for the quality of each facility and service inspected (refer Table 1.5) by every member of the team. The qualifying score for star and apartment hotels is given in Tables 1.6 and 1.7 respectively.

It is not obligatory for hotels in India to seek classification and star ratings. An official award qualifies the properties to avail significant tax and business incentives announced from time to time by the government for the promotion of the sector which is a money spinner in itself. Nonetheless, there are hotel properties in the country and business houses that have made their mark at the global level and are counted among the best in the world. The best indicators or benchmarks of their success are the various awards and international recognition they have earned over the years. Cases in point are the Taj group (Box 1.1) and the ITC Ltd group (Box 1.2).

Table 1.6 Qualifying Score for Star Category Hotels

5*D	90%
5*	80%
4*	75%
3*	65%
2*	55%
1*	50%

Table 1.7 Qualifying Score for Apartment Category Hotels

5*D	90%
5*	80%
4*	75%
3*	65%

Box 1.1   The Taj Group of Hotels: Making a Mark in Global Hospitality

The Taj group of hotels is the largest chain in India with several properties abroad too. The flagship property of the group, the Taj Mahal Palace and Tower in Mumbai (inset), is rated among the 10 best hotels in the world.

Taj Hotels Resort and Palaces comprises more than 60 hotels in 45 locations across India with an additional 15 international hotels in the Malaysia, United Kingdom, United States of America, Bhutan, Sri Lanka, Africa, the Middle East, and Australia.

Taj Mahal Palace and Tower, Mumbai

The Success Story of The Taj Mahal Palace and Tower

The hotel, overlooking the Arabian sea by the side of the Gateway of India, was inaugurated in December 1903 by the founder of the Tata group of industries, Jamshetji Nusserwanji Tata. It was built as a rejoinder to a racial discrimination incident when he was refused entry into the Watson's hotel for being an Indian. Tata founded the Indian Hotels Company Ltd in 1897 and built the exquisite Taj Mahal Palace Hotel. Considered an architectural marvel, it is credited with being the first luxury hotel in the country for the Indians by an Indian.

In 1971, the 220 room hotel was converted into a 325 room hotel, and a multi-storey tower was constructed adjoining the original property. The property is a unique mix of tradition and modernity, and epitomizes the best standards in the industry today in every aspect, be it design features, or the facilities and services offered to the guests

Having made a mark among the finest brands in hospitality for the top segment of the society, the group has turned towards the mid-market and value segments (budget travellers) with its new chain of hotels popular as Ginger hotels and Gateway hotels across India.

Facts about IHCL
- There are 65 hotels in the group, 11 of which are abroad.

- The group commands 20% market share in India.
- It offers nearly 8567 rooms.
- It has 259 food and beverage outlets.
- More than 17000 employees.
- More than 475 executives and managers.
- More than 750 supervisors.

Awards
- Institutional Investor Magazine 2003—The World's Best Hotel Series.
- Galileo Express Travel and Tourism Awards for Best luxury hotel chain in 2003 to The Taj Mahal Palace and Tower
- PATA gold awards for marketing hospitality in 2009 to The Taj Mahal Palace and Tower
- Travel+ leisure 2005 Business Travel Guide—Best business hotel of Mumbai to the Taj Mahal Palace and Tower, Mumbai.
- Jai Mahal Palace was named best spa by Forbes in 2006.
- India Brand Summit Award for Brand Leadership Hospitality presented to Taj Group of Hotels in 2003.

Box 1.2 ITC Group of Hotels: Matching International Standards

One of the eight Indian companies to figure in Forbes A-List for 2004, featuring 400 of 'the world's best big companies', ITC entered the hotel business in 1975. Its 60 hospitality properties across 50 locations in India include some of the best known names such as ITC Maurya Sheraton and Towers, Chola Sheraton, etc. There are various categories of hotels such as five star, heritage palaces, havelis, resorts, budget hotels, and currently 10 hotels are marketed world-wide by Sheraton Corporation, the well known global hospitality chain. ITC-Welcomgroup has strategically customized its hotels and appropriately categorized them to fulfil the service and budgetary needs of travellers. It has forayed into the mid-segment with full service properties for the budget travellers across India, popular as Fortune hotels.

ITC constantly endeavors to benchmark its products, services and processes to global standards. The Company's pursuit of excellence has earned it national and international honours. Some of the milestones in its history include the following

ITC Milestones

- The 484-room Hotel Maurya Sheraton and Towers, New Delhi (inset), has played host to a galaxy of world dignitaries.

- Burkhara restaurant of Maurya Sheraton and Towers, New Delhi has been voted the best restaurant in Asia and is only the Indian restaurant to feature in the list of 50 best restaurants of the World.

- Welcom Hotel Mughal Sheraton at Agra, has been a proud recipient of Asia's first Aga Khan Award for Architecture.

- Welcom Heritage is regarded among India's finest chain of Heritage Hotels.

- ITC-Welcomgroup won PATA Gold Award in Corporate Environmental Category in 2005.

- ITC-Welcomgroup was declared as the Best Premium Hotel Brand for three consecutive years—2005–06, 2006–07 and 2007–2008 by the Indian Express group, who have instituted the Galileo Travel and Tourism award.

- Sheraton New Delhi Hotel won the National Tourism Award for the Best Eco Friendly Hotel in 2004–05

- ITC Maurya, New Delhi won the National Tourism Award for the Best Eco Friendly Hotel 2008

- ITC Grand Central was recognized as the best Private Public Enterprise Providing Facilities for Physically Challenged Persons by Ministry of Tourism in the year 2007–08

- ITC Maratha, Mumbai won FHRAI Green Champion of the year among large hotels in 2004

Maurya Sheraton and Towers, New Delhi

SUMMARY

Tourism industry is the second largest foreign exchange earner in India contributing to 6.36 per cent of the GDP besides being a big job generator. At least 10.17 per cent of employed Indians are estimated to be working in this sector. The industry is also responsible for the development of infrastructure, communication, and environment regeneration in the remote and backward areas. The hotel industry, which is an inseparable part of the tourism sector, is poised for an impressive growth in the coming years. The revenue from the hotel and restaurant industry in India during the financial year 2006–2007 was Rs 604.32 billion, and was expected to reach Rs 826.76 billion by 2010. In 2008, there were about 1,980 hotels approved and classified by the Ministry of Tourism, Government of India, with a total capacity of about 110,000 hotel rooms.

The Union Ministry of Tourism along with various hotel and tourism industry associations like FHRAI, HAI, IHHAI, IATO, etc. formulate the guidelines necessary to maintain the standards of various hotels and food and beverages outlets so that foreign as well as domestic tourists and travellers can enjoy a comfortable stay and good quality food and go home with memorable experiences. In India, hospitality properties are classified into star categories, heritage, and apartment hotels. 90 per cent of hotels opt for the government-approved star rating system, which qualifies them for availing significant tax and business incentives. The available categories range from one star to five star deluxe, while the heritage and apartment categories are very recent concepts in the country.

Classification norms state clearly the minimum requisites of a hotel in terms of its number of rooms, facilities, and services. The Ministry of Tourism has delineated evaluation criteria and guidelines for hotels to check or undertake self evaluation before applying for award of a particular category. There is a proper two-stage procedure for seeking an award of a particular star category, which the hotel managements have to follow from the project planning stage till the commencement of operations.

The government-constituted Hotel and Restaurants Approval and Classification Committee (HRACC) is responsible for assessing the hotels and awarding approval and classification to a property. A team comprising various members, as per the requirement of star category applied for, visits the particular hotel and if satisfied recommends it for the award of the desired category. Otherwise, it issues some recommendations for modifications for the hoteliers to comply with before the award of classification.

Classification of hotels is not mandatory in India but those who want to get benefits of classification have to fulfil certain criteria to maintain the standards of a hotel accordingly. These guidelines are specified by the Ministry of Tourism in coordination with the HRACC and modified from time to time. Thus, it is necessary to remain updated on the subject at all times. The guidelines are specific to the area of the hotel and give an idea to the owner on how to maintain minimum standards of quality service and achieve organizational excellence.

CONCEPT REVIEW QUESTIONS

1. What do you mean by hotel classification? List all the categories under star and heritage hotels.
2. What are the various facilities and services provided in a four star hotel? Compare them with three star hotels.
3. Enumerate the architectural features, facilities and services of a heritage hotel.
4. What are the different benefits that owners of a hotel can avail if their property is approved and classified by HRACC?
5. Why does the Government of India undertake classification of hotels? What purpose is solved by classification?
6. Enlist the points you will consider while submitting a detailed project report for approval of your new five star hotel property.
7. Enlist the possible members of a hotel classification committee.
8. Recreate a format of the following:
   - Approval of a hotel project
   - Hotel classification form
9. Enlist various licenses, permits and no objection certificates required at the time of approval of a project report.
10. What do you mean by Mark sheet for Quality? How many marks/points are awarded for following criteria?
    - Exteriors and approach
    - Pot and dish washing
    - E-mail access
    - State of repair of kitchen equipment
    - Waste management, recycling, and no plastics
    - Facilities for aurally or/and visually handicapped
11. State the criteria necessary for classifying a five star hotel as per the guidelines set by the Government for the classification of hotel industry. State whether the criteria are necessary or desirable.
12. How is a five star apartment hotel different from a five star hotel? Discuss with suitable points.
13. State whether the following statements are true or false:
    (a) Lifts are mandatory for a new four star hotel if the building is more than two floors and local laws permit.
    (b) A five star hotel should have minimum 50 letable rooms.

(c) Minimum size of a single room in a three star should not be less than 120 square feet.

(d) A 5 ampere earthed power socket is desirable in all star categories of hotel.

(e) Mini bar/fridge is a necessary item in a four star hotel.

(f) Head covering for production staff is a desirable feature of a two star hotel.

(g) All the staff is not required to be trained in fire fighting exercise in a one star hotel.

(h) Toilet facilities for staff are desirable features of a two star hotel.

Practical Problem

14. The following observations and comments have been made by a classification committee after visiting a five star hotel (see Table 1.8). Being an advisor to the hotel management assess the report and apply for reclassification. Submit an action plan for the hotel management to ensue so that it is awarded the desired five star category when it applies for reclassification.

Table 1.8

Criteria	Max	Awarded Score	Comments (Division of Marks)
Exterior and grounds	8	6	Exteriors approach 2/landscaping 2/ exterior lighting 1/parking 1
Guest room	10	8	Furniture 2/furnishings 2/décor 1/room facilities and amenities 1/linen 2
Bathroom	8	7	Facilities 1/fitting 2/linen 2/toiletries 2
Public areas	8	5	Furniture 1/furnishing 1/décor 1/restrooms 2
Food and beverage	8	6	Choice of cuisine, menu 1/décor 1/food quality 3
Kitchen	8	7	Equipment 3/state of repair 1/food quality 3
Cleanliness	8	6	Over all impression
Hygiene	8	6	Pot and dish washing 2/drinking water 1/staff facilities 1/pest control 1/garbage disposal 1
Safety and security	8	7	Fire fighting equipment 2/signage 2/awareness of procedures 2/public area and room security 1
Communications	6	5	Phone service 2/e-mail access 1/ Internet access 1/pc and other equipment 1
Guest services	5	4	Overall impression
Eco-friendly practices	5	4	Waste management, recycling, no plastics 1/water conservation, harvesting 1/pollution control-air, water, sound, light 1/alternative energy usage 1

(contd)

Table 1.8 *(contd)*

Criteria	Max	Awarded Score	Comments (Division of Marks)
Facilities for physically challenged persons	5	3	At least a room for physically challenged persons 1/public toilet in lobby 1/telephone in public places 1/ramps, etc. 0/facilities for aurally or visually handicapped 0.
Staff quality	5	3	Overall impression
Total	100	77	Not up to the standards and may apply for reclassification within specified period. Five star categories cannot be awarded.

PROJECT ASSIGNMENTS

1. Visit a three star hotel in your town and evaluate its architectural features, facilities and services provided as per approved government.
2. Interview a member of a classification committee such as Principal of your Institute, Regional Tourist Officer, or a member from HRACC and try to determine the functions of the committee he or she is actively involved in.
3. Check with a local five star hotel and make a list of all the major Necessary and Desirable criteria.
   (*Note:* limit your list to the 50 necessary items and see if they are given any relaxation by the classification committee to these items. If yes then why so?)
4. Constitute a panel from your group and evaluate your institute on the basis of norms according to Board/AICTE/NCHMT/other affiliation agencies and find out its strengths and weaknesses. Make a list of recommendations to improve the architectural features, facilities and services for your Institute.
5. Being a facility planner visualize a five star hotel and prepare a hypothetical profile of the hotel in detail keeping in view the government-delineated checklist of necessary and desirable criteria.
6. Visit a five star hotel in your city and state the facilities offered to the physically challenged persons (special guests) by the hotel.
7. Prepare a report on a heritage hotel near or in your city and make a presentation of the unique features of that heritage property.

REFERENCES

www.incredibleindia.com, accessed on 23 August 2009.
www.tajhotels.com, accessed on 17 November 2009.
www.itc-hotels.com, accessed on 19 November 2009.

ANNEXURES*

General Terms, Conditions, and Application Format for Approval of Hotels at the Project Level and Classification/Reclassification of Operational Hotels

ANNEXURE 1: APPROVAL OF HOTEL AT THE PROJECT STAGE

1. The Ministry of Tourism will approve hotels at project stage based on documentation. Project approval is given to 1, 2, 3, 4, 5 Star and Heritage (Basic) categories. Hotel projects approved under 5 Star and Heritage category after becoming operational may seek classification under 5 Star Deluxe/Heritage Classic/Heritage Grand category if they fulfil the prescribed norms.

2. Project approvals will be valid for 5 years. The project approval would cease 3 months before the date of expiry of project approval or from the date the hotel becomes operational, even if all its rooms are not ready. The hotel must apply for classification within 3 months of commencing operations. The application for project approval will be submitted complete in all respect as per details given below. Incomplete applications will not be accepted.

3. Application form should have the following details:
   (i) Proposed name of the hotel
   (ii) Name of the promoters with a note on the business antecedents in not more than 60 words
   (iii) Complete postal address of the promoter with telephone, fax, and e-mail address
   (iv) Status of the owner/promoter
      (a) If public/private limited company with copies of Memorandum and Articles of Association
      (b) If partnership, a copy of Partnership Deed and Certificate of Registration
      (c) If proprietary concern, name and address of Proprietor/Certificate of Registration
   (v) Location of hotel site with postal address
   (vi) Details of the site
      (a) Area (in sq. m.)
      (b) Title—owned/leased with copies of sale/lease deed
      (c) Copy of Land Use Permit to construct hotel from local authorities
      (d) Distance (in kms) from (a) railway station (b) airport (c) main shopping centre
   (vii) Details of the project
      (a) Copy of feasibility report
      (b) Star category planned

---

* *Source:* www.incredibleindia.com, an official website of the Ministry of Tourism, Government of India

(c) Number of rooms (with attached bathrooms) and size for each type of room (in sq. ft.)

(d) Size of bathrooms (in sq. ft.)

(e) Details of public areas with size in sq. ft.—Lobby/lounge; restaurants; bar; shopping; banquet/conference halls; business centre; health club; swimming pool; parking facilities (no. of vehicles)

(f) Facilities for the differently-abled guests (room with attached bathroom earmarked for this purpose, designated parking, ramps for free accessibility in public areas and to at least one restaurant, designated toilet (unisex) at the lobby level, etc.). All hotels at project stage will require to conform to the requirements by 01.10.2010.

(g) Eco-friendly practices
 - sewage treatment plant
 - rain water harvesting
 - waste management
 - pollution control method for air, water, and light
 - introduction of non-CFC equipment for refrigeration and air-conditioning. All hotels at project stage will require to conform to the requirements by 01.09.2010.

(h) Energy/water conservation (use of CFL lamps, solar energy, water saving devices/taps)

(i) Details of fire fighting measures/hydrants, etc.

(j) Date by which project is expected to be completed and become operational

(k) Any other additional facilities

(l) Security related features

(m) The architecture of the hotel building in hilly and ecologically fragile areas should incorporate creative architecture keeping in mind sustain-ability and energy efficiency and as far as possible in conformity with local art and architecture with use of local materials.

4. Blueprints/building plans signed by the owner, the architect and approved by the competent authority showing
 (i) Site plan
 (ii) Front and side elevation
 (iii) Floor plans for all floors
 (iv) Detail of guest rooms and bathrooms with dimensions in square feet
 (v) Details of fire fighting measures/hydrants, etc.
 (vi) Air-conditioning details for guest rooms, public areas

5. Local approvals by
 (i) Municipal authority
 (ii) Concerned police authority
 (iii) Any other local authority as maybe applicable/required (viz. Pollution Control Board/Ministry of Environment and Forests, etc.)

(iv) Approval/NOC from Airport Authority of India for projects located near the airport

   Note: The above-mentioned approvals/No objection certificates are the responsibility of the promoter/concerned company as the case may be. The Ministry's approval is no substitute for any statutory approval and the approval given is liable to be withdrawn in case of any violation without notice.

6. Proposed capital structure
   (a) Total project cost
   (b) Equity component with details of paid up capital
   (c) Debt—with current and proposed sources of funding
7. Letter of acceptance of regulatory conditions (format enclosed).
8. The application should indicate whether a few rooms or all rooms are to be let out on a timeshare basis. Hotels which propose to let out part of or all its rooms on timeshare basis will not be eligible for classification under this scheme.
9. Application fee in the form of a Demand Draft.
10. In the event of any change in the project plan, the applicant should apply afresh for approval under the desired category.
11. Authorized officers of the Ministry of Tourism should be allowed free access to inspect the premises from time to time without prior notice.
12. The hotel must immediately inform the Ministry of the date from which the hotel becomes operational and apply for classification within 3 months from the date of operation.
13. The fee payable for the project approval and subsequent extension, if required is as under. The Demand Draft may be payable to Pay and Accounts Officer, Department of Tourism, New Delhi. Star category amount in Rs:
    5-star 15,000
    4-star 12,000
    3-star   8,000
    2-star   6,000
    1-star   5,000
    Heritage category 12,000
14. The promoter must forward quarterly progress reports failing which the project approval is liable to be withdrawn.
15. All documents must be valid at the time of application. All copies of documents submitted must be duly attested by a gazette officer/notary. Documents in local language should be accompanied by a translated version in English, which should also be duly certified.
16. Projects, where it is proposed to let out part or whole of the hotel on timeshare basis, will not be covered under these guidelines. (Such facilities, however, will be covered under a separate Guideline of Timeshare Resort).

17. Any change in the project plan or management should be informed to the Ministry of Tourism (for 5-D, 5, 4 Star and Heritage categories) or Regional Director's Office (for 3, 2, and 1 Star categories) within 30 days, failing which the approval will stand withdrawn/terminated.

18. The project approval is only applicable for new hotels coming up and not for additional rooms coming up in existing hotels.

19. The minimum size of rooms and bathrooms for all categories have been specified in the guidelines. Hotels of 1, 2, 3, and 4 Star categories availing subsidy/tax benefits/other benefits from the Central/State Government would be subject to a lock-in period of 8 years so that these hotels continue to serve as budget category hotels. Hotels would be permitted to apply for upgradation to a higher star category after the completion of the lock-in period.

20. Applicants are requested to go through the 'Checklist' of facilities and services contained in this document before applying for project approval of new hotel projects/classification of operational hotels.

21. Application for hotel project approvals forwarded through post will not be accepted if incomplete and applicant will be asked to complete the application and furnish required documents/information.

ANNEXURE 2: CLASSIFICATION/RECLASSIFICATION OF OPERATIONAL HOTELS

1. Classification for newly operational hotels, if approved by the Ministry of Tourism at project stage, must be sought within 3 months of completion of the project. Operating hotels may opt for classification at any stage. However, hotels seeking reclassification should apply for reclassification at least six months prior to the expiry of the current period of classification.

2. If a hotel fails to reapply six months before the expiry of the classification period, the application will be treated as a fresh case of classification.

3. Once a hotel applies for classification/reclassification, it should be ready at all times for inspection by the inspection committee of the HRACC. **No request for deferment of inspection will be entertained.**

4. Classification will be valid for a period of 5 (Five) years from the date of approval of Chairman HRACC or in case of reclassification, from the date of expiry of the last classification, provided that the application has been received within six months prior to the expiry of the current period of classification, along with all valid documents. Incomplete applications will not be accepted.

5. The application should indicate whether a few rooms or all rooms are to be let out on a timeshare basis. Hotels which propose to let out part of or its entire rooms on timeshare basis will not be eligible for classification under this scheme.

6. Hotels applying for classification must provide the following documentation:
   (i)   Name of the hotel
   (ii) Name and address of the promoter/owner with a note on their business antecedent in not more than 60 words
   (iii) Complete postal address of the hotel with telephone, fax, and e-mail address
   (iv) Status of the owner/promoter
        (a) If public/private limited company with copies of Memorandum and Articles of Association
        (b) If partnership, a copy of Partnership Deed and Certificate of Registration
        (c) If proprietary concern, name and address of Proprietor/Certificate of Registration
   (v)   Date on which the hotel became operational
   (vi) Details of hotel site with postal address and distance (in kms) from (a) airport (b) railway station (c) city centre/downtown shopping area
7. Details of the hotel:
   (a) Area of hotel site (in sq. m.) with title—owned/leased with copies of sale/lease deed
   (b) Copy of Land Use Permit from local authorities
   (c) Star category being applied for
   (d) Number of rooms and size for each type of room in square feet (single/double/suites—all rooms to have attached bathrooms)
   (e) Size of bathrooms in square feet
   (f) Air-conditioning details for guest rooms, public areas
   (g) Details of public areas: (1) lobby/lounge (2) restaurants with no. of covers (3) bar (4) shopping area (5) banquet/conference halls (6) health club (7) business centre (8) swimming pool (9) parking facilities (no. of vehicles which can be parked)
   (h) Facilities for the differently-abled guests: dedicated room with attached bathroom, designated parking, ramps, free accessibility in public areas and at least to one restaurant, designated toilet (unisex) at the lobby level, etc. All operational hotels will require to conform to the requirements by 01.09.2010.
   (i) Eco-friendly practices (a) sewage treatment plant (b) rain water harvesting (c) waste management (d) pollution control method for air, water and light (e) introduction of non-CFC equipment for refrigeration and air-conditioning and other eco-friendly measures and initiatives. All operational hotels will require to conform to the requirements by 01.10.2010.
   (j) Measures for energy and water conservation, water harvesting (use of CFL lamps, solar energy, water saving devices/taps, etc.)

(k) Details of fire fighting measures/hydrants

(l) Security features viz. CCTV, X-Ray check, verification of staff, etc.

(m) The architecture of the hotel building in hilly and ecologically fragile areas should incorporate creative architecture keeping in mind sustainability and energy efficiency and as far as possible in conformity with local art and architecture with use of local materials.

(n) Any other additional facilities.

8. Certificates/No objection certificates (current and attested):

(a) Certificate/licence from Municipality/Corporation to show that the establishment is registered as a hotel

(b) Certificate/licence from concerned police department authorizing the running of the hotel

(c) Clearance certificate from Municipal Health Officer/Sanitary Inspector giving clearance to the establishment from sanitary/hygiene point of view

(d) No objection certificate from the Fire Service Department (Local Fire Brigade Authority)

(e) Public liability insurance (optional)

(f) Bar licence (necessary for 4, 5, 5 Star Deluxe, Heritage Classic, and Heritage Grand categories)

(h) Sanctioned building plans and occupancy certificate

(i) If classified earlier, a copy of the classification order issued by Ministry of Tourism

(j) For Heritage property, certificate from the local authority stating the age of the property and showing the new and old built up areas separately

(k) Clearance/NOC/approval required from any other local authority (viz. Pollution Control Board/Ministry of Environment and Forests, etc.) whichever is applicable

(l) Approval/NOC from Airport Authority of India for projects located near the airport

(m) Application fees

The above-mentioned approvals/No objection certificates are the responsibility of the owner/promoter/concerned company as the case may be. The approval of the Ministry of Tourism is no substitute for any statutory approval and the approval given is liable to be withdrawn without notice in case of any violations or misrepresentation of facts.

9. All applications for classification and reclassification must be complete in all respects—application form, application fee, prescribed clearances, no objection certificates, certificates, etc. Incomplete applications will not be accepted.

10. Hotels will qualify for classification as Heritage hotels provided a minimum of 50% of the floor area was built before 1950 and no substantial change has been made in the façade. Hotels that have been classified/reclassified under

heritage categories prior to issue of these guidelines will continue under heritage categories even if they were built between 1935-1950.

11. The application fees payable for classification/reclassification are as follows. The Demand Draft may be payable to 'Pay and Accounts Officer, Department of Tourism, New Delhi'.

Star Category	Classification/Reclassification Fees in Rs
1–Star	6,000
2–Star	8,000
3–Star	10,000
4–Star	15,000
5–Star	20,000
5–Star Deluxe	25,000
Heritage (Grand, Classic, Heritage categories)	15,000

12. Upon receipt of application complete in all respects, the hotel will be inspected by a classification committee which will be constituted as follows:

(a) **For 4, 5, 5 Star Deluxe, and Heritage (Basic, Classic and Grand) categories**
   - Chaired by Additional Director General (Tourism), Govt. of India/ Chairperson (HRACC) or a representative nominated by him
   - Representative from FHRAI
   - Representative from HAI
   - Representative from IATO
   - Representative from TAAI
   - Principal Institute of Hotel Management
   - Regional Director, Indiatourism office/local Indiatourism office
   - Member Secretary HRACC
   - In case of Heritage category, a representative of Indian Heritage Hotels Association (IHHA)

(The HRACC representatives/nominees of FHRAI, HAI, IATO, and TAAI should have requisite expertise and experience of the hospitality, and tourism industry [hands on experience])

(b) **For 1, 2, and 3 Star hotels**
   - Chairperson, Secretary (Tourism) of the concerned State Govt. or his nominee who should not be below the rank of a Deputy Secretary to Government of India. In his absence the Regional Director, India Tourism who is also Member Secretary, Regional HRACC will chair the committee.

- Regional Director, Indiatourism office/local Indiatourism office
- Representative from FHRAI
- Representative from HAI
- Representative from IATO
- Representative from TAAI
- Principal Institute of Hotel Management

(The HRACC representatives/nominees of FHRAI, HAI, IATO and TAAI should have requisite expertise and experience of the hospitality and tourism industry [hands on experience])

(c) The Chairperson and any 3 members will constitute a quorum

(d) The recommendations will be sent to HRACC Division (Ministry of Tourism, Government of India) within 5 working days and the recommendation of the HRACC inspection committee will be approved by the Chairperson (HRACC)/Addl. Director General (Tourism) expeditiously.

(e) **Appellate Authority:** In case of any dissatisfaction with the decision of HRACC, the hotel may appeal to Secretary (Tourism), Government of India for review and reconsideration within 30 days of receiving the communication regarding classification/reclassification. No request will be entertained beyond this period.

13. Hotels will be classified following a two-stage procedure:

(a) The presence of facilities and services will be evaluated against the checklist available (Table 1.2).

(b) The quality of facilities and services will be evaluated (Table 1.5).

14. The hotel is expected to maintain required standards at all times. The Classification Committee may inspect a hotel at any time without previous notice. The committee may request that its members be accommodated overnight to inspect the level of services.

15. Any deficiencies/rectifications pointed out by the HRACC must be complied with within the stipulated time, which has been allotted in consultation with the hotel representatives during inspection. Failure to comply within the stipulated time will result in rejection of the application.

16. The committee may assign a Star category lower but not higher than that applied for.

17. The hotel must be able to convince the committee that they are taking sufficient steps to conserve energy and harvest water, garbage segregation, and disposal/recycling as per Pollution Control Board (PCB) norms and following other eco-friendly measures.

18. For any change in the Star/Heritage category, the promoter must apply afresh along with requisite fee.

19. Any changes in the plans or management of the hotel should be informed to the HRACC, Ministry of Tourism, Govt. of India within 30 days, otherwise the classification will stand withdrawn/terminated.

20. The minimum size of rooms and bathrooms for all categories have been specified in the guidelines. Hotels of 1, 2, 3, and 4 Star categories availing subsidy/tax benefits/other benefits from the Central/State Government would be subject to a lock-in period of 8 years so that these hotels continue to serve as budget category hotels. Hotels would be permitted to apply for upgradation to a higher star category after the completion of the lock-in period.

21. Applicants are requested to go through the 'Checklist' of facilities and services contained in this document before applying.

22. Incomplete applications will not be considered. Efforts will be made to ensure that all cases of classification are inspected within three months from the date of application if complete in all respects and classification order will be issued within 30 days subsequently.

ANNEXURE 3: SPECIMEN FORMAT OF APPLICATION FORM FOR APPROVAL OF APARTMENT HOTEL PROJECT

1. Proposed name of hotel.
2. Name of promoters with a note giving details of business antecedents.
3. Complete postal address of the promoters/tel./fax/e-mail.
4. Status of owners/promoters:
   (i) If public/private limited company with copy of the Memorandum and Articles of Association
   (ii) Partnership firm (if so, a copy of Partnership Deed and Certificate of Registration).
   (iii) Proprietary concern (give name and address of the Proprietor/Certificate of Registration).
5. Location of hotel site along with postal address.
6. Details of the site:
   (i) Area (in sq. m.)
   (ii) Title-owned/leased with copies of sale/lease deed
   (iii) Copy of land-use permit from the concerned local authorities
   (iv) Distance from railway station, airport, main shopping centres (in kms)
7. Details of the hotel project:
   • A copy of the project/feasibility report
   • Star category planned
   • Number of apartments and area for each type of room (in sq. ft.)
   • Number of attached baths and areas (in sq. ft.)
   • Details of public areas: lounge/lobby, restaurants, bars, shopping, banquet/conference halls, health club, swimming pool, parking facilities
   • Facilities for physically challenged persons

- Eco-friendly practices and any other facilities (please indicate area in sq. ft. for each facility mentioned above 5, 6, and 7)
- Date by which project is expected to be completed and operational

8. Blueprints/sketch plans of the project: A complete set duly signed by the promoter and the architect should be furnished, including/showing among other things, the following:
   - Site plan
   - Front and side elevation
   - Floor plan for all floors
   - Details of guest rooms and bathrooms with dimensions in sq. ft.
   - Details of fire fighting measures/hydrants, etc.
   - Details of measures for energy conservation and water harvesting.

9. Air-conditioning details for guest rooms and public areas; facility planning.

10. Local approvals by:
    - Municipal authorities
    - Concerned police authorities
    - Any other local authorities as may be required
    - Approval/NOC from airport authority of India for projects located near airports

The above-mentioned approvals/No objection certificates are the responsibility of the promoters/concerned company as the case may be. The department's approval is no substitute for any statutory and the approval given is liable to be withdrawn in case of any violations without notice.

11. Proposed capital structure:
    - Total project cost:
      (a) Equity component with details of paid up capital
      (b) Debt—with current and proposed sources of funding

12. Letter of acceptance of regulatory conditions.

13. Please indicate whether the promoter intends to give a few rooms or all rooms on a timeshare basis.

14. Application fee:

Star Category	Fee (in Rupees)
Deluxe	25,000.00
5*	20,000.00
4*	15,000.00
3*	10,000.00

(Demand draft for ---------/- in case of hotel project planned for heritage) Draft may be drawn in favor of: Pay and Accounts Officer, Department of Tourism, New Delhi must be attached with the application:

PLACE   SIGNATURE
DATE   (NAME and DESIGNATION OF APPLICANT)

ANNEXURE 4: UNDERTAKING

I have read and understood all the terms and conditions mentioned above with respect to Project Approval/Classification-Reclassification under the Star/ Heritage categories and hereby agree to abide by them. The information and documents provided are correct and authentic to the best of my knowledge.

I understand that the Ministry's approval is no substitute for any statutory approval and the approval given is liable to be withdrawn in case of any violation or misrepresentation of facts or non-compliance of directions that may be issued by the Ministry of Tourism, Govt. of India, without notice. It is to certify that the hotel would not seek upgradation to a higher category for a period of eight (8) years in the event the hotel avails of subsidy/tax benefits/other benefits from the Government. In case of any dispute/legal measure, the same may be eligible in the jurisdiction falling under the NCT of Delhi.

PLACE   **Signature and name in block letters**

DATE   **Seal of the applicant**

CHAPTER 2
Hotel Design

Chapter Outline:

The following topics are covered in this chapter

- Design consideration
- Systematic layout planning (SLP) pattern
- Planning consideration
  - o Guidelines for space determinations
  - o Architectural consideration
  - o Cost of construction estimation
- How to develop a feasibility report
- Guidelines for reading blueprints
- Planning for parking, walks, and drives

Learning Objectives:

This chapter will enable you to understand

- The points to be considered while designing a hotel project
- The flow process of systematic layout planning
- How to determine the space requirement for 100 to 1000 rooms hotel property
- The computation and estimation of project cost
- How to read the blueprints of various facilities with their features
- How to prepare the feasibility report of a hotel
- The difference between carpet area and plinth area

INTRODUCTION

The main aim of any business organization is to earn profit. This not only depends on the working of an organization but also on its presentation; more so in the hotel and hospitality sector. The prime motive or objective of any hotel property is to attract more and more clients and guests and make their visits a memorable experience. It, thus, becomes a priority to give special consideration to their accommodation and needs while showcasing the best of the local traditions and culture. A great deal of this depends on the architecture and designing of a property.

Architecture is the art or science of designing and constructing buildings. A good piece of architecture is one which succeeds in satisfying its intended uses—that it should be technically sound as well as aesthetically appealing. Any building design is invariably influenced by the technologies applied. The process of planning, designing, and construction of a hotel is known as its *integration.* The designing of the building, hotel facilities, and services sets the scene for a lively atmosphere. Throughout the hotel, the designers and architects create a subliminal ambience of elegance and opulence right from the exterior, to the lobby and public areas, the guest rooms, and every section of the property. The designs are generally at their creative best in the specialty restaurants and nightclubs, as also the guest rooms.

According to noted hotel architect Morris Lapidus, hotel guests fall into two categories: Business travellers and other travellers. While the business travellers require a comfortable bed, easily accessible food, drawers space, good lighting for reading, and quick service, the other category appreciates all these necessities, but wants the atmosphere of their room and hotel to reflect the culture of the city or country they are visiting. All these travellers expect something different in a hotel than what they find in their homes.

The architecture of a hotel depends not only on the way its owner or entrepreneur wants, but also on the creativity and imagination of the architect. The final construction of the building is reflective of the skills and experience of the architect.

DESIGN CONSIDERATIONS

A project is an investment, which can be analysed and appraised independently. It refers to a series of activities whose goal is to bring into existence a business organization based on a viable economic opportunity within an established cost and time framework. The basic characteristics of a project are as follows:

- It involves a current capital investment;
- It ensures a yield of benefits in the future;
- It has a specific life span; and
- It calls for teamwork, the members of which are drawn from various disciplines of management.

For example, a company may take up a project for the construction of a motel in a tourist resort. This may involve an investment of Rs 50 lakh. The company expects to earn a return of Rs 8 lakh after-tax per annum for the next 15 years from restaurant sales and room rentals. The completion of this project would entail the coordination of engineering, marketing and financial experts.

However, before even planning or working on a hotel project, or for that matter any project, an entrepreneur or an aspiring hotelier, in our case, ought to have the ability to identify an 'investment opportunity' which can be converted into a viable business proposition (after careful and systematic consideration). There are a number of sources from which an entrepreneur can gain knowledge about project ideas. The following are some of them.

(a) A study of the performance of existing units in an industry with particular reference to profitability of units and capacity utilization would allow an entrepreneur to identify relatively risk-free opportunities. For example, if a majority of the hotels in a town enjoy an 80 per cent occupancy rate, it indicates that there is still a need for lodging facilities.

(b) A study of projects being encouraged by financial institutions indicates that those sectors are deemed highly viable and hold promise. This is because the financial institutions back projects after careful and thorough analyses.

(c) A study of economic trends and consumption patterns of individuals also helps generate new project ideas. In the context of the hospitality industry, for example, the increasing affluence of the middle class, and growing expenditure on tourism, travel, and leisure indicates a vast potential for travel agencies.

(d) An enquiry into the prevailing social and cultural trends of a society may provide valuable insights. For example, the search for Indian identity has caused a boom in the sales of ethnic fashion designers in the country.

(e) An enquiry into the business practices in foreign countries may also provide valuable clues for business opportunities in the hospitality market. For example, adventure sports as part of tourism has been essentially borrowed from Western countries.

(f)   An investigation into locally available resources and raw materials and skills may indicate the availability of business opportunities. For instance, puppets are made in Jaipur, Rajasthan, which enjoys a worldwide market, and opportunities still exist for marketing them within the country.

(g)   A study of developments in technology may also provide new products ideas. Often, new technologies allow a better utilization locally available raw material as witnessed in the coir industry.

(h)   A constant search for the unfulfilled needs of the market allows identification of a series of business opportunities. The development of any product/service which satisfies a human need not catered to earlier ensures a steady market. This phenomenon is observed in the quick success of fast food joints, pre-school nurseries, and labour saving kitchen devices.

(i)   In a country like India, where the government plays a significant role in the economic development of the nation as a regulator as well as a promoter, the policies of the state must be taken into consideration while scouting for new ideas. Quiet often, the plans of the government provide new business opportunities for an alert entrepreneur. For instance, the hosting of the 2010 Commonwealth games in Delhi has triggered the construction of many star category as well as budget class hotels, restaurants, and fast food joints in the national capital region.

(j)   Various incentives given to small-scale industries, units set up in backward regions; tax exemptions for specific products, etc. create new business opportunities. For example, the scheme of export incentives, financing the project at low rate of interest through Tourism Financial Corporation of India (TFCI), tax free holidays, single window clearance for hotel projects, introduced by the government has led to a boom in the development of new hotel projects throughout the country.

The above-mentioned steps should be carefully considered and borne in mind while meeting the specific goals and objectives related to design considerations when conceiving a project. The basic function of a design is to facilitate the flow of work with satisfaction keeping in mind the needs and wants of the end user. Therefore, a new design should be formulated keeping in mind the user friendliness and operational efficiency.

Designing and constructing a hotel is an uphill task. The overall design and décor of a property should exude warmth and hospitality making guests feel at home the moment they step into it. The overall ambience may generate a feeling of sophistication to make a guest feel special, but it should in no way be imposing or intimidating. The basic building design, layout and planning of facilities and services have to be planned very carefully with an eye on the pocket of the promoter, the profile of the targeted clientele, and the expected returns on investment. The following are the points that need to be considered while designing a hotel.

1. Good location and site
2. Architectural features and plans
3. Efficient plan schedule
4. Analysis of raw material available at cheapest rate
5. Good workmanship
6. Sound financing
7. Structural regulations laid by town and country planning department

Good Location and Site

Selection of location and site is a key issue in the development of a hotel project. The selection of suitable sites for hotels is a complex job. It is usually a matter of choosing from among a number of possible sites the one that has the highest number of positive features or the fewest defects. This is because no site is likely to have all the desired merits. The main factors to look for while singling upon a given site are as under.

Financial aspects of the site This pertains to the cost of land, construction costs, costs related to developing the building systems, cost of furniture fixture, equipment, research and development costs, maintenance costs, etc.

General aspects These relate to general features such as accessibility of transport, distance from key commercial hubs, etc., which could have a direct bearing on the business, and thus, selection of sites. Some such aspects are as follows:

- Accessibility of transport, especially from airports and railway stations.
- Existence of present and planned future social centers.
- Special attraction in locations, such as proximity to parks or open space.
- Proximity to business houses and amusement centres.
- Residential or non-residential areas.
- Level of sound during night.
- Access for service deliveries.
- Suitability of ground-floor street frontages for shops.
- Class of surrounding property, whether free from industrial buildings.

- Good sub-soil to eliminate excessive foundation costs.
- Possibility of providing garage and/or parking arrangements.

Each of the above factors must be weighed before the final decision is made after a thorough analysis as to whether the site is suitable for a hotel, and if so, for what type of hotel.

Architectural Features and Plans

For a sector that thrives on showcasing virtually anything under the sun to its visitors, a building of a hotel must be as impressive as its interiors. Its distinctive features should, as we learnt in the last chapter, begin from the designing itself. The Greeks are generally credited with pioneering the concept of designing a building that 'could be viewed as a precious object externally too'. Box 2.1 briefly describes the distinctive characteristics of various building designs or architectural styles that evolved in various civilizations over the ages, and their influence can be seen in some modern structures even today. The principal guiding factor for any hotelier is ensuring maximum occupancy at minimum maintenance cost.

Box 2.1   Architectural Styles of Various Civilizations

Hindu Architecture

Indian architecture found its earliest expression in brick buildings that were contemporary to buildings that were constructed of wood. The wooden structures disappeared over the centuries, but they were succeeded and imitated in stone buildings, which have survived. This kind of architecture usually includes hemispherical mounds, domes, with more concern for sculptural mass than for enclosed volume. There are many old forts in India that have been converted into hotels. Hotels like Amarvilas, Agra, Rajvilas, Udaivilas, etc. are some examples of typical Hindu architecture.

The Hindu style is closely related to the Jain style. It is divided into three general categories: northern, central, and southern. In all these three types, the style is marked by great ornamentality and the use of pyramidal roofs. Spire like domes terminate in delicate finials. Other features include the elaborate, grand-scale gates, and the ceremonial halls.

Modern Indian Style

Notable architectural features of modern Indian style include the vaulted structure, topped by a huge, concrete roof umbrella, and the use of concrete grille and bright pastel colours.

Greek Architecture

Greeks put their walls inside to protect the *cella* and their columns on the outside, where they could articulate exterior space. Perhaps for the first time, the overriding concern is for the building seen as a beautiful object externally, while at the same time containing precious and sacred inner space. Greek architects have been commended for not crushing the viewer with over monumentality.

Roman Architecture

Romans widely used domes and vaults in their architectural style. Cylindrical and spherical spaces are the elements of design. The domes that the

(contd)

Box 2.1   *(contd)*

Romans introduced proved to be more stable. The second important invention of the Romans was vaults formed by the intersection of two identical barrel vaults over a square plan.

Christian Architecture

In early Christian architecture, buildings were of two types—the longitudinal hall, or basilica, and the centralized building, frequently a baptistery or a mausoleum. The buildings mostly consisted of sloping roofs supported by wooden framework and a series of pillars. It was generally made out of bricks.

Romanseque Architecture

The structures were often crude and of relatively modest proportions. The buildings were often composed of elements or decorated with parts, called spoils, looted from Roman structures. One of the characteristics of Romanesque architecture is the circular and polygonal domed structure.

An outstanding achievement of Romanesque architects was the development of architecture of stone vaulted buildings. A major reason for the development of masonry vaulting was the need to replace the highly flammable wooden roofs of the pre-Romanesque structures. The attempts to solve new structural problems resulting from the use of vaults, especially barrel vaults, were endlessly varied. The dome, round and pointed vaults, and plain and ribbed groined vaulting were used.

Islamic Architecture

The basic structural elements of the Islamic architecture are arches and domes. Islam forbade the representation of persons and animals; yet craftsmen created highly ornate buildings. The motifs are geometrical designs, floral arabesques, and Arabic calligraphy. The materials are glazed tile, wood joinery and parquetry, marble, mosaic,

sandstone, stucco carving, and white marble inlaid with dark marbles and gemstones. Plaster, patterned brickwork, and tile were used as decorative media in and on Islamic buildings. Tiles in various shapes, such as stars, were fitted together into wall panels.

Renaissance Architecture

In early renaissance period the elements are combined in rather static compositions; classic design implies a serene balance among the several components, and spaces locked into the geometry of perspective. The buildings mostly consist of files of columns, and domes, all assembled in a restrained and elegant harmony in strong contrast to the spirited elaboration of forms in the medieval North.

Gothic Architecture

The aesthetic qualities of Gothic architecture depend on a structural development: the ribbed vault, the solid stone vaults, these were extremely heavy structures and tended to push the walls outward, which could lead to the collapse of the building. In turn, walls had to be heavy and thick enough to bear the weight of the stone vaults. Early in the 12th century, masons developed the ribbed vault, which consists of thin arches of stone, running diagonally, transversely, and longitudinally. The new vault, which was thinner, lighter, and more versatile, allowed a number of architectural developments to take place.

Art Nouveau

It had simple shapes of the brick and stone exterior clearly indicating the division of space within the building, while large expanses of glass provided a strong visual connection between the interior spaces and the outside world. This style basically aimed at rejection of earlier architectural styles with the view of introducing something new.

(contd)

Box 2.1   *(contd)*

Modern Architecture

Modern architecture introduced use of concrete, steel and iron and construction of skyscrapers facilitated by the introduction of the electric elevator and the sudden abundance of steel. A successful transition was made from the masonry-bearing wall to the steel frame, which assumed all the load-bearing functions. The building's skeleton could be erected quickly and the remaining components hung on it to complete it, an immense advantage for high-rise buildings on busy city streets.

Innovative Architecture

Innovative architecture introduced construction of molding spaces with utmost sophistication, great care in the distribution of light, and the use of materials—stone, wood, and copper—with familiar and sympathetic tactile qualities.

International Architecture

This style is geometric and asymmetrical and features such modern materials as concrete, steel, and glass. Functional, logical floor plans and simple unornamented walls of glass and concrete are emphasized. This method is extremely efficient for large-scale construction, in which the same module could be repeated indefinitely. Inner spaces became standardized, predictable, and profitable, and exteriors reflected the monotony of the interiors; the blank glass box became ubiquitous.

Source: www.greatbuildings.com, accessed on 14 December 2009.

Building plans   The modern day constructions, including hotel properties, by and large fall in the innovative and international architectural styles, described in Box 2.1. Over the years some building designs and construction plans have withstood the test of time and become so popular that they are emulated by many players in the industry. Some of the popular types of modern hotel plans are as follows:

- Modular construction
- Slip forming
- Arch design
- Cylinder-like structure

Modular construction   This is the most recent and promising development in the construction of hotel buildings. The technique has cut down the construction time and costs by as much as 40 per cent as compared to traditional construction methods. In this method, room units are constructed separately and hoisted into place with the help of cranes. The procedure entails putting in place all the necessary electrical and plumbing conduits with reinforcing steel, and then pouring concrete to form the room module. After curing, the unit is ready to be trucked to the site and placed in the required position. Buildings constructed with this technique are relatively low cost, time-saving in construction, fire resistant and virtually sound proof as well. An example of this type of construction is the Travelodge as showed in Figure 2.1.

Figure 2.1 Travelodge: An Example of Modular Construction

Slip forming Slip form construction was first used in the 1930s in the building and erection of grain-storage silos and other similar structures. Early slip forming techniques relied on hydraulic jacks and the pouring of concrete into a form work made of timber. Slip forming was also used to eventually build lighthouse towers. Today, slip forming is used to build everything from silo complexes, chimneys, reservoirs, medium- to high-rise housing developments, to office buildings, hotels, hospitals, bridge support piers, in-ground shafts to dams and power stations. It is also still used to build elevator cores and batch houses. This technique is another recent variant involving reinforced concrete extension in hotel construction (Figure 2.2). It was used to raise the exterior walls and some of the interior structures of a 15-storey hotel in Petersburg, Florida. It enabled the hotel to be 'topped out' (constructed till the top storey) in just eight days. In Norfolk, Virginia, the slip forming technique, which was used in the construction of a 14-storey motor-inn, enabled the builders to cut three months from the normal construction time for a property of that size. In that property, a three inch thick reinforced slab was poured for the foundation. Then, a specially constructed slip made of steel and wood

Figure 2.2   Hotel SoMa: An Example of Slip Forming Design

were placed, and concrete was poured into it continuously at the rate of 9.5″ per hour. At the same time the form was raised by a number of electrically operated hydraulic jacks while steel reinforcing rods were inserted into the concrete to give it shape.

Arch design   Arch building designs have hundred per cent useable clear span space and do not have any beams, poles and trusses. They are easy to construct and most of the buildings are erected in just a few days. These buildings are well ventilated and have better air flow than other building types. These buildings are very cost effective and have very low cost in developing heating, ventilation and air-conditioning system. The maintenance cost of these buildings is also very low and they are fire resistant.

The idea of tri-arc design style was introduced by Travelodge International. In this case, [Figure 2.4(f)] the wings of the building are arch-shaped, with the guest rooms being laid on the concave face of the arch, while the facilities are planned in the central core formed at the intersection of the convex face of the arches. The main advantages of this type of designing are as follows:

- Each room has a view.
- The wedge shape of guest rooms permits each to have an unusually large bath and dressing area.
- The control core containing elevators, linen room, utilities and ice cube machines, facilitates economies in construction and operations.

Cylinder-like structure   The cylinder-like design of a hotel building has a distinctive appearance as seen in the Radisson property in Berlin (see Figure 2.3). It has the following advantages:

Figure 2.3   Cylindrical Design: Radisson Blue, Berlin

- Concentration of service and utility equipment at the centre core.
- Lower construction and operating costs.
- All guest rooms on the outer-side with view.
- Ready-made for the popular roof top revolving restaurant or lounge.
- Minimum resistance to wind.
- Suitable for site where land costs are high and minimum area is available.
- Compatibility with circumferential ramps leading to parking.

Curtain wall   In this system, the exterior wall of each floor is hung on the iron or steel frame so that the wall supports only its own weight and not the floors above it. This method of construction reduces the overall weight of a building, which allows it to be built higher, and permits the extensive use of glass on the facade.

Rooms   As guest rooms or bedrooms constitute a major part of hotel construction, the key to economical design lies largely in layout of the guest room block. Some of the variants in the design layout of guest rooms (Figure 2.4) are as follows:

Double-loaded block   Considered the most economical layout, this is capable of development into courtyard plan. It requires two staircases. [Figure 2.4(a)].

Double-loaded T shaped block   This is capable of being developed into cross; also economical, but 3 staircases required. [Figure 2.4(b)]

Single-loaded block   This is capable of being developed into courtyard plan; not an economical solution but may be desirable. [Figure 2.4(c)].

Square block   This comprises a central core containing all vertical services, such as maids rooms, etc. It is compact and useful for small sites where tower development may be desirable. [Figure 2.4(d)].

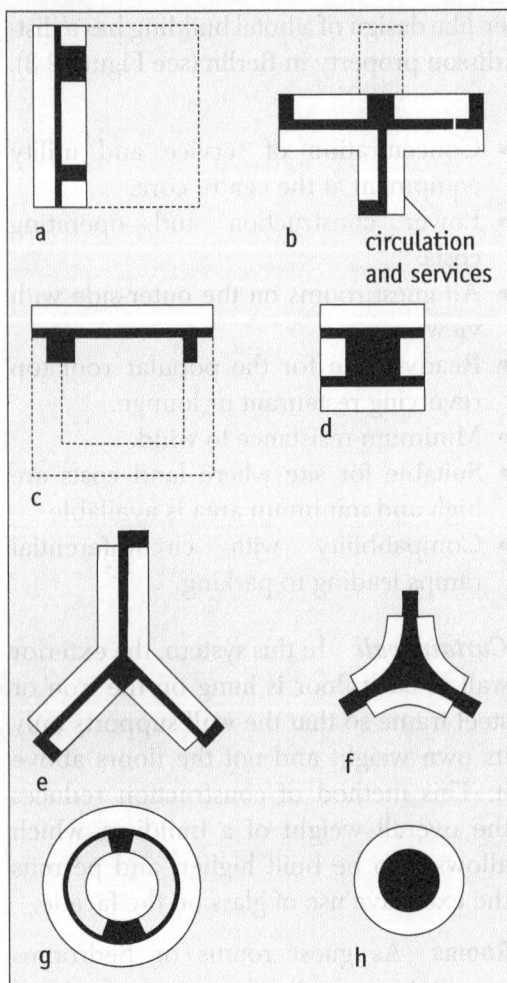

Figure 2.4   Design Plans for Room Layout

Y plan   It has more complicated structure than straight blocks, and requires three staircases. The disadvantage, however, is that this structural system may cause problems in public areas. [Figure 2.4(e)].

Tri-arc plan   This is similar to the 'Y' plan, but more space is taken up by circulation; concave curve results in a bedroom wider at bath room end providing opportunity for larger bathroom and dressing area. [Figure 2.4(f)].

Circular plan   This requires careful handling; avoid awkward and inward facing rooms; not capable of extension. [Figure 2.4(g)].

Circular with central core   This design is similar to the square block one. However, this too requires careful handling to avoid awkward room. [Figure 2.4(h)].

Table 2.1 provides useful insight into the optimum number of guest rooms that can be accommodated on each floor depending on the design layout.

Efficient Plan Schedule

Establishing a schedule of project implementation ensures that the project is completed within the planned time and commences operations on schedule. Delays in the implementation of

Table 2.1   Guide Table for Number of Rooms

Structure	No. of Double Rooms Per Floor	Dimensions	Remarks
Single load	12–30	32' x l	Long corridor
Double load	16–24	60' x l	Long corridor
Offset slab	24–40	80' x l	Split corridor
Rectangular	16–24	110' x 110'	Space in centre enhances room appearance
Circular	16–24	130'	Less rooms/floor
Atrium	24	90' x l	Beautification capsule lift can be provided. Space in the centre enhances the appearance

project quite often create cost over-runs and may affect the profitability of the enterprise or hotel property. In the case of large and complex projects, advanced scheduling techniques like Programme Evaluation and Review Technique (PERT) are utilized. This is discussed in detail in Chapter 7 on Project Management.

Analysis of Raw Material Available at Cheapest Rates

Availability of raw materials and other inputs is essential for successful implementation of the project. The requirement of various inputs like raw material and labour must be estimated on the basis of estimated turnover. The availability of inputs of the right quantity and the right quality on a regular and continuous basis is essential for continuity of operations. Wherever necessary, the enterprise must enter into supply contracts to ensure availability of essential inputs. The enterprises may also create their own sources of supply.

The various building materials that are commonly used in modern construction are as follows:

Brick   A brick may be defined as a block of clay or other ceramic used for construction and decorative facing. These cost relatively little, resist dampness and heat, and can last longer than stone. The colour varies according to the clay used and in proportions according to architectural tradition. Some bricks are made of special fireclays for use in fireplaces or ovens. Others may be made of glass, or they may be textured, or glazed. Bricks may be arranged in various patterns called bonds according to the way the long sides (stretchers) or short sides (headers) are placed. They can be laid in a variety of intricate patterns, such as checker, herringbone, basket weave, or Flemish bond.

Concrete   It is the most widely used construction material in the world. Concrete is the only major building material that can be delivered to the job site in a plastic state. This unique quality makes concrete desirable as a building material because it can be moulded to virtually any form or shape. Qualities of concrete as a building material are its strength, economy, and durability.

Polymer concrete   Another composite material used in architectural elements is polymer concrete, a formulation of thermo set resins and aggregate that simulates stone. In some applications, particularly those within the reach of pedestrians, a heavy material may be desirable to provide both the look and feel of stone or concrete. The polymer concrete surface also has several advantages over real stone because it does not absorb moisture, dirt or graffiti. Stone-like polymer concrete surfaces can also be created on lightweight fibreglass panels.

Steel Introduction of steel for construction purposes was done by the Americans. Steel not only acts as a frame but also provides tensile strength to the building. It doesn't rot and can be easily moulded.

Glass It is widely used for construction purpose nowadays. Frames that can be of wood or steel support them. It is common to see buildings which are made entirely of glass from all sides. This has become possible due to production of more durable glasses.

Fibreglass For specialty applications, fibreglass decorative architectural elements are fast becoming the first choice among building owners and architects. Not only is the installed cost of fibreglass less than that of traditional materials, but also composites are easier to install and maintain. Technological advances such as new finishes that better simulate traditional material make fibre-reinforced plastic (FRP) nearly indistinguishable from the real thing. Fibreglass decorative elements make it possible to achieve certain ornate styles. Fibreglass can be moulded into a number of different finishes to mimic wood, stone, terracotta, concrete, steel or other materials.

Good Workmanship

This entails the selection of appropriate technology, and plant and machinery which ensures efficient and economical operations. Technology must be chosen on the basis of specific requirements of the enterprise. A very important decision in the area of plant and machinery refers to the size or capacity of the facilities to be created. This decision must be taken after a careful consideration of demand and fluctuations in the market demand.

Sound Financing

A proper determination of the cost of project is essential for determining its viability and profitability. An entrepreneur generally approaches financial institutions for loans on the basis of the cost estimates of the project. If there is any cost over-run, the entrepreneur would find it difficult to raise the extra funds required for completion of the project. This in turn would lead to a time over-run thereby affecting all estimates of funds flows too. Hence, there is a need for proper determination of cost of capital. The following are the essential elements of project cost:

- Land and site development
- Building and civil works
- Plant and machinery
- Engineering fees for acquisition of technology

- Miscellaneous fixed assets: These include the following:
  - o Furniture
  - o Office equipment
  - o Cars and trucks
  - o Power equipment
  - o Air conditioning systems
  - o Fire-fighting systems
  - o Pollution control systems and other such systems
- An exhaustive schedule of such fixed assets must be prepared and their prices ascertained for estimation of the cost
- Preliminary and capital issue expenses
- Provision for contingencies
- Margin money for working capital

A sample summary of project cost is provided in Box 2.2.

Box 2.2   Sample of Summary of Project Cost

Item	Cost (in Rs)
Site	
Building	
Plant and machinery	
Furniture, furnishing, and interior	
Food and beverage equipment	
Laundry and housekeeping equipment	
Specialized equipment	
Misc. accessories	
Linen and uniform	
Architectural fee 4%	
Interior designing fee 10%	
Facilities planning fee 10%	
Project management and supervision 1.5%	
Contingency 2.5%	
Pre-opening expenses	
Cost of finance	
Total	

Structural Regulations Laid by Municipal Authorities

Every town and city planning authority generally lays down structural regulations and guidelines to be followed scrupulously in the event of any mishap such as a fire, or an emergency such as bomb scare. It is obligatory for hotel managements to incorporate such structural regulations while designing their properties. For example, in case of a fire or a terror attack, safe evacuation of building occupants may present serious problems unless a plan for orderly and systematic evacuation is prepared in advance and all staff well trained through evacuation drills. Guidelines on the following aspects of an emergency are intended to assist the staff in this task.

Alarms Any person discovering fire, heat, or smoke should immediately report such condition to the fire brigade unless he or she has personal knowledge that such a report has been made. No person shall make, issue, post, or maintain any regulation or order, written or verbal, that would require any person to take any unnecessary delaying action prior to reporting such condition to the fire brigade.

Drills Fire drills must be conducted, in accordance with the fire safety plan, at least once every three months for existing buildings during the first two years after the effective date of these rules, or for new building during the first two years after the issuance of the certificate of occupancy. Thereafter, fire drills must be conducted at least once in six months.

All occupants of the building must participate in the fire drill. However, occupants of the building, other than building service employees, are not required to leave the floor or use the exits during the drill. A written record of such drill has to be kept on the premises for a three year period and produced readily for fire brigade inspection.

Signs and plans

Signs at lift landings A sign shall be posted and maintained at a conspicuous place on every floor, or near the lift landing, indicating that in case of fire, occupants shall use the stairs unless instructed otherwise. The sign shall contain a diagram showing the location of the stairways, and it must be pasted at conspicuous places on every floor. It should have the caption, 'in case of fire, use stairs unless instructed otherwise'. The font size has to be at least 1.25 cm block letters in red against a white background. The lettering has to be properly spaced to provide good legibility. The sign shall be at least 25x30 cm, where the diagram is also incorporated in it, and 6.25x25cm where the diagram is omitted. In the latter case, the diagram sign shall be at least 20x30cm. The sign should be located directly above a call-button, and squarely attached to the wall or partition. The top of the sign should not be more than 2 metres from the floor level.

Floor numbering signs A sign indicating the floor level has to be pasted and maintained within each stair enclosure on every floor. The numbering has to be distinct and conform to the stated specifications. The numerals have to be bold type and at least 7.5 cm high. The numerals and background shall be in contrasting colours. These signs should be prominently displayed on the stair-side of the door.

Staircase and elevator identification signs Each stairway and each elevator have to be identified by an alphabetical letter. A sign to this effect should be posted and maintained at each elevator landing and on the side of the stairway door that leads to the exit. The lettering on the sign shall be at least 7.5 cm high, of bold type and in a contrasting colour from the background.

Staircase re-entry signs A sign shall be posted and maintained on each floor within each stairway and on the occupancy side of the stairway where required, indicating whether re-entry is provided into the building and the floor where such re-entry is provided, in accordance with the requirements given below. The lettering and numerals of the signs should be at least 1.25cm high of bold type. The lettering and background should be of contrasting colour and be displayed at approximately 1.5 m from the floor level. The Fire command station should be provided with the floor plan of the building and other pertinent information related to the service equipment of the building.

Eco-friendly practices In view of increasing environmental concern and governmental regulations in this regard, the technical feasibility study must also outline the systems for safe and non-polluting disposal of solid and liquid effluents like solid and liquid wastes. Use of non-conventional energy resources like renewable energy from sun, windmills, etc. can also be considered, as these now carry extra points when seeking approval/classification for new or on-going projects (Table 1.5).

SYSTEMATIC LAYOUT PLANNING (SLP)

Systematic refers to an organized, disciplined, and rational approach to a problem or assigned task. This entails a sequential procedure to decide a course of action based on facts and analyses to fulfil a given objective. Systematic planning process involves conceptualization, planning, analysis, designing and implementation, with interrelationships of people, materials, information, equipment and method in a flow with an objective of efficient

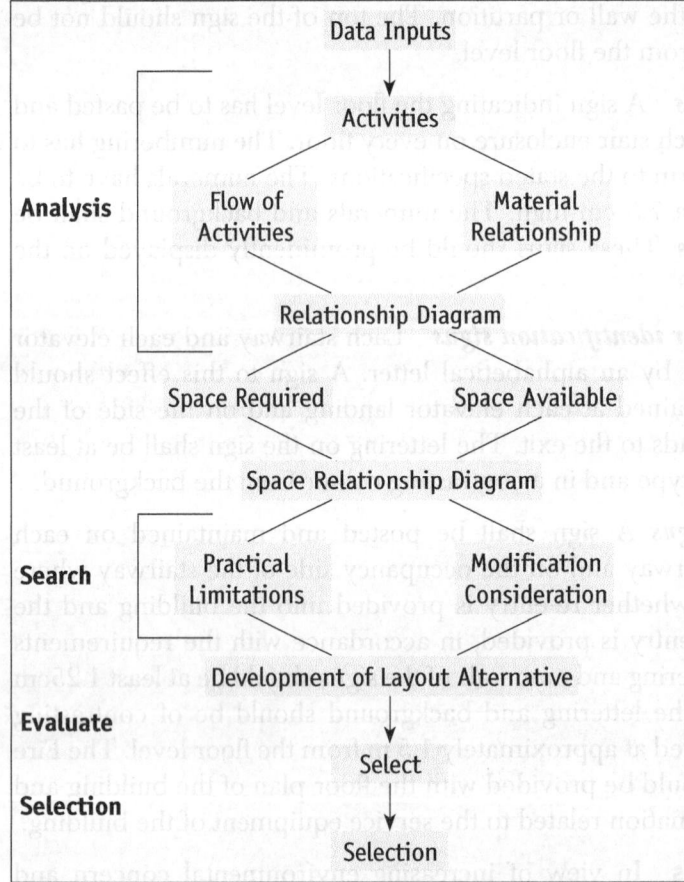

Figure 2.5   Flow Diagram of Systematic Layout Plan

layout. Figure 2.5 depicts the various activities of systematic planning in a sequential manner.

Systematic Layout Planning is a framework of four planning phases: analysis, evaluation, search and selection. There are 20 steps in the systematic layout pattern/SLP of facilities design procedure, which are as follows:

1. Procure data
2. Analyse data
3. Design production process
4. Design material flow pattern
5. Select/design material handling plan
6. Calculate requirement of equipment
7. Plan work areas
8. Select material handling equipment
9. Plan groups of related operations
10. Design activity relationships
11. Calculate space requirement
12. Plan service activities
13. Calculate total space requirements
14. Allocate activities to space
15. Consider building types
16. Construct model layout
17. Evaluate, adjust, and check layout
18. Justify
19. Install layout
20. Nurture layout

THUMB RULES FOR ALLOCATION OF SPACE IN A HOTEL

Where and how much space should be allocated for a particular facility such as a restaurant, or lobby, or guest rooms in a hotel is a complex and tricky job. Space allocation of various facilities is an important aspect of designing and planning a hotel project. Nonetheless, there are certain ground rules or principles that have evolved in the industry over the years. Tables 2.2 and 2.3 present a summary of some widely followed norms in space allocation in hotels.

Table 2.2   Space Allocation Norms in Hotels According to Their Room Size

	Size of Hotel			
No. of rooms	100	200	500	1000
Guest rooms				
King 43%	43	86	215	430
Double 50%	50	100	250	500
Handicapped 2%	2	4	10	20
Suites 5%	5	10	25	50
Lobby		(In square feet.)		
Floor area	1000	2000	4000	7000
Seating	100	200	500	1000
Retail	100	100	800	2000
Asst managers	0	0	100	100
General cashier	0	125	150	200
Bellman station	40	50	50	50
Count room	0	40	100	150
Work area for mail storage	0	40	80	120
Food and Beverage		In square feet		
Coffee shop	1200	2400	3500	4400
Specialty restaurant	0	0	2800	4000
Theme restaurant	0	0	0	4000
Roof top restaurant	0	0	0	3000
Snack bar	0	0	0	0
Cocktail lounge	800	1600	1920	2400
Lobby bar	400	800	2000	2800
Entertainment	0	0	3150	0
Night club	0	0	0	5000
Pool bar	0	0	0	450
Support-dressing rooms, bar storage/toilets, coats/telephones	0	75	100	100

(contd)

Table 2.2   *(contd)*

Function Area	Size of Hotel			
	In square feet			
Ball room	1400	3500	8000	20000
Ballroom foyer	450	900	200	500
Junior ballroom	0	0	4000	12000
Junior ballroom foyer	0	0	2400	6000
Banquet rooms	0	1200	2400	6000
Meetings rooms	0	0	600	1200
Board rooms	0	0	1200	1500
Lecture theatre	0	0	1200	1500
Exhibits hall	0	0	100	15000
Support	In square feet			
Function room storage	100	500	2500	5000
A.V. equipment storage	0	0	100	200
Convention registration	0	0	0	200
Projection booth	0	0	250	400
Translation booth	0	0	0	0
Banquet captain's office	0	0	100	200
Food Preparation	In square feet			
Main kitchen	1100	2000	9000	18000
Banquet pantry	0	0	1200	1200
Coffee shop pantry	0	0	0	0
Specialty restaurant pantry	0	0	1200	1200
Baker's shop	0	0	850	1000
Room service area	75	75	300	500
Chef's office	100	100	120	120
Dry food storage	150	300	1000	1800
Refrigerated food storage	100	200	500	1000
Beverage storage	150	150	500	1000
Refrigerated beverage storage	50	100	250	400
Food controller's office	100	100	120	120
China, silver glass storage	100	200	500	1000
Toilets	100	100	150	150

(contd)

Table 2.2   *(contd)*

	Size of Hotel			
Executive Office	In square feet			
Reception/waiting	0	200	250	300
General manager	0	150	200	200
Executive assistant manager	0	0	180	180
Resident manager	0	0	0	180
F and B manager	0	120	150	175
Secretary	0	100	150	200
Conference room	0	0	200	250
Copying and storage	0	40	100	100
Sales and Catering	In square feet			
Reception/waiting	0	150	200	300
Directors of sales	0	150	150	200
Sales representatives	0	0	330	550
Director of public relations	0	0	150	150
Secretary	0	0	225	375
Catering manager	0	0	150	200
Banquet manager	0	0	150	175
Function booking room	0	0	80	100
Banquet representative	0	0	100	200
Beverage manager	0	0	120	120
Convention services	0	0	120	240
Secretary	0	0	225	400
Copying and storage	0	50	150	200
Accounting	In square feet			
Reception/waiting	0	0	100	100
Controller	0	120	150	200
Asst controller	0	0	100	100
Accounting work area + secretary + copying	0	150+ 100	900	1200
Payroll manager	0	120	120	120
Computer room	0	0	100	200
Receiving and Storage	In square feet			
Loading dock	100	200	400	800

(contd)

Table 2.2 *(contd)*

	Size of Hotel			
Receiving area	180	250	500	1000
R. office	100	120	150	150
Purchasing office	100	120	175	200
Locked storage	100	125	175	200
Empty bottle storage	100	100	125	150
Trash holding area	100	150	200	250
Refrigerated garbage	80	80	100	120
Compactor	150	150	200	250
Ground equipment storage	200	200	300	400
General store	500	1000	2000	4000
Laundry and Housekeeping	In square feet			
Soiled linen room	0	100	150	250
Laundry	0	1000	2500	4000
Laundry supervisor	0	0	100	120
Valet	0	100	150	200
Supplies storage	0	50	125	175
Housekeeping	In square feet			
Housekeeper	100	100	125	150
Asst housekeeper	0	0	100	120
Secretary	0	0	100	100
Linen storage	300	500	1500	3000
Uniform issue storage	100	250	500	800
Supplies storage	100	100	100	200
Lost and found	0	100	150	200
Sewing room	0	0	100	200
Engineering	In square feet			
Engineer	100	100	125	150
Asst engineer	0	0	100	120
Secretarial	0	0	100	100
Carpentry shop	0	0	200	250
Plumbing shop	0	0	200	250
Electrical shop	0	0	200	250
Paint shop	100	100	200	250
TV repair shop	100	100	150	200
Key shop	80	80	80	100

(contd)

Table 2.2   *(contd)*

	Size of Hotel			
Energy management computer	0	0	120	120
Storeroom	200	300	800	1000
Mechanical	In square feet			
Plant	1200	1200	3000	6000
Transformer room	100	150	1000	1500
Emergency generator	100	100	300	500
Meter room	50	50	100	150
Fire pump	0	0	100	200
Electrical switch board	150	200	750	1000
Elevator room	100	100	400	800
Telephone equipment room	100	100	500	800
Recreation and Administration	In square feet			
Swimming pool	0	800	1200	1500
Pool deck	0	2000	3000	4000
Lockers/toilets/sauna	0	300	500	1000
Executive room	0	0	500	800
Whirlpool	0	0	100	200
Game room	0	300	300	500
Manager's office	0	0	100	200
Attendant	0	0	80	200
Equipment storage	0	100	250	400
Pool pump/filter	0	100	200	200
Children play room	0	0	0	500
Safe deposit locker	0	30	60	60
Bell captain storage	0	150	200	300
Front desk	0	160	250	420
Front office manager	0	120	120	120
Asst manager	0	0	120	120
Credit manager	0	100	100	100
Director room	0	0	150	150
Reception secretary	0	100	100	100
Reservation manager	0	80	120	120
Telephone operator	0	80	150	200
Reservation area	0	80	200	250
Fire control room	0	80	120	120

Table 2.3 Allocation Norms for a Three Star Hotel

Hotel Component	Plinth Area
Rooms including toilets, internal lobby corridors, etc.	20–33 sq. m.
Restaurants (Bar and coffee shop)	1.5 sq. m. per seat
Conference/party hall	1.0 sq. m. per person
Kitchen	75% of dining areas
	25% banquet areas
F and B stores	60% of kitchen
Laundry	0.75 sq. m. per room
Work shop	0.60 sq. m. per room
Staff lockers and toilets	0.75 sq. m per room
Boiler room and fuel storage	0.75 sq. m. per room
Substation	0.10 sq. m. per room
Water pumping station	0.10 sq. m per room
Staff canteen and staff kitchen	0.20 sq. m. per room
Lounge including reception, etc.	1.5 sq. m. per room
Administration	1.00 sq. m. per room
Air conditioning plant room	0.75 sq. m. per room
Garbage room	0.10 sq. m. per room
Air handling units	0.1 sq. m. per room
Telephone equipment and battery room	10.50 sq. m. total
Sound control room	10.25 sq. m. total
Lifts	15 sq. m. per floor
Stairs	15 sq. m. per floor
Floor pantries	10 sq. m. per floor

Noted hotel architect William. B. Tabler coined some important criteria for designing and space allocation. His thumb rules in this regard are as follows:

- Construction cost must not exceed Rs 1,000 per Re 1 of average room rate.
- The market and competition determine the room rate. If the ARR (Average room rate) is Rs 1,000 then Rs 10,00,000 should be the maximum construction cost for the finished but unfurnished room, including public space and service areas.
- The total area of bedrooms and floors should be at least as much as total public space and service areas.
- The total allowance for all facilities should not exceed 6,000 sq.ft. (162m^2 per guest room).

- Not over one employee/per room. Payrolls must be kept to minimum. The requisite number of staff is determined by the basic design which involves the number of kitchens, methods of food handling, the routine of guest and built in maintenance stores.
- Land cost must not exceed 10 per cent of the cost of the building.
- Profit ratio: Profit mix of a hotel business may be summarized as follows: Contribution of profit from the guest rooms is average 70 per cent and remaining revenue comes from other departments such as food and beverage, shopping arcade, business centres, health club, etc. Generally a small profit is shown on food but often this does not include space rental value, cost of kitchen equipment, utility services, repairs and maintenance.
- Breakeven point at 65 per cent is a highly controversial figure. The design should permit operating costs to be reduced, proportionately if possible, when business declines by shutting down guest floors using only segments of the total kitchen facilities.

FORMULATION OF PROJECT REPORT/FEASIBILITY REPORT

Formulation of a project generally culminates in the preparation of a project report. *A project report is a document setting out the nature of the activity proposed and the justification for selection and commitment of resources (men, materials, money) to the activity.*

A project report, generally, contains the following:

1. Promoters and their track record with specific emphasis on their experience and the activity selected for the project.
2. Particulars of the project with specific reference to:

    (a) Technology and technical arrangements
    (b) Location and land and buildings
    (c) Plant and machinery
    (d) Raw materials
    (e) Utilities like power, water supply, transportation, etc.
    (f) Labour
    (g) Schedule of implementation
    (h) Cost of the project
    (i) Means of financing
    (j) Marketing and selling arrangement
    (k) Profitability and cash flow
    (l) Economic considerations
    (m) Government consent
    (n) Declaration of the promoter

A well prepared Project Report ensures that every aspect of the project is well considered. It allows the promoter to embark on the project with total confidence. In addition, financial institutions appraise the financial viability of a project, primarily on the basis of the project report. For preparing a project report any of the following options can be considered.

- Where the organization promoting the project is well-versed with all aspects of the project, it may get the report prepared by its own employees. However, financial institutions insist on the services of specialists like chartered accountants for the preparation of certain aspects of the project report.
- The organization may hire the services of professional consultants or consultancy firms to prepare the project report.
- The organization may primarily depend on project reports prepared by financial/professional institutions. They may make suitable modifications/alterations in the reports depending on local conditions and circumstances.

BLUEPRINT

A blueprint of a building is a series of drawings showing the layout of the parts of the building: the rooms, their sizes and shapes, doors and windows, and details that would otherwise take thousands of words to communicate to a reader. There are chances of getting misled if one is unable to read a blueprint. Reading a blueprint for the first time is a great learning experience. Lines, numbers, symbols, and a few words are all that it takes to make a blueprint. A good blueprint should convey all the technical details to its readers. Developing a blueprint is the key responsibility of an architect, who develops the promoter's ideas and conveys them to a draftsman. The draftsman makes the first drafts original drawings that are reproduced as blueprints. Nowadays, computers are generally used to develop blueprints.

Purpose of Blueprints

A blueprint is an important document, especially in construction as it is the starting point of any building activity related to a project. It serves the following purposes.

- It acts as a 'basic talking point' between the owner and the architect.
- It conveys detailed information to the people in the trade (mostly contractors) so that they can read, understand, and construct a building according to specifications contained in these documents.

- A plumber looks at a blueprint to study and install the appropriate types and sizes of plumbing fittings and fixtures at exact locations and points. In the same manner electricians, audio-video mechanics, gas-pipe mechanics use the blueprints for their doing their jobs to precision.
- Managers use blueprint to check the level of performance of the work performed by contractor/plumber/electricians/mechanics, etc.
- Blueprint can also be used to determine the quantity of materials required for refurbishing and redecorating. The estimates regarding the amount or sizes of floor coverings, wall coverings, paint, plaster, wallboard and drapery can be developed from blueprints.
- Blueprints can also be used to determine manpower requirements in housekeeping and maintenance.
- A blueprint may also be used as a basic tool in energy management. An energy saving renovation plan can be developed by reviewing blueprints.

Types of Blueprint

One drawing cannot show all the details of the construction procedure for a building or even a restaurant/linen room/guest room. If there is only one drawing, then it would become cluttered with too many lines, notes, and symbols. That would also increase the chances of serious errors. Therefore, a series or number of blueprints is used for every building. Each drawing is labelled and shows specific information of interest to workers in a particular field. Information which cannot be depicted graphically can be included in written specifications. The combination of blueprints and written documents is called a *construction document.*

The more common types of drawing are: plan, elevation, detail, perspective, section, mechanical, and plot and survey views. Some of these are very specialized, such as heating mechanical views, heating detail views, heating plan views, or perspective details views. It is the prerogative of an architect which views he/she should focus up on to instruct the variously skilled labour on the installation procedures to be followed. The various kinds of blueprints are explained as follows.

Plan views   It is the most common view and is used very frequently. A plan view is akin to seeing a room from the top. If you were looking down from above a room or area with no ceiling or roof, the view you would get is a plan view. The primary use of such a view is to show room layouts. More importantly, the plan view serves as a basis for various calculations, such as, electrical outlets, security alarm system requirements, sizes and number of furnishings, and determination of HVAC (heating, ventilation and air-conditioning).

Elevation views   If you were to stand outside a building and look at it and drew a picture of the building, you would get an elevation view. Elevation views help in deciding how the exterior wall would be done up. What percentage of glass would be used for windows, the types of windows, the kind of material to be used on the wall, orientation of wall, balcony areas, and most importantly, if the balcony will provide an awing effect for the lower level. This view is very important for architects, who prepare a number of alternative elevation views to let the owner or client take a final decision.

Detail views   Detail views serve as a vital communication link between the architect and the builder. It can be a plan view or an interior elevation drawing of an item that cannot be depicted in sufficient detail in other views. Detailed views of interior walls, location of equipment or position of permanent assets and their utility can be of special importance for future renovation of the building.

Perspective views and models   This is an impressive technique for selling ideas. It is basically a three dimensional view of a proposed building generally showed to the owners. It may be dressed up further by showing the location of trees, parking zones, side walks, etc. The purpose of model is to help the onlookers visualize and place themselves in the proposed settings.

Section views   A section view may be a vertical or sometimes horizontal cutaway view of a wall, roof, or foundation of a building. This is a critical from the point of view of the manager/s because it indicates the type of construction material to be used, where insulation is planned in roofs or near foundation walls. A section view is very important for energy conservation planning because the thickness of insulation is very important in reducing energy costs. An economical insulation thickness for the present may be inadequate for the future. It is important to have exterior structural walls and roofs with low heat-transmission coefficients.

Mechanical views   This is the most frequently used blueprint which gives the idea of all mechanical/electrical systems in the building separately. Each mechanical view may use a special set of symbols. System of air-conditioning, plumbing, closed circuit television, fire safety, security system, etc. may be shown on separate mechanical views.

Plot and survey views   These drawings are made by registered surveyors. They show the legal boundaries of the property. In most areas, a plot view is required before building permits are issued.

Computer-aided Design and Drafting (CADD)

The CADD is a relatively new technique which provides tremendous potential for cost-effective drafting and design. A typical CADD system includes a stand alone mainframe or microprocessor computer, workstations with one or two terminals offering graphic and/or alphanumeric capabilities. The strength of a CADD system is its ability to recall enormous amounts of unwieldy information. Thus, turnaround time of CADD drawings is much faster than of drawings done by hand. A building system can be quickly located when questions concerning maintenance, repair and renovation must be explored. An architect can also perform a number of experiments to explore a unique building design due to unique features offered by CADD systems. Walls, partitions, doors, and furnishing can be moved in a matter of seconds to depict alternative uses of space.

PARKING, WALKS, AND DRIVES

Safe and secure parking facility for their vehicles is a fundamental right of all visitors to a hotel property. Although such provisions have to be made by hotel owner, yet most of the hotels are unable to provide sufficient parking space for their guests. Planning for car parking totally depends on the availability of the space, size, configuration, and contours of a site. Parking facilities are of different types, such as the following:

- On-grade
- Above-grade
- Below-grade
- Composite

On-grade Parking

This is the most common and least expensive car parking facility and is totally dependent on the availability of space and its configuration. The most valuable point to consider is cost of land which generally exceeds the cost of a parking structure and in this case a parking deck will prove more economical. Low costs of land always support the on-grade parking. If land cost is too high and does not support on-grade parking such as in high density area/commercial plot then structured parking is the only choice left with the owner of the hotel. On-grade parking requires a lot of maintenance in respect of property management.

All parking lots deteriorate with the passage of the time so early detection and immediate action for rectifying the defects is important. Small cracks and break of surface are common problems, which are unnoticeable and may become serious defects if not repaired immediately. There should be a preventive maintenance programme to ensure that all walks and drives are clean and in good condition. Among the general precautions that may be taken are avoiding the use of salt to melt snow or ice on concrete surface and avoiding spillage of oil/kerosene or other such liquids on asphalt surfaces. Inspection of the parking space should be undertaken twice a year and records detailing the maintenance history of the parking surface should be maintained. A special inspection programme may be designed to detect shrinkage, slippage, potholes and skid hazard on driveways.

Above-grade Parking

Above-grade structured parking is a free standing parking deck of two or more levels. It provides maximum efficiency in terms of area, structure, and circulation and is least expensive after on-grade parking.

Below-grade Parking

Below-grade parking, commonly called underground parking, is more expensive because of structure and mechanical systems required to construct it. Below-grade parking garages are commonly found in large commercial buildings such as apartments, mall buildings, hotel buildings and are used for parking and access to the above-grade floors of the building. Below-grade parking is considered a basement. A *basement is defined as any area of a building having its floor sub grade (below ground level) on all sides.* A careful design consideration is required while planning for below-grade parking in the areas where chances of flooding are more. Flooding of these areas may result in significant damage to the building and any mechanical, electrical or other utility equipments located there such as HVAC, lighting, elevator equipment, and drainage pumps, etc. The garage walls, which often are major structural components of building foundation are also susceptible to flood damage, therefore, hydrostatic or hydrodynamic forces must be considered at the time of planning for below-grade parking. A critical element in any flood proofing design for a below-grade parking is the point where the garage entrance ramp meets the street grade. The best method of protecting a dry flood proofed garage from flood waters is to design garage entry to the above BFE (Base flood elevation).

Composite Parking

It basically integrates above and below-grade parking types with the building above the structure. It requires special ventilation and sprinkler systems and a more elaborate façade.

Zoning Laws

Zoning laws determine the requirement of the parking space but as a thumb rule 1000 square feet is sufficient enough to park three cars in a suburban area and 10 per cent lesser space can solve the problem of parking three cars in urban areas, that is 900 square feet.

Parking space standards The following are the standards pertaining to parking spaces in various kinds of parking lots in hotels in the country.

Standard off-street Parking spaces for standard automobiles shall be a minimum width of nine feet (9') and a minimum length of eighteen feet (18'), except for parallel stalls.

Compact off-street Parking spaces for compact automobiles shall be a minimum width of eight and one-half feet (8.5') and minimum length of sixteen feet (16'). A maximum of ten per cent (10%) of the total parking spaces may be compact spaces.

Long-term off-street Parking spaces for long-term parking for employees or others expected to park a minimum of four or more hours shall be a minimum width of eight and one-half feet (8.5') and a minimum length of eighteen feet (18').

Height Above-grade parking structures shall conform to height limits for the zoning districts in which they are located, except that in districts where building height may exceed three storeys, no parking structure shall exceed four levels of parking or thirty-five feet in height, measured from grade level to the top of the parapet, if any. Lighting standards and mechanical equipment or other appurtenances, shall not be counted in assessing building height. However, special attention shall be paid to the mechanical screening requirements of the zoning ordinance.

Access The distance from parking structure entry and exit points to a corner of a street intersection shall, where possible, occur from an interior street, and shall conform to city standards for access points. To minimize conflicts between exiting or entering cars and pedestrians a minimum of two car lengths (approximately forty feet) shall be provided between an exit or an entrance control gate and the inside edge of a sidewalk.

Ramps
- Protected ramps shall not be constructed with slopes exceeding 12.5 per cent gradient.
- Unprotected ramps shall not be constructed with slopes exceeding 10 per cent gradient.

- Ramp slopes exceeding ten per cent shall have a transition area of not less than fifteen feet in length at the top and bottom of the ramp, and the slope of the transition ramp shall be approximately one-half of the main portions of the ramp.
- Single lane entrances shall not be less than 15 feet wide at the street. However, as the lane approaches the access control point for a garage or lot, the lane shall be necked down to an appropriate width.

Design
- Openings for parking structure façades shall be designed and constructed in accordance with the National Building Code.
- Full enclosure of any level of a parking structure may be permitted only if all applicable building code requirements are met.
- Landscaping and architectural urban design building elements shall be utilized to reduce the overall mass of the structure, and to make the structure attractive and aesthetically pleasing.
- Architectural detail elements shall give depth and visual relief to the entry and corners of the structure that face the street and/or property zoned for residential use.

Landscaping
- The landscaping shall conceal 40 per cent of the structure façades from residential and street views. The screening shall maintain such level of concealment during periods of deciduous leaf loss.
- All drawings shall show the actual size of landscaping at the time of installation.

Lighting
- Interior light levels shall be maintained at an average equal to or greater than five foot candles to enhance security and safety.
- Lighting for rooftop parking shall be placed in the parapet or interior of the parking area. All parking structure lighting shall be designed so as not to reflect or shine on adjacent properties.

SOME KEY DEFINITIONS IN BUILDING CONSTRUCTION

Plinth Area

It is the built up covered area of a building measured at floor level of any storey. Plinth area is calculated by external dimensions of the building at the floor level excluding plinth offsets if any, and the courtyard, open area, balcony and cantilever projections are not included in the plinth area. Supported porch (cantilevered) is included in the plinth area.

The following are included in the plinth area:

- All floors, area of walls at the floor level excluding plinth off sets, if any
- Internal shaft for sanitary installations, provided these do not exceed 2 square metres area in air conditioning ducts
- The area of *barsati* and the area of *mumty* at terrace level
- Area of porch other than cantilever

The following are not included in the plinth area:

- Area of loft
- Internal sanitary shaft provided these are not more than 2 square metres in area
- Unenclosed balconies
- Towers, turrets, domes projecting above the turret level, not forming a storey at the terrace level
- Sunshades, vertical sun breaker, or box louvers projecting out.

Floor Area

Floor area of a building is the total area of the floor in between walls and consists of the floor and all rooms, verandah, passage, corridors, staircases, entrance hall, kitchen, store, bath, and W.C. Sills of door and opening are not included in the floor area.

Area occupied by walls, pillars, plasters, other immediate supports is not included in the floor area.

In short, **Floor area = Plinth area − Area occupied by walls**

For deduction of wall area from plinth area to obtain floor area, the area should include:

- Door and other opening in the walls
- Intermediate pillars and support
- Plasters along walls excluding 300 sq. cm. in area
- Flues, which are within the walls. But the following shall not be excluded from the wall area:

  1. Plaster along walls not exceeding 300 sq. m. in area
  2. Fire place projecting beyond the face of walls in living room
  3. Kitchen platform projecting beyond the face of wall in kitchen

The floor area of each storey and different types of floor should be measured separately. Floor area of basement, mezzanines, *barsati*, and porches should also be measured separately.

Floor Area Ratio (FAR)

It is calculated by dividing the total covered area that is plinth area of all the floors by the area of the plot.

Floor Area Ratio (FAR) = Total covered area of all floors / Plot Area

Example: If total covered area of all floors of a building is 30,000 sq. ft. and Plot Area of the building is 15000 Sq. Ft. then FAR will be as follows:

FAR = Total covered area of all floors/Plot Area
     = 30,000/15000
     = 2 .00

FAR or Floor Space Index (FSI)

This is the ratio of the total floor area of buildings on a certain location to the size of the land of that location, or the limit imposed on such a ratio.

The Floor Area Ratio is the total building square footage (building area) divided by the site size square footage (site area).

As a formula: Floor Area Ratio = (Total covered area on all floors of all buildings on a certain plot)/(Area of the plot)

Thus, an FSI of 2.0 would indicate that the total floor area of a building is two times the gross area of the plot on which it is constructed, as would be found in a multiple-storey building.

Carpet Area

The carpet area of a building is the useful area or liveable or letable area. This is the total floor area minus circulation area, verandah, corridors, passages, staircase, lift, entrance halls, etc. minus other non-useable areas such as sanitary accommodation (bath + W.C.), air-conditioning room, etc. For office buildings, carpet area is the letable area or useable area and for residential buildings carpet area is the liveable area and should exclude the kitchen, pantry, stores and similar other types of rooms which are not used for living purpose. The carpet area of a building for any storey shall be floor area excluding the following:

- sanitary accommodation, verandah, corridor, and passages
- kitchen and pantries, entrance halls, porches stores
- staircases, shafts for lifts, *barsatis* and garages
- canteens, AC ducts and plant room

Thumb Rules for Carpet Area

- Carpet area of an office building is generally 60%–75% of the plinth area.
- Carpet area of a residential building is 50%–65% of the plinth area.

- For a multi-storeyed building with frames, the area occupied by walls may be 5%–10% of the plinth area (a standard 3% for external + 2% for = internal)
- For an ordinary building without frame, the area occupied by walls may be 10% to 15% of the plinth area.
- The carpet area, plinth area, floor area should be measured or taken separately for each floor.

Circulation Area

It is the area of verandahs, passages, corridor, balconies, entrance hall, porches, and staircases, etc., which are used for movement of people using the building. The circulation area of any floor comprises the following:

- Verandah
- Balconies
- Passages and corridors
- Entrance halls
- Staircases and mumties
- Shafts for lifts

The circulation area may be divided into two parts:

- Horizontal area
- Vertical area

Horizontal area   The horizontal area of a building is the area of verandah, passages, corridors, balconies, porch, etc., which are required for horizontal movement of the users of building. This may be 10% to 15% of the area of building.

Vertical circulation area   Vertical circulation area of a building is the area or space occupied by staircases, lifts, and entrance halls adjacent to them, which are required for vertical movement of users of the building. This may be 4%–5% of the building.

ROLE OF VAASTU SHASTRA IN BUILDING DESIGN

The word *Vaastu* is derived from the Sanskrit word *Vasati* which means house. In fact many Indian languages have the sound *vaas* in words denoting a house or a dwelling unit. For example, in Tamil, *vasam* means entrance. Practically, Vaastu is the science of building or science of structure.

Vaastu is essentially an oriental science and is more widely-accepted and practised in the Orient. A similar science is known as *Feng Shui* in Hong Kong, China, Japan, Thailand, and Singapore. *Feng Shui* in Chinese means 'wind- water'. It is the Chinese science and art of placement whereby human beings can place themselves in a manner so as to live in harmony with the environment.

In India, the principles of *Vaastu* have been formulated on the basis of five natural elements or *panchbhutas*, namely earth, water, light (sun or fire), air, and sky. The philosophy underlying the principles of *Vaastu Shastra* is that the whole environment in which we live is permeated with a cosmic force which breathes life into the atmosphere around us, and thus, everything around us influences everything else. As a result, how an individual faces or lives in relation to a house, a door, a window, the air, the water, etc., has a definitive influence on their well being and future.

Vaastu plays an important role in planning the following:

- Site selection: shape, location, slopes, and orientation of the site.
- Layout of the building as per site.
- Location, direction, sizes, shapes of various elements, for example, furniture of a room.
- Placing, direction, sizes, shapes of toilets, kitchen, water sources, and septic tanks.
- Proportions, sizes, shapes, numbers of doors, windows and other openings, especially main entrance.
- Position, number, and sizes of columns.
- Area of various elements in planning.

The common rules that apply to any hotel site facing any direction according to *Vaastu* are as under:

- The shape of a building should either be a perfect square or rectangular.
- Plan single or double rooms in northern and eastern sides as there has to be lesser weight. King size rooms, suites, etc. should be built in the southern and western sides.
- Planning a kitchen should always be in the south-west.
- Wells, bore wells, and underground storage facilities should always be constructed in the north-east.
- Always plan main entrance on higher side.

SUMMARY

Hotel project planning is a very complex and technical topic that requires a high level of expertise from various fields of engineering and architecture. The basic building design, layout, and planning of facilities and services have to be planned very carefully with an eye on the pocket of the promoter, the profile of the targeted clientele as also the expected returns on the investment. Some of the points that need to be considered while designing a hotel are: good location and site, attractive appearance, efficient plan schedule, analysis of raw material available at cheapest rate material, good workmanship, sound financing, structural regulation laid by town and country planning, survey and market analysis, and paying capacity of population to ensure adequate return on capital. Over the years, some building designs and plans have withstood the test of time and become so popular that they are emulated by many players in the industry. Some popular plans are modular construction, slip form, tri-arc design, and cylinder-like structure. Space allocation of rooms and other facilities is also a complex task, but there are certain ground rules that need to be followed to make the activity a successful venture.

CONCEPT REVIEW QUESTIONS

1. Enlist the points to be considered while designing a hotel.
2. Write short notes on the following:
   - Modular Construction
   - Slip Forming
   - Tri-arc Design
   - Cylinder-like Structure
3. 'Location and site play a major role in the success of a hotel.' Justify the statement with suitable examples.
4. Differentiate between the following:
   (a) Carpet area and plinth area
   (b) Floor area and circulation area
   (c) Mechanical view blueprint and section view blueprint
   (d) Floor area ratio and floor space index
5. Estimate the cost of a 100-room five star hotel in your city.
6. Complete the following table: (Area required in a hotel property)

Key Area	100 Rooms	200 Rooms	500 Rooms	1000 Rooms
Lobby				
Coffee shop				
Florist				
Beauty parlor				
GM's office				

PROJECT ASSIGNMENTS

Student's exercise based on a feasibility report of a hotel

Note: A group of 5–6 students can perform this activity by using a hypothetical hotel project in the classroom to understand the topic in depth. The format of the exercise has been outlined as under. Each stage, which corresponds to a week, represents the activity to be undertaken and accomplished during the allotted time.

Stage 1: Formulation of a group

Stage 2: Develop a hotel profile
- Location and site
- Size
- Area
- Type
- Facilities offered
- Services provided

Stage 3: Formation of promoters
- Promoter's profile
- Business volume

Stage 4: Development of organization structure

Stage 5: Preparation of market feasibility report
- Check arrivals in the town according to type of hotel
- Growth rate
- Existing accommodation available
- Need analysis of the size and type
- Future needs

Stage 6: Preparation of financial feasibility
- Funding and financing of the project
- Budgets
- Profit and loss statement
- Work out repayment strategy
- Sales forecast for next 10 years
- Breakeven analysis

Stage 7: Preparation of basic architectural plans (discuss with professionals and experts)

Stage 8: Preparation of network program for the entire process of development (apply application of PERT and CPM)

Stage 9: Legal requirements (enlist and find out the hurdles for location/site development from the local and municipal authorities for approval)

Stage 10: Prepare the drafts on prescribed formats for approval of the project to the relevant government department.

Stage11:
- Submission of the architectural plans to the local and municipal authorities for approval.
- Submission of application for project approval to the relevant government department.
- Submission of application and negotiation for mobilizing finance.

Note: For approval, we can call the faculty experts to play the role representing ministry of tourism, bank/financial institutions, and local authorities. After getting the approval ensure your documentation.

Stage 12:
- Preparation of detailed architectural plans (working drawings) and conduct an exercise for asking quotations/tenders for construction, scrutinizing and negotiating with the contractors (discuss with the field experts/contractors)
- Preparation of design for interior and furniture
- Planning of facilities with layout and specification of equipment and accessories
- Planning of systems
- Planning for affiliation, arrangement for management contracts.

Stage 13:
- Develop strategy for management co-ordination and supervision of the project for construction, procurement and installation
- Develop marketing/promotional/advertising strategy and programme

Stage 14:
- Planning for food and beverage (refer restaurant planning exercise)
- Develop standard operating procedures and administrative set up
- Develop accounting and control system

Stage 15:
1. Develop formats, specimen for various departments/outlets
2. Preparation of operating graphics and stationery

Stage 16:
- Planning for human resource
- Develop recruitment policies and draft
- Preparation of service condition and job descriptions

Stage 17:
- Develop uniforms for the staff of the hotel
- Chalk out training and induction programme
- Establishing operating system

Stage 18:
- Organize a presentation session with a model of hotel and documentation
- Get feed back and incorporate

Stage 19: Review the entire exercise and prepare a final project report

Stage 20: Final presentation

Note:

Students are advised to restrict their work according to the format given as above with due regards to their faculty and take expert advice from time to time. This assignment will basically will help them revise the entire curriculum of their hospitality education because a lot of inputs are required from other core areas of their course viz: strategic management, human resource management, marketing management, financial management, accounts, front office, hotel engineering, food production, housekeeping, and of course, facility planning.

REFERENCES

Bihari, Dr. Girish (2006), *Materials and Machine Management*, IISE, Lucknow.

Kumar, Kapil (1994), TS 3 (study material available for Bachelors in Tourism Management Programme for IGNOU courses), Indira Gandhi National Open University, New Delhi.

Pandit, S.N. (1998), *Hotel Venture Management*, Hotex Publishers, New Delhi.

Sherlekar and Sherlekar (1984), *Principles of Business Management*, Himalaya Publishing House, New Delhi.

CHAPTER 3

Restaurant Design

Chapter Outline:

The following topics are covered in this chapter

- History of restaurants
- Types of restaurants
- Guidelines for restaurant planning and designing
- Myths about restaurant designing
- Role of props for various theme restaurants
- Bar designing

Learning Objectives:

This chapter will enable you to understand

- The definition of a restaurant
- The various facilities that are offered to guests in a restaurant of good class
- The points to be considered while designing a new restaurant
- The role of colours in creating an atmosphere of a food and beverage facility
- The kind of list of props required for theme restaurants
- How to calculate space for various food and beverage facilities
- How to design food and beverage facilities
- The designing of a bar counter

INTRODUCTION

A food service facility's design and layout have a great impact on its appeal not only on guests but also on employees. If a facility is poorly designed, the guests will be inconvenienced and could receive slow service. Production employees will lose precious time in having to walk and move more while preparing food, while service employees may have to walk further between food pick up areas and guest tables. A good design and layout, like the right equipment, improves employee productivity and food quality manifold.

As an operation's design, layout, and equipment directly influence profitability, these factors are also the prime concern of the owners. Design and layout affect capital cost. If more space is designed into the facility than is needed, capital and labour cost will be greater than necessary. Unnecessary operating cost for servicing the extra space (heating, ventilating, air conditioning, cleaning and maintenance, etc.) will be incurred. Government agencies too have a role to play, in that they coin the regulatory laws for design, layout, and equipment that managers adhere to.

One would obviously like the food service facility to be used for a long time. What if a menu change requires a new and different type of equipment? Are there ways to design flexibility into the facility? The best design and layout are the ones that are flexible. You probably did not help design the facility in which you now work. However, you may be involved in remodelling projects. Even simple rearrangements of production equipment or dining room tables should be based on some very basic principles. Therefore, regardless of your management role, some knowledge about design and layout is helpful. In this chapter, we shall focus on the planning, designing, and layout of restaurants.

HISTORY OF RESTAURANT

A restaurant is a type of establishment where people can obtain refreshments or meals on demand and according to their needs. The public dining room that ultimately came to be known as the restaurant originated in France, and the French have continued to make major contributions to the development of restaurants. The first restaurant proprietor is believed to have been A. Boulanger, a soup vendor, who set shop in Paris in 1765. The signboard outside his facility read restoratives, or restaurants, referring to the soups and broths offered. The institution took its name from that sign, and 'restaurant' now denotes a public eating-place in English, French, Dutch, Danish, Norwegian, Romanian, and many other European languages, with some variations.

In Spanish and Portuguese, the word becomes *restaurante*; in Italian it is *ristorante*; in Swedish, *restaurang*; in Russian, *restoran*; and in Polish, *restauracia*.

Although inns and hostelries often served paying guests meals from the host's table, or *table d'hôte* (a French term which literally means table of host), and beverages were sold in cafés, Boulanger's restaurant was probably the first public place where any diner could order a meal from a menu offering a choice of dishes. Boulanger operated a modest establishment; it was not until 1782 that *La Grande Taverne de Londres*, the first luxury restaurant, was founded in Paris.

TYPES OF RESTAURANT AND THEIR THEMES

The food and beverage facility of a hotel has a significant role to play in revenue generation. Food and beverage sale contribute approximately forty to forty-five per cent in total volume of hotel sales and in most cases, food and beverage outlets are the main reason for the success of hotels around the world. For example: *Bukhara* of ITC Maurya Sheraton and Towers, *kebab factory* of Radisson and so on.

Commercial

As the name suggests, these outlets are meant for profit generation and are situated at vantage or profitable locations in the city to cater to the needs of its patrons. Depending on the type of dishes and the services offered, commercial restaurants are categorized into the following types.

Coffee shops These are generally outlets within the premises of large hotels serving food and beverages round the clock. Unlike their formal meals serving counterparts in the premises, coffee shops offer pre-plated service and menu too is not so much elaborate. Light meals are served, and provision of buffet can be made. Seat turnover is high.

Specialty restaurants These are mostly the formal dining spaces in large hotels or even independent outlets in commercial urban hubs serving authentic specialized cuisine with style and class but for a price. The dishes are priced on the higher side. The menu is elaborate, food is served by uniformed staff, and the silverware too is carefully chosen to make dining a visually pleasing and satisfying experience. Seat turnover is high during dinner time.

Ethnic restaurants These are almost similar to specialty restaurants and provide atmosphere according to the culture of the region that they are based on. Apart from the cuisine, which is exclusively ethnic to the advertised region, even the dress code of the serving staff and the way of serving is traditional. There could be a live performance which is also invariably from the region. Needless to say, exclusivity and showcasing of the culture come for a price. Like their specialty counterparts, ethnic restaurants could be an outlet of a hotel or run by single ownership firms. Seat turnover is often high during dinner time.

Fast food joints   These joints, as the name suggests, are based on the quick turnover of guests. There could be self service too, as is seen in leading food joints such as Domino's and McDonald's. These are normally frequented by guests on a regular, or even daily basis. At a fast food restaurant, guests breeze in for a quick bite and leave equally quickly. The décor here is thus, more functional. Everything is organized and arranged in a streamlined manner to facilitate quick and hassle free constant flow of guest traffic. The emphasis being on the functional part, there are standing tables and a few high-seat chairs without back rests. The décor is spartan and the colours staid which are not designed to distract the guest. They should just blend in the backdrop. All these form a part of a functional décor. At times, there are big wall-mounted televisions that help the guests keep up with the latest in sports, news, and entertainment world.

Fast food joints have their origins in *The cafeteria*, an American contribution to restaurant development, that opened in San Francisco during the 1849 gold rush. Featuring self-service, it offered a wide variety of food displayed on counters. The customers made their selections, paying for each item as they chose it or paid for the entire meal at the end of the line. The cafeterias gave way to other quick-food serving joints such as the drugstore counter—serving sandwiches or other snacks; the lunch counter, where the diner is served from a limited quick-order menu at the counter; and the drive-in, 'drive-thru,' or drive-up restaurants, where patrons are served in their automobiles. The so-called fast-food restaurants, usually operated in chains or as franchises and offer limited menus—typically comprising hamburgers, hot dogs, fried chicken, or pizza and their complements—and also offer speed, convenience, and familiarity to diners who may eat in the restaurant or take their food home.

In India, fast food restaurants are very popular and these outlets serve one or two specialty regional dishes that have become popular throughout the country. Most of these outlets are still in the small scale sector but corner a major chunk the food and beverage market. In a bid to blunt their competitive edge, some large Indian players are trying to rope in the small scale sector by offering franchises and expert opinion.

Grill room and barbecues It may be a part of a restaurant with that section of the restaurant separated by a glass so the guest can have a look at the preparation or order the dish according to his/her choice. They can select a meat portion. A *barbecue* is always in an open space with the same features.

Bars and pubs In bars, the underlying principle is provision of privacy to the guests. For this reason, a bar is normally furnished and done up in such a manner that the guests can relax and have their drinks without any hindrance. At the same time, there could some guests who come seeking company. For them there are bar stools are at the counter. The noise level is low and illumination near dark to enhance the feeling of privacy. So a combination of primary and solid/striking colours are used.

Compared to bars, the turnover is expected to be high and fast in a pub. The guests are supposed to come, have a couple of drinks quickly and move out. Privacy is not an important factor. The illumination is normal and the noise level too is higher though not loud. The origin of the pub concept can be traced to the ranches of the American continent, reminiscent of cow boys and the wild West. It is thus common to see designers trying to recreate such an ambience by hanging saddles, guns, guitars, etc. The furniture is typically wooden.

Theme-based Restaurants

Not only the food but also the theme of a restaurant is the starting point or the basis for planning, designing and decorating a restaurant. These are midway between specialty and ethnic restaurants in that they may serve a fair variety of special dishes peculiar to the region or the selected theme of the joint. The décor would also match the theme, but not necessarily to the minutest detail of an ethnic restaurant. The theme can be Indian, classical French, Chinese, Middle Eastern, etc. Some theme restaurants are briefly discussed as follows.

Indian theme Restaurants based on various ethnic groups in the country, that showcase the ambience and authentic cuisine of a particular region, are collectively known as Indian theme restaurants. The most widely prevalent among them are the South Indian and North Indian themes.

South Indian theme The basic concept of the South Indian theme is openness, and it is central courtyard based. A South Indian theme generally conjures up images of lush coconut trees, rice fields, bamboos and plantain leaf *thalis*. The designer keeps these basic concepts in mind. At the same time they are aware that eating on a plantain leaf may not be feasible, or appeal to all the guests. It might not be an economically viable proposition outside local regions. Thus, ideally speaking a South Indian restaurant should have a courtyard decoration in the center, with dining tables laid around the place.

The furniture could be of cane or bamboo in ethnic style to create the right kind of atmosphere.

North Indian theme   This is generally a typical village theme, with a bit of ruggedness. The normal idea is that of a thatched roof hut. This décor is generally done up in one of the corners of a restaurant. The furniture is mainly of wood, the colour is bold

Classical French theme   Showcasing the 19th century elegance and charm of Europe, the classical French restaurant is characterized by light and sober shades in furnishing enhanced with a lot of natural illumination. The furniture is normally simple and elegant. They have murals and paintings on the walls are sought to be highlighted with concealed spotlights.

Middle Eastern theme   In the *tavérnas* of Greece, customers are served such beverages as retsina, a resinated wine, and ouzo, an anise-flavoured apéritif, while they listen to the music of the *bouzouki*. Like other Mediterranean countries, Greece has the grocery-tavérna where one can buy food or eat. The Turkish *iskembeci* is a restaurant featuring tripe soup and other tripe dishes; *muhallebici* shops serve boiled chicken and rice in a soup and milk pudding.

Japanese theme   A characteristic of Japanese restaurants is *sushi* bars that serve *sashimi* (raw fish slices) and *sushi* (fish or other ingredients with vinegared rice) at a counter. Other food bars serve such dishes as noodles and *tempura* (deep-fried shrimp and vegetables). *Yudofu* restaurants build their meals around varieties of *tofu* (bean curd), and the elegant tea houses serve formal *Kaiseki* table d'hôte meals.

Chinese theme   Notwithstanding the political relations between the two countries, Chinese cuisine is among the most popular international foods in India. Thus, restaurants with logos of the dragon and the mandarin script could easily outnumber other international theme based eating joints in the country. The main features of a Chinese theme restaurant are dim lighting heightened by the dark red and green colours. Natural lighting is less. The illumination in the dining hall is low, although direct. A usual Chinese décor has red or green as predominant colours. The tables and chairs are generally low. Ceramic vases and traditional folding fans with traditional oriental motifs, and statues add to the décor. Normally tables are separated with wooden partitions to provide privacy. In the up-market classy restaurants, one would even find porcelain crockery, which China is renowned for.

In China, restaurants serving the local cuisine offer a wide variety of noodles and soups. The dim-sum shops provide a never-ending supply of assorted steamed, stuffed dumplings and other steamed or fried delicacies. A common sight in most parts of Asia is a kind of portable restaurant, operated by a single person or family from a wagon or litter set up at a particular street location, where specialties are cooked on the spot. Also, cooking utensils vary widely in Asia.

Although there is no hard and fast rule that states that theme restaurants have to follow a particular style, most of designers and decorators, by and large retain some basic style features of the theme in question and rely on their creative skills and imagination for adding the touch of exclusivity.

DESIGNING AND PLANNING A RESTAURANT

A restaurant is among the most profitable areas of any hotel operation—but it is also among the most neglected. A well-designed facility contributes in a big way to the profitability of the organization in more ways than one, although the architect and other designers make a facility unique with their imagination and creativity.

Guidelines and Design Considerations

Following are the basic principles and guidelines which should not be ignored while making a restaurant.

- There should be maximum return on investment.
- There should be an efficient flow of people and products within the facility and equipment should be well placed.
- The facility must provide safe working space for employees and public access space to guests.
- Design and layout must take sanitation issues into account.
- The facility should lend itself to employees work efficiency so that fewer employees are needed to meet quality standards and labour costs are lowered.
- Equipment should be energy efficient for making facility maintenance costs low.
- Facility design should render employee supervision and other management activity easy.

Planning

Effective planning takes time and generally requires the specialized knowledge of people such as contractors, food service suppliers, and interior designers.

Preliminary considerations There are many steps and people involved in the planning process of a restaurant. The commitment of capital fund is likely to be substantial; the amount of planning to help ensure that project goals are met without surprises also involves a substantial time commitment. Efficient planning comprises the following sequence of actions.

The planning team   The first step is to form a planning team. The restaurant manager and the owner must be members of the team. In most cases, an architect is needed. Unless the promoters are thoroughly familiar with the complex task of interior space design, a food service facility consultant should also be included in the team.

After the planning team is in place, it must develop the concepts and ideas for the facility. It should seek to answer questions such as 'Does the remodeling project involve the exterior and/or the interior of the facility? or 'Does it include the entire kitchen or just one particular area?' The other factors helping the crystallization of concepts and ideas are as follows.

- Type of facility (commercial, institutional)
- Its size in terms of capacity
- Operating hours
- Type of menu (*à la carte* or *table d'hôte* or combination of both)
- Quality requirements of productions,
- Style of service,
- Types of manpower (skilled/semi-skilled/unskilled)
- Atmosphere and décor

The development of a thorough idea of the project ensures its successful completion. It is important to conceptualize the exact activities proposed to be performed in a given area before designing it. While it is not possible to look ahead many years, it is still important to think about general functional activities and provide some flexibility in the design.

Equipment and space needs   The menu is a primary factor in dictating the kind of required equipment and space needs. Other factors include employee skills and the variety and volume of food and beverages the operation produces.

A food service operation is usually designed or redesigned by first considering individual workstations. *A workstation* is a place where one employee works, or where one menu item is prepared. Workstations are put together to form work sections, that are then organized into the larger work area. For example, the workstation for one bartender may be designed first. It can then be matched with a similar bartender workstation to form a work section—the bar. This work section must be appropriately placed in the work area—the lounge.

Preliminary layout and equipment plans help with space allocations; floor plans can show the general arrangement the equipment, work aisles and the relationship of one work area to another. Cost estimates can be based on these plans. If estimated costs are greater than the amount budgeted for, it may necessitate redesigning and renovations, and readjusting the plans.

Space allowance for seating Some guidelines have been established for different types of food services. These are summarized in Tables 3.1 and 3.2.

Table 3.1 Guidelines for Space Allocation for Seating in Various Types of Restaurants

Type of Establishment	Space Allowance per Cover* Seat (in Square Feet)
Restaurant luxury	18
Medium restaurant	12–14
Coffee shop	10–12
Bar and lounge	6–8
Staff canteen	6
Formal service	10–12
Counter service	6–10
Table service (club)	14–16
Cafeteria (commercial)	6–8
Cocktail parties and reception	4–6
Banqueting rounds	12
Banqueting sprigs	10
Theatre seating	8
Desk seating arrangement	16

Note: The above allowances take into account the area within dining rooms used for service and seating. These, however, do not include toilet, wash room, and other customer facilities.

* Cover means a person/pax. In food and beverage terminology it means a space allotted to keep crockery, cutlery, glassware and linen so that a person can consume his/her meal in a comfortable condition. Pax is generally used in function catering (banquet) to denote its capacity.

Table 3.2 Suggested Minimum Aisle Dimensions

Area	Customer Access Aisles (in Inches)	Service Aisles (in Inches)	Main Aisles (in Inches)
Institutional banquets	18	24	48
Lunch room cafeteria	18	30	48
Fine dining	18	36	54

Redesign goals Managers must determine what they want the redesigning activity to accomplish. For example, managers of an elegant facility may want the dining room to project an atmosphere of luxury; a fast food establishment that depends on a high guest turnover may use bright, hot colours in its dining room as a subtle means of persuading guests not to linger over their meals.

Managers must also keep government safety regulations in mind when redesigning food service areas. These laws may restrict equipment placement in the kitchen, the number of guests that can be seated in the dining room, emergency lighting, the placement and the number of exits, and so on.

Blueprints and specifications   When preliminary information has been reviewed and approved, the final blueprints can be drawn and equipment specifications prepared. These are used to solicit price quotations and make decisions about hiring contractors and suppliers. Construction and installations tasks follow. Contractors, equipment suppliers, and the operation's planning or management team should be agreed on a time frame or schedule and must stick to it.

Ambience and Décor

A restaurant is visited by maximum local clientele. That is the reason the design of a restaurant has an immense effect on the marketing of the food and beverage services of an outlet. One should be very particular about the atmosphere and standard of the food and service to be provided. It is often a mistake to plan the décor and the menu as well as other standards separately, since the final product and ambience thus created usually lead to a mismatch. There have been instances wherein restaurants of even five star hotels have an Indian name with a Western décor serving Chinese food. Careful planning of the style of the restaurant is, therefore, extremely essential from the very outset and should not be based on the whims and fancies of the owner, but on a realistic market survey of the requirements as well as competition from restaurants in the neighborhood, if any.

The ambience of a restaurant contributes greatly to its success. Atmosphere is often what the guests come back for. The atmosphere is as important as food. Today it is the accepted attitude that a restaurant's ambience reflects the character of the organization; its owners and their popularity directly influences the clientele. Hence, in order to succeed, the restaurant must strike the right balance between atmosphere and quality of food, drink and service.

An important point is establishment of clear guidelines on the seating capacity, hours of opening, traffic pattern, and service standard for the interiors. Though there are various norms for seating on a per square foot basis, these norms only serve as general guidelines. Some restaurants have a tremendous atmosphere and are very popular, even though they may seem more overcrowded than other successful restaurants that have a spacious layout.

A common mistake often made is totality and imitation of the seating capacity and the standard of well-established restaurants in the neighborhood. Such a policy usually proves to be counter productive, since prospective clients are usually attracted to a new restaurant, if it is different from the others.

The *service standard* should indicate the need for counters, service stations, trolleys and similar equipment within the restaurant, which would have to harmonize with the décor. It would also be advantageous to decide on the type and number of staff of the restaurant, such as hostess, headwaiter, captain, steward, bartender, etc. The uniform graphics, linen, chinaware and silverware should be thought of from the beginning, so that they form part of the interior décor.

Once the basic criteria have been clearly established, detailed planning can commence. The next step is to try and utilize the advantage of the building such as corners, low ceiling, intervening columns, and differences in floor levels area of window glazing, entrances and exits, etc. to the maximum and to the advantage of the facility.

External factors Factors such as direct sunlight, traffic noise and other environmental factors should also be carefully considered. It is often a desirable practice—especially if there is to be live music, dance performances of dancing—to design the restaurants with a clear cut demarcation of the different atmosphere necessary for lunch and dinner. For lunchtime, a cheerful ambience is necessary and natural light is a distinctive advantage. However, for dinner a more inward looking restaurant is necessary. Problems such as glazing can be treated in a number of ways by providing beads, fabric and curtains, sliding wooden screens or bamboo blinds which can be opened or raised to let in different quantum of light, and change the atmosphere for the different meals. Using reflective light often suitably treats low ceilings. Angles and corners within the restaurant can be put to advantageous uses by segregating different areas to provide more privacy.

It is always better to sub-divide the restaurant into smaller areas which may be visually distinct, but have the definite benefit of making the restaurant look full, even when it is half empty.

Intervening columns can also be treated in several ways, either with the use of mirror (in case one does not want the column to be highly visible) or by decorating paneling, if the columns are to be a feature of the restaurant.

Very often fixed seating banquets can be placed around the columns, as well as along the walls, for maximum utilization of the space. The seating plan, however, must carefully incorporate in sight-lines, so that each guest gets a clear view of the stage, if there is to be any live performance.

Noise control This is also essential since many restaurants are designed with extremely hard surfaces, and often the clatter of cutlery, chinaware, etc. is very disturbing. To ensure effective control of noise, sound absorbent materials should be used on walls, floors and ceilings. For floors, there is no better substitute for carpeting (if the budget permits). Whereas fabric paneling over a thin layer of foam is ideal for the walls. Chilling could ideally be treated with acoustic boards, fabric or even thin carpeting in an aesthetic pattern.

Lastly, attention should be given to the electrical, air conditioning and other services, as well as adequate fire prevention and control measures. All lighting should be on a dimmer control to vary the mood of the restaurant during the meal, and on differently planned circuits so that the entire illumination can be changed at will.

In case of air-conditioning, if music is also required, all grills as well as speakers must be incorporated into the ceiling plant from the outset, so that they do not protrude into the décor. Fire exits must be clearly indicated and a sprinkle system as well as fire hoses and extinguishers should be discreetly placed, yet easily accessible. The use of water fountains and indoor plants can also give a cooling effect in a hot climate, though this would of course, depend on the rest of the restaurant interior.

Keeping the above points in view, a carefully coordinated interior is possible though every interior is, of course subservient to the quality of the food and service. It is seldom that a guest would repeatedly come to a restaurant to the admire interior, though he/she may definitely visit it again, if the food and service is excellent. This aspect must always be predominant when thinking about a good restaurant. Box 3.1 provides an insight into the points that need to be factored while selecting a designer.

Box 3.1 Selecting a Designer

How does a dining room manager select a designer?

Among the factors that should be considered are the following:

- Professional membership
- Education
- Experience
- Portfolio
- First impressions
- Contacts
- Budget
- Design fee

Building the Character and Ambience

Competition has driven restaurants to create character and ambience through décor. Bright rooms encourage sociability and they make the surrounding inviting. Dark rooms signify coziness and privacy. Thus a restaurant should be designed and decorated with a specific set of diners or theme in mind. The attention to detail in matter of ambience should be given accordingly. However, ambience can be an elusive goal as it often defines conventional standards.

Thumb rules for lighting   More than any other design element, lighting creates the mood of a space. The following are some guiding principles in this regard.

- Sparkle enhances the appetite and encourages conversation. Chandeliers or multiple pin lights help achieve sparkle. Light also bounces off mirrored surfaces, wet looking finishes, and shiny service ware also help to create sparkle.
- Dark shadows appear hostile; small patterns of light appear friendly.
- Brightly lit architectural surfaces tend to move people and are, therefore, good for high-volume facilities.
- Direct light must be counteracted with indirect lighting to avoid a boring look and achieve environmental comfort.
- Candles between people draw them together.
- Strong down lighting is unbecoming to people.
- If lighting makes flesh tones look good, it also tends to make food look good.
- Surround people with light rather than spotlighting them.
- Design lighting in transition zones so guests don't feel blinded when they enter a room from sunlight, or get disoriented when they exit into darkness.
- Use a dimming system in food rooms to permit mood changes:
  - Brightness and cheer for breakfast
  - Restfulness for lunch
  - Animation for cocktails
  - Romance for dinner

Role of colour schemes in creating atmosphere   The colours used in dining areas obviously affect the atmosphere sought to be portrayed or projected. As is true with most decisions, the restaurant manager makes the important consideration as to what the guest wants? The answer to that question may be far different from the feelings he/or she has about specific colours and combinations of colours. Interior designers use a wide range of colours. For this and many other reasons, it is often wise to involve a professional interior designers/decorator in the designing of dining areas and to depend on them for colour coordination ideas.

Violets, blues, and light greens are cool colours and tend to make guests feel relaxed. Facilities emphasizing leisurely dining may want to use these colours or a combination of these colours. In contrast, warm colours such as, red, yellow, and orange, are stimulating—they encourage activity. Therefore, these colours are generally used to encourage fast table turnover as in fast food facilities.

Many of us are aware that rooms which receive little sunlight should have light and warm colours, while those receiving a lot of sunlight should utilize cool, dark colours. Colours also have an impact on perceived room size. Light colours make the room appear large; dark colours tend to make a room look small. Dark colours also make ceilings look lower than they actually are. The broken effect created by painting one wall then putting wall paper on the next should be available. When one wall is very brightly coloured, the other wall should be more neutral, perhaps in the same shade or tint.

Small pictures, wall hangings, and other decorations should be used in small rooms. Larger items should be used with care, even in large rooms. When decorations from various periods or with different styles are selected, a unified effect can be created if their colours are coordinated. Such decorations should be selected carefully if they are to portray a theme. For example, various items that could be chosen to portray a nautical theme include models of ships, anchors, oars, buoys, fishing nets, and shells. To add to an old Western theme, such items as copper cooking utensils, saloon signs, whiskey barrels, and branding iron might be appropriate. Careful thought and often considerable expenses are necessary to decorate dining area effectively.

Role of props in creating theme in the Restaurants Props constitute an important element in the enhancing the décor of theme restaurants. Table 3.3 provides a list of props that are generally seen in special theme restaurants.

Restaurant safety The restaurant manager should be concerned about the safety of both employees and guests. Some aspects of safety actually relate to the property's ongoing security and safety programme.

Safety implies preventing accidents that can harm both employees and guests. Security relates to other emergencies and methods to handle them.

Accidents are caused by someone's carelessness; they are unplanned and unforeseen events. Using safety principles can prevent many accidents. The restaurant manager's most important concern when developing and implementing safety programmes are to protect human resources. However, these programmes will also reduce the possibilities of losses in revenue, equipment, and the facility itself. Management and food service personnel

Table 3.3   Some Widely Used Props Seen in Theme Restaurants

Nautical Theme	Early American Theme
Anchors	Dueling pistols
Lobster traps	Indian figures
Harpoon-whalers	Barrel tables
Manila rope	Barrel stool
Spanish cork	Boots
Portholes	Drums
Glass floats	Gun racks
Fish nets harpoons	Colonial clamps
Anchor lights	Williamsburg plaques
Buoys	Early American notices
Men of the sea plaques	Sal don signs
Ship models	Café doors
Ship wheels	Advertising mirrors
Block and tackle	Beer and soda
Nautical telescopes	Mirrors
Ships flags	Wagon wheels
Divers helmets	Whisky barrels
Life preservers	Old west clocks
Ensign room artifacts	Yoke wall fixtures
Harpoons	Copper pots and pans
Wire fish basket harpoons	Colonial shovel
Mexican Theme	**Western Theme**
Metal light fixtures	Steer hide and steer skull
Bull light scenes	Cigar store Indians
Matadors	Indian blankets
Street scenes	Pot belly stove
Aztec clocks	Oak barrels
Street musician	Boots
Spanish ladies	Horse shoes
Violin	Oxen yoke
Guitar	Coveted wagon plaques
Trumpet	Horse collar mirror
Wrought iron	Early tools
Donkeys	Western street scenes
Poncho	Wanted signs and bulletin board

must make a commitment to consider safety programmes as important. In this regard, managers can do the following.

- Help develop work procedures that recognize safety concerns.
- Train employees to use safe working procedures.
- Conduct continuous inspection of food service areas to ensure that the equipment and facilities lend themselves to safe work practices.
- Complete accident reports, assist in accident investigations, and do all that is necessary to quickly correct problems causing accidents.
- Provide medical assistance to injured employees and guests, and, if qualified, administer first aid.
- Report needed repairs, maintenance, changes in work procedures, or other conditions which can potentially cause accidents.
- Regularly conduct schedule safety meetings and other programmes for dining service staff.
- Space allotment must bear in mind the need of changing layouts for service and dining areas in response to changing demand of customers, their ages and body sizes. *Flexibility is therefore, the essence of good space allocation.*

Checklist for Effective Design

Properly designed dining areas necessitate a complex planning process to ensure the following.

1. The completed dining area has the proper appeal and ambience.
2. A minimal investment for dining service is made.
3. A maximum return on the investment in space is realized.
4. There is a practical layout to ensure an efficient flow of guests, employees, food products and equipment within dining areas.
5. Simplified procedures for performing required task is possible.
6. Dining areas provide safe work space for employees and public access space for guests.
7. Dining areas adhere to the high sanitation standard which the property requires.
8. Dining areas lend themselves to efficient employees work.
9. Dining areas lend themselves to low maintenance costs.
10. Dining areas are energy-efficient.
11. The design makes the supervision of dining service employees and other management activities easy.
12. The design provides guests with the 'comfort zone' they desire.

Designing tips

- Avoid too much distance from the service counter and guest.
- Too vast a menu causes delays on the part of customers in selecting their dishes.
- Ensure proper size and positioning of service stations.
- Lighting that falls on the ceiling makes spaces look larger.
- Use of glass panels, mirrors, paintings with a deep perspective or sceneries on walls which suggest to the viewer something distant.
- A lighted wall panel gives a feeling of spaciousness.
- Use cool and light colours on walls, floors, and ceilings of the restaurant.
- Clear plastic or glass tops of tables through which floors are visible make them appear larger instead of being cut into small segments with piece of furniture.
- If floor coverings are continued over parts of walls, this also gives an impression of larger spaces because of continuity of floorings.
- Use proper degree of illumination in different parts of an area.

Recommended levels of illumination for service areas

- Coffee shop = 150 Flux
- Dining room/grills/restaurant =100 Flux
- Food production area = 500 Flux

Myths about Restaurant Designing

There are many myths or misconceptions about restaurant designing which need to be exploded so as to avoid glaring errors that could affect their business to a great extent. Following are some of them.

Décor of a restaurant is similar to interior of the drawing room of a house. Normally, a house interior is very sober. However, the décor of a restaurant has to be eye catching and striking, but relaxing at the same time. The décor of the restaurant mainly depends on the concept or theme.

It is very simple to plan lighting, ventilation, air-conditioning and other features. Contrary to popular perception among owners, it is very difficult to plant the right kind of illumination, air-conditioning and ventilation for a restaurant. Elements like light, colour, materials used, ventilation/air circulation, curtains and furniture depend a lot on the theme or the concept to the extent that the desired effect has to be created. All these elements have some set standards, which are not to exact measurement but in a certain range. An inappropriate choice in the overall combination of these elements could severely mar the ambience of the restaurant.

Restaurants are only food points where customers come to feed themselves. There is a common misconception among people that restaurant is just a food point where people come to feed themselves, and ambience does not matter much. As a result, they impose their own likes and preferences while designing with scant respect for underlying principles. It must be ensured while designing that the restaurant is a public place where guests with different moods, behaviour, likes and dislikes come not just for dining but also to enjoy the dining experience.

BAR DESIGN

The design of the bar area is very important. A professional bartender and server know that the bar design and available equipment play a significant role in their productivity and performance, which, in turn, affects their service to a guest. Thus, when bar area is designed, those responsible should consider the sequence of the activity necessary to prepare drinks, properly locate equipment required for these tasks, design workstations so that employees can share expensive and space-consuming equipment, and provide ample space for drinks that are ready to be picked up.

Points to be Considered while Planning a Bar

Like a restaurant, a bar is also an important revenue generation facility of a hotel property. Clients, be they of any class, frequent bars for unwinding and cherishing their drinks. Bar designing, thus, has to be sensitive to their moods and preferences, while at the same time ensuring maximum returns on investment to the organization at minimal possible costs. The following factors need to be considered while planning and designing a good bar.

- Budget
- Area
- Clientele
- Points of service
- Shape and size of bar counter
- Guest preferences
- Seat turnover
- Average spending power
- Timings
- Location and site
- Décor, ambience, and colours
- Style of service

Figure 3.1 shows one possible layout/design for a combination of public and service bar as well as the placement of equipment in it.

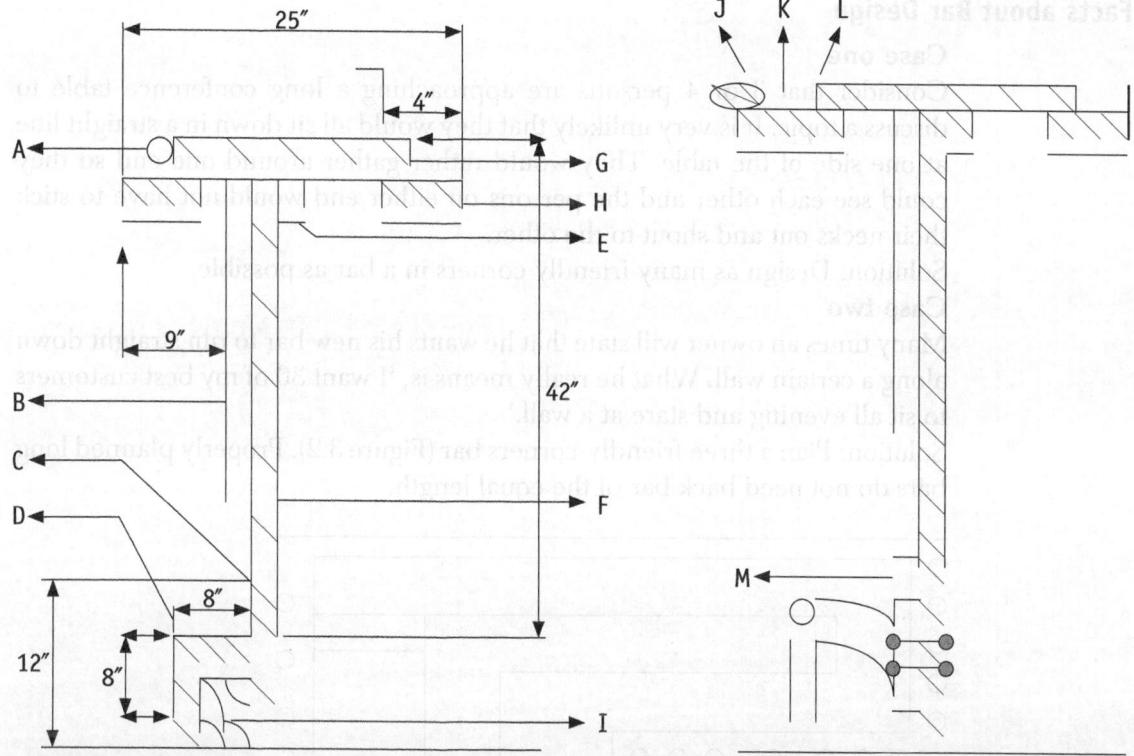

Standard bar details

A- Arm rest-typical wood shape shown-many styles available including finishes

B- Decorative finish – wood panel, tongue and groove board, carpet, upholstery, ceramic tile, etc.

C- Kick plate- linoleum, formica, etc.

D- Foot rest- linoleum, slate, hard wood. etc.

E- Cleat-for securing top to die, varies by manufacturer.

F- Bar Die-usually ¾" plywood.

G- Liquor gutter – usually constricted as shown, Maybe formed in one piece mahogany bar top.

H- Water stop-1/4" thick black formica or wood. Cut down for cleaning at ends.

I- Shoe–To prevent moisture from separating laminations of the plywood die, a solid wood base strip or metal channel shoe is desirable

J- Extended arm rest-wood, Formica or upholstery. Many styles are available.

K- Extension bar- brass or black iron

L- Water stop-same as "I"

M- Brass foot rest-rail usually 2" diameter. Swing away support to floor optional. Check thickness of brass rail proposed by supplier. They are rather expensive.

Figure 3.1   Cross Section Diagram of a Bar Counter

Facts about Bar Design

Case one

Consider that 3 or 4 persons are approaching a long conference table to discuss a topic. It is very unlikely that they would all sit down in a straight line at one side of the table. They would rather gather around one end so they could see each other and the persons on either end would not have to stick their necks out and shout to the other.

Solution: Design as many friendly corners in a bar as possible.

Case two

Many times an owner will state that he wants his new bar to run straight down along a certain wall. What he really means is, 'I want 30 of my best customers to sit all evening and stare at a wall.'

Solution: Plan a three-friendly-corners bar (Figure 3.2). Properly planned long bars do not need back bar of the equal length.

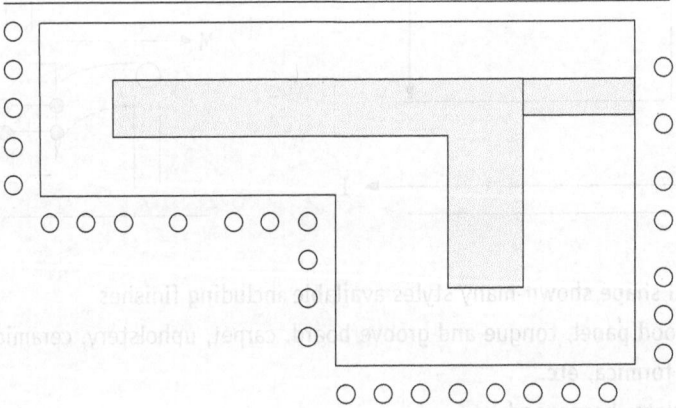

Figure 3.2   Floor Plan of a Three Friendly-Corners Bar

Suggestions or Useful Tips while Planning and Designing a Bar

1. When planning large island type bars, consider the slow periods when only one bartender is on duty. Divide the islands into sections leaving walk through space.
2. If your preference is for serpentine, round ends or curved bars, weigh carefully the aesthetic value against the much higher construction costs and remember the under bar sinks and coolers. To place a long bottle box, or draft beer unit under a curved bar, not having an exceptionally large radius, could make it impossible for the bar tender to reach far enough to be able to serve a customer sitting in front of the under bar unit.

3. A fat expenditure on the bar front should be incurred only if it is an absolute necessary and in keeping with the theme. People seldom pay a lot of attention to it.
4. Inexpensive panelling or applying carpet to the bar front are usually quite satisfactory.
5. Masonry brick fronts provide an attractive rustic appearance.

Dining and unwinding at a bar can be a pleasant and memorable experience if the ambience is tastefully created. A good design is one that is subtle and unobtrusive while at the same time imbuing a degree of affluence and exclusivity. Some of the finest restaurant designs in the world are discussed in Chapter 10 that will give you a fair idea of putting the theory into practice.

SUMMARY

A restaurant is a commercial establishment committed to the sale of food and beverages. It may be a part of a hotel or an individual identity. There are thousands of restaurants in India where diners go not only for quality food and beverage but also for the accompanying entertainment, décor, and ambience that makes dining there a memorable and pleasant experience. Restaurants and bars are also among significant revenue generators for a hospitality property. Hoteliers and entrepreneurs, thus, should go for in-depth planning and designing of their food and beverage outlets so that diners can enjoy their meals in a perfect environment.

Safe, secure, and proper hygiene and sanitation facilities boost the confidence of loyal diners and assists in generating a positive image in the competitive market of catering industry.

More often than not, owners end up designing their food and beverage facilities in accordance with their likes and preferences, which may prove counterproductive in the long run. The beautifully done up interiors of many a fine restaurant have months, or years of hard work of architects and designers, who ensure that an exquisite ambience is equally efficient in the functional and operational aspects for the service providers as well as the guests. Preliminary aspects of restaurant design with an emphasis on space, light, colour, décor, and ambience are explained in the chapter. Blending of colour with lighting may create a wonderful atmosphere for diners, and proper space utilization adds to the profitability of the restaurants.

The best way to work on this topic is to visit a number of food and beverage facilities and conduct one's own analysis about the merits and demerits thereon. It is thus, necessary for the owners as also designers to be aware of the standards and best practices in designing and layout of their facilities.

CONCEPT REVIEW QUESTIONS

1. Discuss the points to be considered while designing a food and beverage outlet.
2. Colours play a vital role in creating the atmosphere of a restaurant. Justify the statement with suitable examples.
3. Enumerate different parts of a bar counter with the help of a cross section diagram.
4. Décor and ambience gives life to a specialty restaurant. In keeping with this view, propose the décor and ambience of a 100 covers Chinese restaurant.
5. Space is a very expensive commodity today. How will you manage space requirement in a coffee shop?
6. How will you deal with the following problems in your food and beverage facility?
   - Noise
   - Poor lighting levels at entrance
   - Foul smell
   - Direct sunlight on corner table
   - Slippery floors
   - Pillars on the floor
   - No perfect shape

NUMERICAL PROBLEMS

1. Determine the space requirement for the following kinds of food and beverage facilities:
   - 500 covers banquet hall
   - 120 covers coffee shop
   - 60 covers staff cafeteria
   - 80 covers bar
   - 100 covers multi-cuisine restaurant
   - 200 pax cocktail parties
   - 60 covers barbecue

PROJECT ASSIGNMENTS

1. Visit various food and beverage outlets in your city and prepare a report of comparative analysis on the following key factors:
   - Space management
   - Floor plan
   - Lighting arrangement

- Atmosphere, décor, and ambience
- Interiors and colour scheme
- Manpower ratio
- Type of menu and cuisine
- Average spending power
- Guest's preference

2. Do a SWOT analysis of the food and beverage outlets of your institute or area and prepare a report on how you can redesign these outlets.

REFERENCES

Anthony M., Rey Ferdinand, and E.I. Wieland (1976), *Planning Your Kitchen,* MANSER (Jose) and MANSER (Michael) London.

Borsenik, Frank D. and Alan T. Stuffs (1996), *The Management of Maintenance and Engineering Systems in the Hospitality Industry,* John Wiley & Sons, Inc., New York.

Gen Takeshi Saito (1994), *Restaurant Design,* Graphic Sha Publishing Co. Japan.

Watson, Olive B. (1968), *School and Institutional Lunchroom Management,* Parker, New York.

CHAPTER 4
Kitchen Design

Chapter Outline:

The following topics are covered in this chapter
- Physical layout
- Space requirement
- Work area requirement
- Role of chef in kitchen planning
- Work and method study
- Flow of work
- Commercial kitchen configurations
- Environmental conditions
- Role of human engineering

Learning Objectives:

This chapter will enable you to understand
- The principles of kitchen planning
- The various kitchen configurations
- The role of work flow in kitchen planning
- And compute requirement of area
- The role of chef in kitchen planning

INTRODUCTION

A food facility is a complex organization performing specialized functions in the manufacture, sales, and service of food. The choice of equipment, the layout, and the physical factors supporting these functions directly influence the success with which the facility operates. In the previous chapter, the discussion concentrated on the designing of the dining space and the finer points to be considered in its layout. It is equally important, if not more, to ensure that the cooking space is designed scientifically to ensure maximum productivity, for it is the kitchen where the all important food is prepared and upon which all the revenue hinges. An orderly and logical study of essential functions and the development of facilities to promote their accomplishment with maximum efficiency and high standards form the basis for layout planning. The needs, resources, and characteristics of a specific situation govern the functions to be performed. The essential functions, in turn, influence the flow or sequence of operations, the equipment needed, and the space requirements. When the flow of work, the equipment and space as well as physical factors are considered together, the layout is largely determined. This chapter focuses on the designing aspects of a kitchen, with emphasis on the elements that need to be considered while planning a food preparation facility.

BASIS OF PHYSICAL LAYOUT

A kitchen plan or layout should be determined by the catering policy, even though a plan may often be limited by space available. The policy adopted, and the space and layout required for a kitchen to carry forward that policy, is affected by many factors such as the following.

1. Type of business
2. Type of customer
3. Seasonal pressures
4. Possibility of expansions
5. Type of meal
6. Number of covers (guests) to be offered
7. Timings of meals (will it be a lunch or dinner service, or day service)
8. Cover turnover
9. Facilities of equipment in still room
10. Is allowance to be made for special functions?
11. To what extent will 'convenience' foods be used?
12. Floor space
13. Position of windows, ventilation, drainage, water supply, etc.

14. Type of service proposed—self-service, cafeteria, waiter or waitress service

The above mentioned points that must be considered when a catering establishment including its kitchen is in the project stage. This because caterers often complain that the kitchen seems to be added to hotels or hospitals, as an afterthought and is given insufficient or the least attention in early planning stages.

While determining the kitchen layout as well as organizing subsequent work within it, certain fundamental intentions remain constant whatever the operation. It is possible that traditional kitchen organizations along sectional or partie (sub-section in the kitchen, for example Indian kitchen may have various sections such as tandoori, curry, sweet sections, etc.) line may be compatible with the achievement of fundamental aims but it is unwise to start with such an assumption.

Kitchen planning must not be dictated by traditional thinking and preconceived notions of systems or organizations should give way to a clinical approach. Principles applicable in designing any production or assembly plant should be applied to kitchens also. Old style production has in some cases been replaced by new systems including 'cook freeze' or 'cook chill'. Industrial and institutional caterers seek to reduce equipment, commodities and method. The constant endeavours are to smooth out the peaks of production during meal times everyday or during longer periods of season. This is often achieved by continuous production and subsequent 'holding' in frozen or chilled condition for service at 'peak' demand hours.

As renowned French chef, restaurateur, and culinary writer Georges Auguste Escoffier, observed in a guide to modern cookery: 'social custom and methods of life alter so rapidly that a few years now suffice to change completely the face of usages which at their inception bade fair to outlive their age'. Continuing cost inflation affects every industry, more so catering, which involves labour, food commodities, and fuel. It is very sensitive to price escalation. High payroll costs, dearer food and energy sources spur caterers to seek new answers to production problems.

LAYOUT OF KITCHEN

The term 'layout' means positioning of work centres and their arrangement with respect to equipment and necessary services like drainage, fuel supply, etc. in the kitchen. Planning layouts requires knowledge and expertise in four different areas such as the following.

Management or administration of kitchens   It is not always necessary to be a specialist, but a person must possess the ability to view a kitchen in terms of its functional efficiency, as far as meeting the objective of the catering establishment is concerned. It is also important for the administrator to be able to identify resources and constraints or limiting factors, and to make policy and other strategic decisions.

Operation   The expert in this field must be able to present the essential data accurately, completely, and in an easily understandable form. He or she has to be a food specialist because they have to approve the plan in the end on behalf of the users. The food service manager must, therefore, play an active role in the planning of layouts, as the direction of the food preparation and service activities within the layout are solely their responsibility.

Architecture   The expertise of an architect is vital to kitchen planning regarding construction features, timing of contracts, and desirable building materials, in terms of providing the facility with structures and equipment that conform to prevailing standards laid down for the safety of users. Very often it becomes necessary to change a fancy architectural plan because it is not feasible as far as the extension of local amenities to the building like the provision of extra lines for drainage and electricity load, etc., are concerned.

Present trends in kitchen layout are designed to lead to closer contact between actual points of food service and customers. This stimulates demand for quicker cooking appliances and conversely render some hot food holding equipment or hot storage redundant. More frequent preparation of food in small quantities for immediate service finds favour with customers. Frozen or chilled 'held' food can, however, dovetail effectively into such forms of catering.

The menu is 'marketing action' and a guide to meal merchandising. The menu is also the blueprint of the catering operation and 'menu justification' may be accepted as the starting point when designing kitchens and selecting appliances. Determining menu policy hinges on decisions made about what is the scope of operation and what shall be and its style of catering.

Convenience foods are used by most hoteliers, caterers and chefs. Meat, fish, poultry, vegetables and fruits are obtainable quick frozen and in prepared and/ or portioned forms. Canned goods have been joined by dehydrated products, bakery premixes, prepared soups and sauces. Packaging liquids in plastics and continuing experiment with new methods of preservations, new forms of vegetable protein, meat analogue, use of less familiar fish suggest that changes in commodity forms continue. Convenience commodities displacing or supplementing unprocessed foods continue to affect planning and equipment. Certain type of equipments such as those for vegetable or preparation may be reduced or eliminated. Storage facilities require adjustment. Dehydration and other forms of processing enable storage areas to be reduced. The use of quick-frozen products demands adjusted provision of sub-zero storage and refrigeration. Thus, modern kitchen operations are planned not only in accordance with concepts of work flow and culinary principles, but also to take technological changes into accounts.

AREA REQUIRED

Kitchens are sometimes reduced in size in order to provide more space and increased seating in the restaurant. This reduction does not necessarily increase the trading capacity of restaurants, for a kitchen, as much as a dining room can determine what number can be served during a service period. Reduction in kitchen size must, therefore, be planned to maintain (and even increased) productivity and still result in a satisfactory work place for employee. Cramped kitchen leads to delays and faults in service. These flaws may ultimately deter customers. Apart from adversely influencing volume of trade and repeat business inadequate kitchen facilities lower staff efficiency.

Many elements make calculating kitchen areas controversial and even experts differ. Briefly stated, kitchen areas vary according to the type and number of meals provided. As the number of patrons increase, the kitchen area relative to seating capacity may tend to be reduced. Accordingly, information about number alone is not sufficient to plan a kitchen or to calculate its area. Knowledge of peak load is essential and this must either be based on experience, or in the case of new establishment, intelligent forecasting.

Hotel and restaurant premises once tended to require kitchen's out of all proportion in size to actual dining seat capacity. This is mainly due to the length of time meals are available during conventional meal time arrangements. Under certain circumstances, hotel and restaurant kitchens have been as much as 40% of total restaurant area.

Something between 0.93 and 1.10 sq. m (10 and 12 sq. ft.) has been conventionally allowed for each customer per meal in calculating restaurant space. But the rate of meal service or 'customer turnover time' affects such calculations. According to an architects' journal of 1960, kitchen space estimates have been as low as 0.23–0.37 sq. m. (2.5 to 4 sq. ft.) per catering unit for a kitchen catering to 1000 guests to as much as 0.84–.093 sq. m. (or 10 sq. ft) per head per meal served in small establishments as for example, fifteen to twenty bedroom guest houses, though some consider such a figure appropriate even for more substantial hotels.

There are no hard and fast rules for calculating kitchen areas or space. However, as a suggestion 'rule of thumb' is 0.56 sq. m. or 6 sq. ft. of floor area per person should be accommodated in the dining room at the sketch plan stage. This figure is arrived at by assuming that 50 per cent of the area allowed in assessing the size of the dining room is 1.10 sq.m. or 12 sq. ft.) per person, which includes tables, passageways, etc. For example, if the floor area of the restaurant is 2000 sq. ft., then kitchen space should be approximately 1000 sq. ft.

Because of such variable factors it is unrealistic to deal with the kitchens of hotels and restaurants as a group. Small à la carte restaurants may have relatively tiny kitchens, whilst some hotels may have large ones compared to the dining areas. Coffee shops and similar catering facilities available round the clock in hotels permit considerable economics in kitchen area allocation.

All that can be said with certainty is that a lower per head area suffices for straight forward kitchens such as those planned primarily for a single purpose such as banqueting, or an institutional fixed meal. A higher rate for calculating floor space must be used when preparation and cooking becomes more complex as in a high class hotel, or in certain hospital kitchens where several types of diets may be required.

No firm rules as to area can, thus, be given but Tables 4.1, 4.2, and 4.3 provide a rough idea about the kitchen space normally required for hotels and restaurants offering waiter or waitress serviced meals. In attempting to estimate kitchen area on the basis of total daily catering capacity, it is similarly impracticable to lay down a hard and fast scale. The tables are thus intended for board guidance only.

Table 4.1 Approximate Indication of Kitchen Requirements

Numbers Eating during Business Hours	Kitchen Area Desirable per Person (in sq. ft.)
100	5–9
100–250	4–6
250–500	4–5
500–1000	3–4
Over 1000	2.5–3

Note: Area reduction may be made when convenience foods (frozen) are fully exploited. The lower figures relate to such simpler operations while the higher for complete catering.

Table 4.2 Possible Area on a Daily Basis of Catering Capacity (Area in sq. ft.)

Total Meals per Day	Restaurant Area	Kitchen Area	Total Catering Floor Space
100	375	150	525
250	560	215	775
500	950	300	1250
1000	1500	500	2000

Table 4.3 Possible Area on a Daily Basis of Seating Capacity (Area in sq. ft.)

Seating Capacity	Restaurant Aea	Kitchen Area	Estimated Possible No. of Meals per Hour
50	700	300	75
75	1000	400	115
100	1250	500	150
125	1750	750	190
200	2750	1200	300

Out of a hotel kitchen area anything between 15 and 25 per cent may be required for storage depending up on the nature of operations and its form of supplies. The remaining space can be devoted to food preparation, cooking and serving. Due to variations even between similar establishments, the calculation of areas cannot be reduced to an exact science. Architects and kitchen engineers adopt their own formulae for calculating requirements and may follow thumb rules for adjustments for flexibility in scope of food production operations.

In case of catering area, initial planning is not the concern of a single person. It normally involves a project planning team or committee which includes the user (chefs), hotelier, and restaurateur, and possibly, his chef and maitre de hotel. Their needs have to be reconciled with site limitations and the views of other members of the team such as consultants, kitchen engineer, all of whose activities are coordinated by the architect.

Chef's Role in Kitchen Planning

A chef is not likely to ever have a decisive voice in determining the space allotted for his or her activities. Despite managerial representation on the planning team, planners may still not consult a chef adequately with regard to various aspects of kitchen design. Despite such conditions, chefs should take a keen interest in the whole kitchen concept and be prepared to help provide briefing on culinary aspects in the planning, constructing and equipment of their work place. Architects, engineers, and hotel directors are often criticized by the chefs and other catering executives for faults in design and planning, but some of the blame can be ascribed to chefs who are inarticulate. Wisdom after the event is no substitute for intelligent anticipation by a trained and experienced person.

Work and Method Study

A layout is based on a good work flow from the receipt of raw materials at goods entry to the dishes finally brought by servers for the guests. Over familiarity with processing sometimes inhibits radical thinking.

Flow of work   Intelligent disposition of preparation machinery, sinks and work, benchmark and reduce the total daily 'kitchen mileage' covered by foot and cut down unnecessary 'travelling' by staff. Thus, a perfect kitchen from this point of view is one in which the raw and cooked materials have minimum movement and only cover the same route once. When each section or *parties* is satisfactorily planned, they must be linked to comply as nearly as possible to the work flow illustrated in Figure 4.1.

This may seem simple but in many cases the task involves modernizing an existing old kitchen or laying out a new kitchen within existing premises.

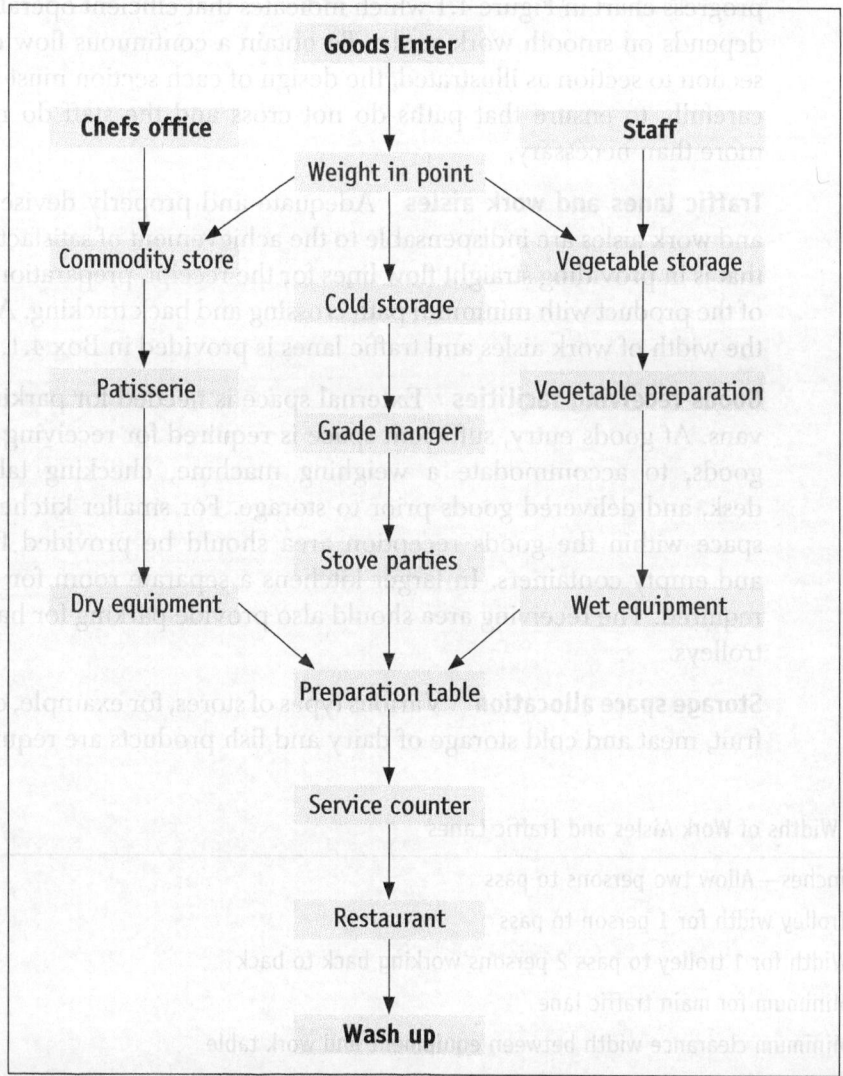

Figure 4.1   Goods and Work Flow

A well planned layout largely depends on the following requirements which if properly provided for, establish good basic kitchen conditions.

1. Incoming supplies and raw materials (checking and weighing)
2. Food storage
3. Cooking
4. Server arrangements
5. Pan wash arrangements
6. Crockery and cutlery wash up

Kitchen design fundamentals may be illustrated by the diagrammatic progress chart in Figure 4.1 which indicates that efficient operation of kitchen depends on smooth work study. To obtain a continuous flow of goods from section to section as illustrated, the design of each section must be considered carefully to ensure that paths do not cross and the staff do not back-track more than necessary.

Traffic lanes and work aisles   Adequate and properly devised traffic lanes and work aisles are indispensable to the achievement of satisfactory work flow that is in providing straight flow lines for the receipt, preparation, and cooking of the product with minimum path crossing and back tracking. A broad idea of the width of work aisles and traffic lanes is provided in Box 4.1.

Goods receiving facilities   External space is needed for parking of delivery vans. At goods entry, sufficient space is required for receiving and checking goods, to accommodate a weighing machine, checking table, stand up desk, and delivered goods prior to storage. For smaller kitchens, a separate space within the goods reception area should be provided for waste bins and empty containers. In larger kitchens a separate room for waste may be required. The receiving area should also provide parking for hand trucks and trolleys.

Storage space allocation   Various types of stores, for example, dry, vegetable, fruit, meat and cold storage of dairy and fish products are required in a good

Box 4.1   Widths of Work Aisles and Traffic Lanes

2 feet 6 inches—Allow two persons to pass
2 feet—Trolley width for 1 person to pass
5 feet—Width for 1 trolley to pass 2 persons working back to back
5 feet—Minimum for main traffic lane
3 feet—Minimum clearance width between equipment and work table
3 feet 6 inches–4 feet—Minimum in front of cooking equipment (to which food is conveyed by trolley

kitchen. Total storage space should not exceed one quarter of the kitchen area for storing of food and equipment. We can calculate space required for a dry goods store on the basis of 8 to 10 per cent of total kitchen space.

Effects of Changing Food Technology on Kitchen Planning

As manpower and space is becoming expensive day by day, kitchen layout is gradually coming closer to the actual point of service and guests. Rapid advancement in food technology has resulted in more efficient equipment becoming available in the market. This enables meeting the demand for faster cooking and quicker service. Guests' demands and tastes are changing rapidly, and accordingly caterers have to change their kitchen plan to cope with changing trends.

In new kitchen planning, more weight is given to space, fuel and man-hour saving. People too are becoming more health conscious, thanks to the popularity of the microwave and infra-red ovens. This has seen the introduction of new equipment that takes care of nutritional value of the dishes. To help serve food faster, conveyer belts, mobile buffets, self-service counters, etc. have been introduced in catering establishments. See through and interactive kitchens are becoming more popular nowadays.

Key Steps for Designing a Kitchen

The following are the main steps involved in designing a good kitchen.

1. Determine a basic menu design or pattern.
2. Estimate menu items to be prepared according to demand.
3. Consider food purchasing policies.
4. Ascertain the size, number, and type of equipment needed to process the menu style and type of dishes chosen.
5. From the specification of equipment compute the amount of space required to house the equipment required.
6. Determine layout equipment departmentally according to food flow analysis and frequency of use.
7. The peak food purchasing requirement must be determined.
8. Determine and allocate floor space required for refrigeration and dry store purposes as a ratio to total space available.
9. Estimate the dining room space by analyzing the peak patron loads and average seat turnover during these periods for any given restaurant.
10. Allocate service area space within the kitchen by considering menu, peak load requirements, patron's needs and type of service offered.
11. Determine the number of employees needed and their distribution in the various departments from study of hours of operation and peak production, and serving requirements.

12. Calculate the amount of space needed for work and traffic aisles by studying equipment layout and employee duties.

COMMERCIAL KITCHEN CONFIGURATIONS/SHAPES

Kitchens may take different shapes according to how much space is available in a building for the production and service of food, and where this space happens to be. Kitchens vary from square, rectangular, U-shaped, L-shaped, parallel to a single or straight line, with dimensions varying according to the need of particular catering establishments. Figures 4.2 (a-g) give an idea of the shapes that can be used for a kitchen.

Square Kitchen

This shape is not very common as the amount of area in the centre is more [Figure 4.2 (a)], and it requires much walking to reach from one wall to another. It is also difficult to use the central space effectively except for an aisle or for odd jobs, which too might come in the way of the main cooking and preparation activity. All plumbing, electricity and gas connections are best brought to wall ends rather than have the pipe and drains under the floors in the centre of the kitchen.

Rectangular Kitchen

This is a very common shape among kitchens and is generally used in establishments where a lot of activity is undertaken for most of the day [Figure. 4.2(b)]. In large establishments, where many different types of menus are served, and more space is required, a rectangular kitchen proves useful. Rectangular configuration is very common in hospitals, large restaurants and central kitchens.

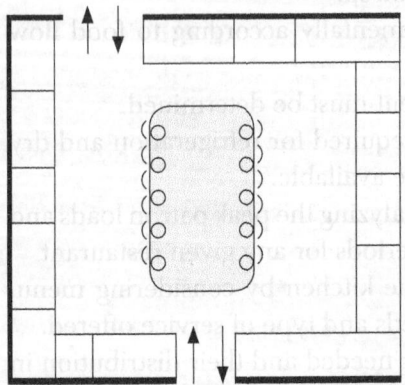

Figure 4.2a Square-shaped Kitchen

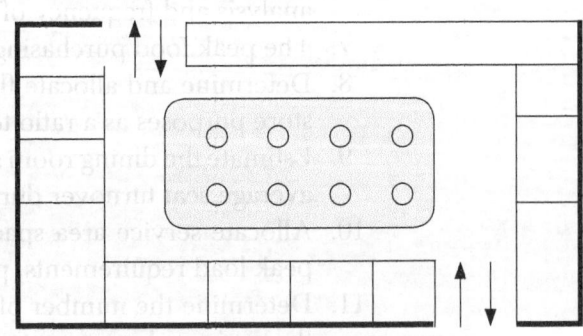

Figure 4.2b Rectangular-shaped Kitchen

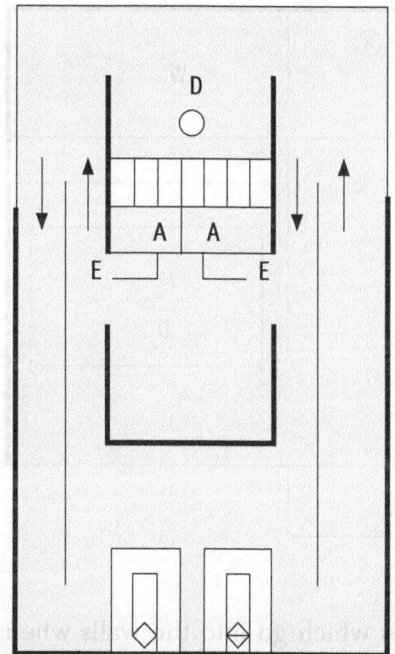

A indicates Wall fixed counters on either side which come up to form an additional counter for service

Figure 4.2c   U-shaped Kitchen

U-Shaped Kitchen

This is the most efficient type, being compact and step-saving, as shown in [Figure 4.2(c)]. Doors are located at the end of the 'U' and the cooking/working area along the three sides of the room. The sink unit is placed in the end wall or inside the U, with a window over it. There is no chance of crisscrossing such that work flows easily from one centre to the next.

L-shaped Kitchen

This kitchen makes use of two adjoining walls at right angles [Figure 4.2(d)]. It is an efficient design in cases where floor space is limited. The figure shows the arrangement of a refrigerator, sink, and cooking unit. Extra space can be created by use of revolving shelves installed in a cabinet at the base of cooking and sink units. It is a very useful shape for small canteens, kiosks and tea, and coffee shops.

Parallel Kitchen

In this type of kitchen, the sides of passages may be utilized while the central space acts as an aisle. The passage may be slightly screened off on one side for service during peak hours. This sort of plan is best suited to cafeterias of the self service type. [Figure 4.2(e)] shows a parallel

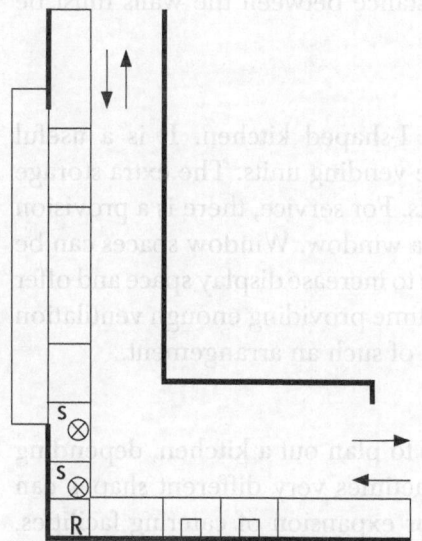

Figure 4.2d   L-shaped Kitchen

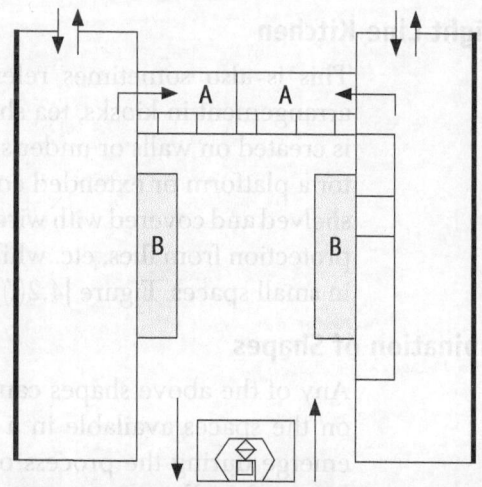

Figure 4.2e   Parallel Kitchen

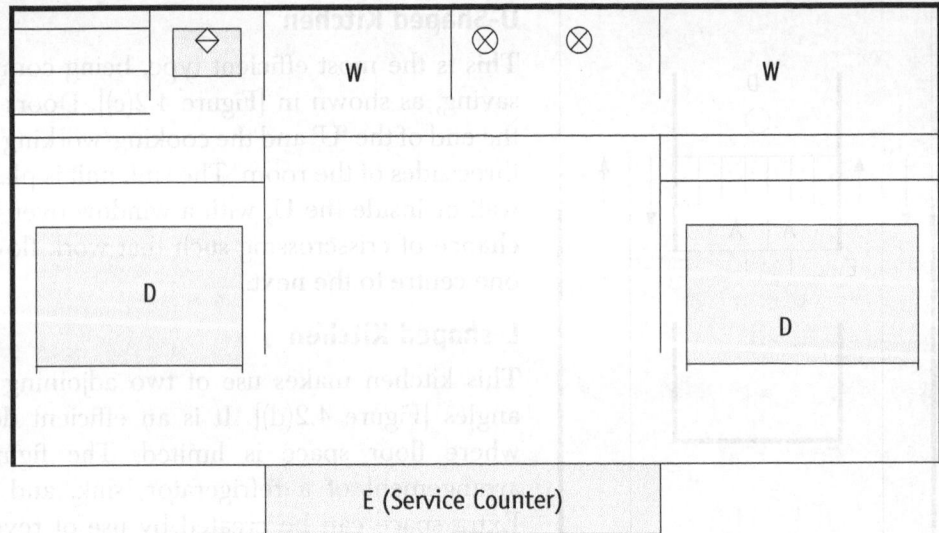

Figure 4.2f   Straight Line Kitchen

arrangement. 'AA' in the figure shows tables which go into the walls when the service is not open. 'BB' indicates extendable counters opening into the passage during service hours.

This type of kitchen is suitable for midday meals in schools where dining facilities are not possible. The central passage can be used for children to squat on mattresses and eat the food served in plates. Generally, children like to eat while standing or playing and prefer to carry the food away from the areas of service. For such a kitchen the distance between the walls must be between 1.2 and 1.5 metres.

Straight Line Kitchen

This is also sometimes referred to as an I-shaped kitchen. It is a useful arrangement in kiosks, tea shops, or mobile vending units. The extra storage is created on walls or under sinks in cabinets. For service, there is a provision for a platform or extended counter outside a window. Window spaces can be shelved and covered with wire mesh shutters to increase display space and offer protection from flies, etc. while at the same time providing enough ventilation in small spaces. Figure [4.2(f)] gives an idea of such an arrangement.

Combination of Shapes

Any of the above shapes can be combined to plan out a kitchen, depending on the spaces available in a building. Sometimes very different shapes can emerge during the process of renovation or expansion of catering facilities. [Figure 4.2(g)] gives an example of one such configuration.

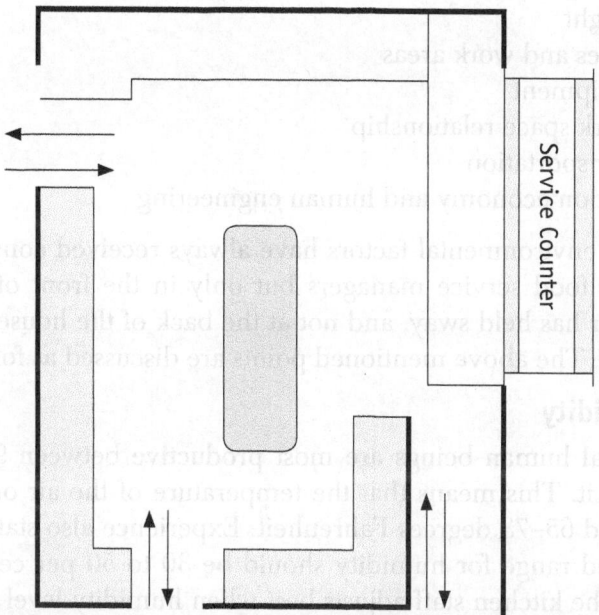

Figure 4.2g   Combined Shapes Kitchen

ENVIRONMENTAL CONDITIONS

It is of utmost importance that the environmental conditions be considered at length before initiating the exercise of kitchen planning. It is a well-established fact that living organisms perform better in proper environment. There is scientific data to back the fact that a cow yields more milk, and a hen lays better quality eggs when proper light and air are provided. Similarly, the productivity of human beings improves remarkably in proper environs. Thus, it becomes necessary for us in the food service operations to design and equip our kitchens in conformity with environmental conditions in which human productivity is at its best.

The following points should generally be considered as contributors to making the working conditions or the environment of the kitchen utterly convenient and comfortable to work in.

- Performance
- Temperature and humidity
- Lighting
- Colour
- Sound
- Odour
- Work area

- Height
- Aisles and work areas
- Equipment
- Work space relationship
- Transportation
- Motion economy and human engineering

These environmental factors have always received considerable attention from the food service managers but only in the front of house where the hotel user has held sway, and not at the back of the house where the food is prepared. The above mentioned points are discussed as follows:

Temperature and Humidity

In general human beings are most productive between 91 and 93 degrees Fahrenheit. This means that the temperature of the air or the room should be around 65–73 degrees Fahrenheit. Experience also states that though the prescribed range for humidity should be 30 to 50 per cent, in our country most of the kitchen staff adjusts best when humidity level is between 50 and 60 per cent. If the temperature gets above 85 degree Fahrenheit and relative humidity 70 per cent, productivity falls rapidly. High temperature and high humidity have a tendency towards increased accident rates, reluctance towards using standards, increased short tempers. According to a study, 50 per cent of the heat that comes into the kitchen never finds its way into the food. 'It is poured into the air where it boils the cook not the food.' As a general rule, a comfortable worker is usually a more careful one.

A solution to reducing heat loss in the kitchen is application of air conditioning systems. Hotels and restaurants that have air conditioned kitchens are known to be yielding 10 to 15 per cent better productivity and better product line. Insulation is also advisable as it reduces heat input into the fryer by 33 per cent and reduces heat radiation into the kitchen even more. Some more ways by which heat loss into the kitchen room can be prevented or decreased are:

- Insulated coffee urns
- Better venting of mechanical dishwasher
- Use of rapid heating, hard surfaced aluminum griddle

According to well known kitchen planning expert Richard Lambert, soft, yellow lights are attractive to kitchen staff and make the commis more productive.

The main thing to remember about colour is to get away from the depressing effect of hospital white. While it may seem to give the feeling of absolute cleanliness, it also gives an oppressive walled effect—an effect that would perhaps make the worker feel that he or she cannot wait to escape.

Sound

Too much sound in the kitchen also has an unnerving effect on the workers. If not properly controlled, noise becomes a leading cause of high sickness rates, mistakes and quarrelling. When noise becomes excessive, it continues to build up as people have to speak louder and louder to be heard over the humdrum. If the noise level persists between 80 and 90 decibels for a long time period, it causes deterioration in a worker's performance. In such cases the use of acoustic tiles are preferred. They help to reduce the noise level. Nowadays, acoustic paints are also available. Sound absorbing enclosures with glass wool or other absorbents similar to that used around noisy motors and compressors can be installed in the kitchen area. Asphalt or similar undercoating can be used on the underside of the preparation tables. Soft tiles can be used on the floor. Heavy plastic dishes dull the clatter and plastic dish racks also subdue noise. Refrigerator compressors can be located remotely. And usually most important of all, workers can be cautioned to talk rather than shout.

Odour

In most facilities, good air turnover and circulation within the work spaces are efficient enough such that odour does not become a problem for the food service workers as it does in a more close environment. Unpleasant odour can result in poor food intake, disturbed sleep, and even affect the mind. High humidity intensifies reaction to undesirable odours.

Work Space Relationship

There is a greater need to understand how much happier a cook would be when you are trying to work out the work-space relationship of the kitchen. There are some designers who do not consider the cook's interaction with the food inside and outside the cooking device. They seem to have an impression that cooking is a process that demands little more attention than placing the food into the device; and when the dish is done the cook gets around to it, takes the food out in an optimum cooked condition. Such is not the case. It is as important for a cook to face his food constantly as it is for a surgeon to face his patient. One never knows what is going to happen, and the cook must always be in a position to quickly note the unexpected happenings in order to prevent damage to the cooking food.

The Role of Human Engineering

The science of enhancing human productivity through control of the work-place or environment is known as 'human engineering' or 'human dynamics'. Its goals are improvement of work and human welfare. Simply put, it means adaptation of human work and working environment to the sensory, perpetual, mental, physical, and other attributes of human beings.

When a person works, he or she prefers to carry out the entire task as easily as possible in a set logical pattern with minimum physical and mental disturbance. Generally speaking, the operation or the chores should move from left to right (as the cook faces the equipment) because majority of people are right-handed. It has been found in motion studies that workers find it easy and comfortable to reach to the left for their raw material, operate on it in front of them with both hands, and deposit the finished product to their right.

Height   The height of the work table should be 37 to 39 inches where women work, and 41 inches for men. Heavy work tables should not be more than 36 inches in height. Each permanent work area should have definite places for every hand tool, condiment, and utensils that the worker can reach out and grasp them blindly as a matter of routine. All items should be placed between waist and shoulder height directly in front of the worker, with those tools used by the left hand side of the work area on the left, and those used by right hand placed on the right side. Particularly every thing used by the worker should be between 26 inches and 52 inches from the floor.

Those items below waist height should be on pull-out and those things stored above eye level should be on open shelves, preferably tilted forward. These provisions are desirable as human nature limits useful storage space to what a person can see from a standing position. In most cupboards of below waist height with fixed shelves, only 5–6 inches on the shelves can be used.

Thankfully, nowadays equipment are designed in such a manner that these fulfil all imaginable needs of the kitchen staff. A lot of human engineering is applied by equipment manufacturers to ensure that cooking becomes a pleasure for the kitchen staff. In spite of all these facts, the following points need to be considered while designing, fabricating, or selecting kitchen equipment:

- Use of a single indicating pointer is the least confusing. It should not cover any numbers in its movements and should be of a colour that contrasts sharply with the scale.
- All controls and displays should be above 32 inches from the floor so that workers do not have to bend to reach any control from the normal vertical body reach.
- There should be 10 gradations between numbers and the contrast between numbers or letters and the background should be stark.
- Temperature control should be on the right hand side.

It is no longer considered to be good human engineering now to do any heavy or repetitive lifting for carrying raw material, equipment or utensils. The wheels now have the carrying to do where the task is intermittent and the destination uncertain, and conveyors are used where the path and type of load is known and the trip is repetitive.

Motion economy The industrial engineer was one of the first to perceive the worker as a mechanical component of the manufacturing process. If maximum efficiency was to be achieved in their services, it was necessary to have a complete understanding of their physical and mental attributes and limitations so as to plan the tasks around their knowledge and skills.

The following are some of the basic elements of motion economy, the grand-old-daddy of industrial engineering, which would help you to understand their applications to the subject we have been discussing.

1. Both hands should begin as well as complete their motions at the same time.
2. Hands should not be idle except during rest periods.
3. Motion of arms should be made simultaneously and in opposite and symmetrical directions.
4. Motion sequence that has fewest basic divisions of accomplishments is best for performing a given task.
5. Hands should be relieved of all work which can be performed more advantageously by the feet or other parts of the body.
6. Tools, materials and controls should be located in an arc around work space and as close to the worker as possible.
7. Tools and materials should be pre-positioned to eliminate searching and selecting.
8. Two or more tools should be positioned together, wherever possible.
9. Wherever applicable, height of work space and chair should be arranged so that sitting and standing at work is possible.

DEVELOPING KITCHEN PLANS

Before any kitchen plan can be developed, it is important to follow four main steps discussed as under.

Step 1

Formulate a list of activities that are to be performed in the kitchen. In the process of scheduling, the activities may be organized into a 'production cycle' which shows the sequence in which the listed activities are to be performed.

Step 2

Each part of the production cycle is then broken up into 'jobs' or 'tasks' which need to be performed in a particular order to achieve the objective of food service establishments. For example, if the menu for a canteen consists of small cakes, hot and cold beverages, a plated meal and sandwiches, each activity can be broken down into specific 'tasks' for every item on the menu.

Step 3

Once the tasks have been defined, one has to think of the simplest ways in which they can be performed.

Step 4

The tasks are then arranged in a sequence so that one task can smoothly follow another to establish what is termed as 'work flow' in any operation. In other words, the work planned to be in the domain of the kitchen space flows from one area of activity to another with the least expenditure of time and energy.

Trends Stemming from Modern Day Economic Challenges

The modern hotels are complex facilities which aim at yield management that is maximization of profits through optimum utilization of resources. In order to do so they have to comply with the prevailing trends. They aim at the fulfilment of the guests' needs with maximum precision, resulting in quality service and a satisfied customer. These trends emphasize on the following:

- Greater mechanization.
- Simpler operations.
- Increased use of 'convenience' foods.
- Use of new commodities (for example, vegetable protein, or increased use of low cost protein (e.g. 'new' types of fish: coaly, blue whiting, etc.).
- Development of new cooking appliances and methods.
- Reduced size of food production areas (kitchens).
- Use of conveyors to save on staff, who previously carried or wheeled items from place to place. Conveyors may also deal with dirty crockery particularly where customers clear their own tables. A conveyor can then be integrated into a system feeding crockery into the dishwasher. More applications for conveyors are possible in field service within kitchens and food preparation areas.
- Greater emphasis on marketing and merchandising is reflected in selling prices based less on meal production costs and more on value to customers of the total food service offered.
- Development of specialties either of dishes or form of service imparting a character to an establishment.
- Luxury hotels and restaurants may appear to be the least affected by these considerations, but even at their level, the kitchens are designed to deal with higher paid and scarcer staff. Coffee shops, especially restaurants, self serving and self help buffets are some manifestations of change. This is reflected in kitchen plans which involve fewer staff and more prepared commodities.

SUMMARY

If we in the food service industry are to put out high quality food at reasonable prices, we must hold on to our good men and obtain maximum productivity from them. This can be achieved with an enlightened management coupled with maintenance of a pleasant working environment and an efficient kitchen design to make the best use of each worker's physical and mental capabilities. The basic considerations of kitchen planning are discussed but a careful thought is to be given to your conceptual skills. There is a myth about kitchen design that entrepreneurs generally start working on their own without taking advice from experts in this field. More often than not such designing of the kitchen proves to be an obstacle to the growth of catering business. Depending on the space available and allocated, various configurations of kitchen designs have crystallized over the years. These provide useful tips on space utility and motion economy for the food preparation staff. Mostly kitchens are located on the back side of food and beverage service facility and generally neglected with respect to environmental conditions even though it makes a vast difference in the efficiency of a kitchen worker. So always consider the role of environment on the efficiency of kitchen staff. Human engineering too plays an important role in designing a proper kitchen layout.

CONCEPT REVIEW QUESTIONS

1. Enumerate the points to be considered while planning for a kitchen.
2. Why is there a need to take advice from the chef while designing a kitchen facility?
3. Illustrate the work flow in a kitchen and discuss its importance in kitchen layout.
4. With the help of neat diagrams, suggest possible kitchen configurations.
5. Discuss environmental conditions which affect kitchen planning.
6. Write short notes on the following:
   (a) Lighting of the kitchen
   (b) Noise control in the kitchen
   (c) Human engineering
   (d) Floor finishes
   (e) Production cycle

PROJECT ASSIGNMENTS

1. Discuss the details of the kitchen given in the following diagram.

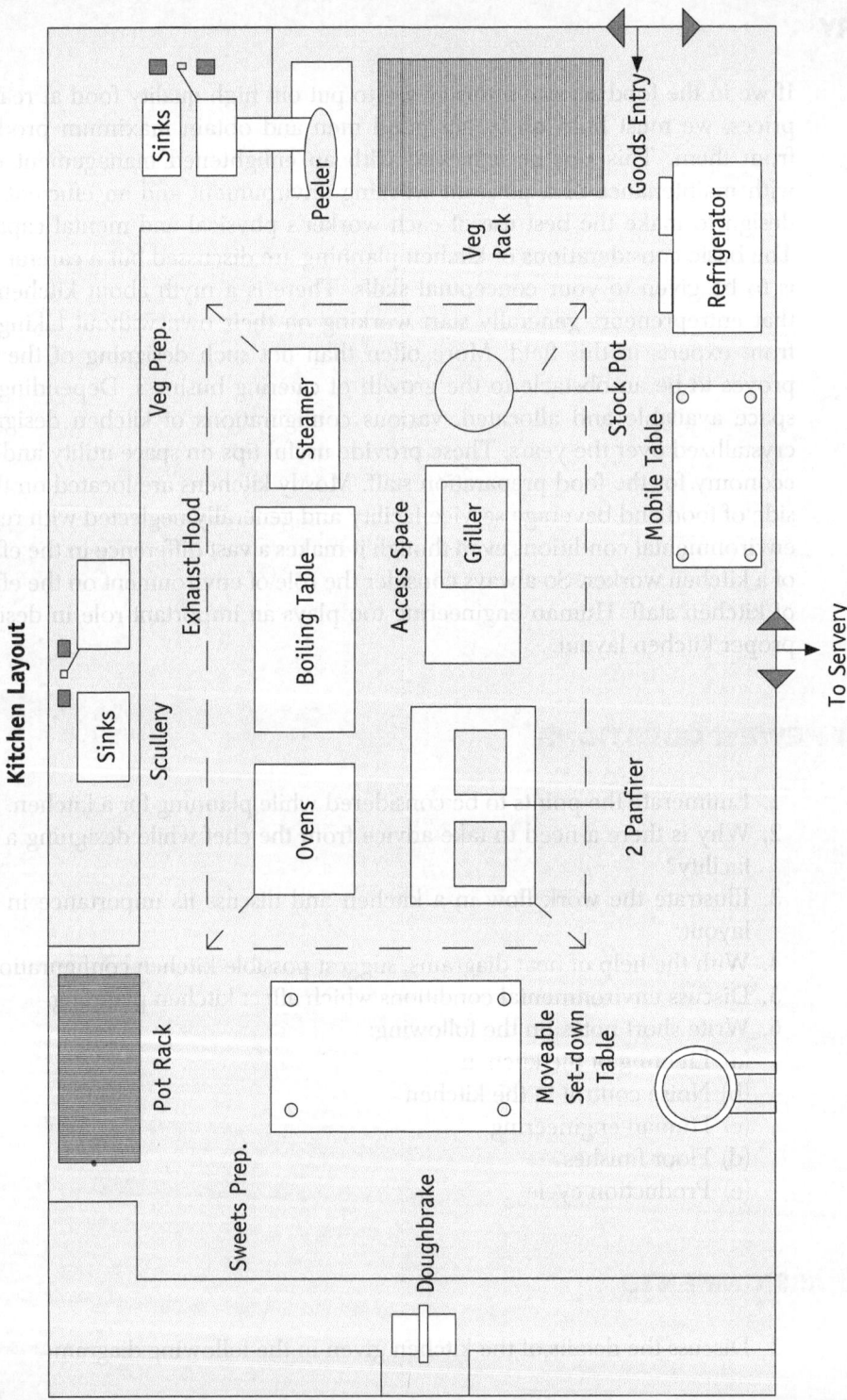

Figure 4.3   Diagram for Project Assignment

2. Visit a kitchen in a five star hotel of your city and determine its merits and demerits keeping in view the work flow.
3. Plan a kitchen for a 100 cover Indian specialty restaurant.
4. Visit a kitchen of a large hospital and compare it with the kitchens of five star hotels.
5. Prepare a report on why you want to redesign the kitchen of your institute.
6. Prepare a comparative report on fast food kitchens located in your city.
7. Organize a seminar on 'Effects of changing food technology on kitchen planning'.

REFERENCES

Dana, Arthur W. (1988), *Kitchen Planning for Quantity Food Service*, Harper and Bros., New York.

Kinton and Ceserani (1980), *Theory of Catering*, Fourth edition, Edward Arnold Publishers Ltd, London.

Morel, J.J. (1957), *Scientific Catering in Hotel Operations*, Isaac Pitman, London.

Salmon, Geoffrey (1967), *Storage*, Design Centre, Macdonald and Co., London.

Scriven, Carl and James Stevens (1989), *Food Equipment Facts*, Van Nostrand Reinhold, New York.

Sethi, Mohini and Surjieet Malhan (1984), *Catering Management,* Willey Eastern Limited, New Delhi.

Swanson, Bettye B. (1981), *Introduction to Home Management*, Macmillan, New York.

Watson, Olive B. (1968), *School and Institutional Lunchroom Management*, Parker, New York.

West-Wood and V.F. Harger (1977), *Food Service in Institutions*, Fifth edition, John Wiley, New York.

CHAPTER 5

Specifications for Equipment, Ventilation, and Kitchen Safety

Chapter Outline:

The following topics are covered in this chapter
- Features of a good kitchen
- Floor finishes
- Modes of ventilation
- Designing for safety
- Care and maintenance
- Checklist of equipment for commercial kitchen
- Specification for kitchen equipment

Learning Objectives:

This chapter will enable you to understand
- The features of a good kitchen and compute the list of kitchen equipment
- What the specifications for kitchen equipment are
- Safety measures in kitchen design
- The maintenance schedule of large kitchen equipment

INTRODUCTION

The kitchen being one of the most important components of the hospitality industry should receive its due importance in the early stages of construction itself. Often caterers complain that kitchen seems to be added to hotels or hospitals as an afterthought and is given insufficient or the least attention in early planning stages. Not without reason. Many a time it is seen that a poor kitchen location with respect to the building renders efficient designing and planning very difficult.

As far as possible, the kitchen should be adjacent to the service area, and preferably in one corner of a building, in the north-west direction. This provides two side walls for windows and free access to air and natural light. A corner location also makes it convenient for the purpose of receiving supplies and removal of garbage. The kitchen should be situated over the ground to avoid flooding, drainage backflow, and unnecessary expenses on artificial lighting and ventilation. In basement areas the humidity and heat of kitchen render it prone to dampness, and insect and pest infestation.

FEATURES OF A GOOD KITCHEN

A good kitchen is one in which drainage, electricity, gas connections, and water supply systems are properly installed and taken care of. These are generally provided for before the equipment is installed, although ideally, according to experts of kitchen designing 'the kitchen structure should be built around the equipment and service.' Apart from these essentials, proper lighting, ventilation, design and finish of floors, walls, ceilings and work surface, are features that contribute to the making of a good kitchen or cooking facility. Last, but not the least, the structure must be safe, and provide hygienic and sanitary conditions for those who work in it.

Drainage

The efficiency of the drainage system determines the hygiene and sanitation of the kitchen environment to a large extent. Poor drainage leads to contamination of food with dire consequences. Problems can arise in drainage areas when fat and grease gets collected in the drains restricting the flow of water. All kitchens should, therefore, be fitted with grease traps on all drainage inlets to prevent backflow or blockage. Taking care of this aspect of drainage during the layout planning can prevent unnecessary expenses in clearing blocked drains during the course of operation of the catering establishment. Drains should be at least 10 to 15 cm in diameter.

Electricity and Gas Connections

Electricity and gas points to be provided in a kitchen must coincide with the plan of equipment in the kitchen and future plans for use. Therefore, once the placement of work centres is established and a list of equipment to be used at each centre formulated, the number of gas and electricity connections required can be determined.

Depending on the size of the catering unit, the requirements may vary from one power point and two light points as in a kiosk, to three power and four light points as in the case of a cafeteria kitchen, which may need to use a refrigerator, a mixer, and a juicer, in addition to lighting the area of display for food and dining. For larger kitchens, it is safer and more economical to have a pipeline gas supply which is metered as in the case of electricity, thus avoiding the inconvenience of gas cylinders getting empty in the middle of food preparation. Gas cylinders may be used by very small establishments where the menu does not feature many cooked items. For such establishments it would suffice to provide an inlet from the cylinder to the work top to be positioned correctly for use.

Cabinets must be designed below the work surface to place the cylinder out of sight and away from the source of heat and dirt. Gadgets are now available in the market which when fixed on cylinders can indicate the quantity of fuel in them, so that a replacement can be arranged before it is exhausted.

All pipeline arrangements and wiring should preferably be concealed in the walls, flooring, or ceilings. Any unconcealed sections must be properly insulated and earthed, both for economy and safety. It is wise to make provision for more than one type of fuel in the kitchen to cope with failure and shortages.

Water Supply

In large kitchens, provision for both hot and cold running water is necessary. This has to be made at the structural stage itself. For smaller kitchens, arrangements for fitting a water heater above sink units may be sufficient, whereas in kiosks and coffee shops provisions for the installation of instant water heaters connected to the normal plumbing proves quite effective.

All water supply into kitchens must be from purified sources. Non-purified sources may be used only to wash out swill bins. Overhead water pipes should be avoided as they collect dirt and cause water of condensation to drop on the work areas. All pipes should preferably be concealed. Where storage tanks are necessary, they should be covered and easy to clean periodically. Separate provision for drinking water is necessary where the public supply is not satisfactory, as in most tropical climates.

Floors

Kitchen flooring should be smooth but not slippery, hardwearing, free from joints, not easily damaged by spillage, easy to clean, and preferably in dark plain colours which do not show patches easily. Choice should also take into account appearance and durability.

There are a number of flooring materials available in the market. It is a good policy to avoid any type of tiles as they require a number of joints which are not easy to clean. A comparison of different floor covering is indicated in Table 5.1.

Walls

Hard plaster with an emulsion finish is most suitable because it is smooth and easy to clean as it is without joints that may harbour dirt. Ordinary emulsion

Table 5.1 Comparison of Different Floor Finishes

Flooring	Merits and Demerits
Vinyl	Vinyl sheets are better than tiles.
Plastic	This material is less hard wearing, gets soft with heat, and is, therefore, unsuitable for kitchens.
Rubber	Sheet rubber is easily damaged by spillage, which is a common feature in kitchens. It also gets easily cut with the movement of trolleys or the falling of sharp tools and is, therefore, not generally recommended. Rubber which is ribbed, studded, or patterned is quite hard wearing, and suitable for flooring. May be used effectively where a lot of mobile equipment is not installed, and moved around.
Linoleum	This is smooth and easy to clean, stands wear and tear well. Linoleum is also available in a number of colours land patterns. Dark plain colours are preferable as they do not show patches easily, but at the same time any spillage is visible and should promptly be cleared up.
Floor finishes	A number of floor finishes are available which render the surface easy to clean, make it non-corrosive to the action of mild acids and alkalies generally used in the kitchens.
Terrazzo	This floor covering is expensive, but good.
Tiles	Many types of tiles are available in the market. The non-inflammable ones may be considered for use in kitchens where finishing of foods is the major activity. The only disadvantage is that they crack easily and need to be replaced frequently. The disadvantage of using tiles in general has been pointed out. Tiles are available in cork, ceramic or vinyl and even metal for use on ceiling, covered steam hoods, walls, etc.
Bricks	Well-laid bricks to give a smooth surface to floors, can provide good kitchen flooring as they are hard wearing, washable, and quite comfortable to the feet. They have a pleasant colour and a natural look.

paints are not washable, and removing marks or stains could smudge the wall. Gloss paints are washable, but tend to show faults in old plaster work. In areas where the wall is near steam equipment, a plastic finish is better than tiles as it is non-absorbent and condensation from steam does not damage the surface. Enamel and oil paints are also hardwearing. Any particular type of finish cannot be specified for a kitchen because the manager of the kitchen must decide what properties should be given priority. Each wall covering has its own plus and minus points. Whatever the choice, the walls should be smooth, easy to clean, and impervious to moisture.

Ceilings

Any finish on the ceiling should be heat resistant and not affected by steam or gases. A plaster paint finish is most suitable, though it requires frequent redoing. Gloss paints, on ceilings, however, cause condensation and effect humidity in the kitchen, making working conditions uncomfortable as also unhygienic. If one can afford them, acoustical ceilings are important for absorbing kitchen noise.

In general, while choosing finishing for walls, floors, and ceilings, it would help to remember that dark colours reduce the level of illumination and affect visibility in kitchens. It is also a good policy to invest on quality for long-lasting effects.

Work Surface

All work surfaces should be hard-wearing, smooth, and impervious. Stainless steel is by far the best among work surfaces in the kitchens, though the initial cost is much more than of any other surface topping. Work surface can be covered with laminated plastics, hardwood, or ceramic tiles, with some sections in marble or stainless steel to reduce the cost. Laminated plastic is relatively easy to maintain and not very costly, but it needs to be inspected at regular intervals and replaced if it begins to lift at places. Hardwood work surfaces are a good option, but they need a lacquered finish to be practical in an institutional kitchen. They also get easily stained and marked, and are expensive to install and maintain.

Marble though expensive is ideal as a work surface for food preparation work, because of its hardwearing and hygienic qualities, and also its beauty. It is, however, impractical for small establishments that could go in for simulated marble, which is also a very practical work surface for food preparation activity.

No surface, however, can be protected from knife marks and, therefore, a separate wooden surface or board is a must in any work area where sharp implements need to be used.

Lighting

Kitchen lighting should be designed purely to give the best possible illumination. In addition to overall lightings, fittings need to be placed directly above work tables and food preparation areas. At times, the hoods placed above cookers may interfere with the placement of light fittings.

Types of lighting

Fluorescent lamps Fluorescent lighting is more economical to use than filament lamps, because even though the initial cost is more, their maintenance cost is low. Fluorescent lighting lasts almost six times as much as filament bulbs and gives three to six times more illumination for the same power consumption.

The colour effect of fluorescent lighting is correlated to the colour temperature. High efficiency fluorescent tubes reaching a temperature of 3,000 to 4,300 K do not give particularly good colour effects, and are not recommended for use in kitchens, dining or storage areas where the colour of the food could be masked. Those tubes which do not give a better light output than the high efficiency fittings are better for their colour rendering properties, and therefore more suitable.

Mercury lamps These may be used in kitchens, and are available in ranges of 80-W to 400-W capacities. The colour, appearance, illumination, and life are nearly similar to white fluorescent tube lamps. Enclosed fittings giving diffused light provide greater comfort to eyes, are safer, and also easier to clean. The seal also protects the lamp from moisture and dirt. These fittings can also be easily fixed to false ceilings.

The recommended lighting per square metre of floor area is 30-watts if fluorescent lights are used. If filament lamps are preferred, 80-watts per square metre area are considered optimum. The illumination recommended for performing a task is 500 fluxes. The mounting height should not be less than 2.4 metres above the floor, and the fittings not more than 2.2 metres apart. Additional lighting is necessary under steam canopies; any equipment used should be of rustproof material and be able to withstand moisture and heat.

All fittings should be arranged over work surfaces and not behind the workers. Strip lights should be parallel to the surface and not at right angles to prevent shadows falling onto the work surface.

Ventilation

Ventilation in kitchens is very important to prevent the process of condensation, that is, droplets of moisture forming on equipment, food, surfaces, etc. Condensation leads to formation of moulds and bacteria, resulting in contamination of food. Good ventilation helps to replace oxygen used by workers during respiration, and sets up a current of fresh air which drives out kitchen odours, fumes, etc. through suitable outlets. It also eliminates excessive heat from the cooking environment, regulating the temperature and making the work place more comfortable. In kitchens catering to large numbers, insufficient attention paid to good ventilation and introduction of fresh air into food preparation area, is mainly responsible for the unnecessary high temperature of the working environment. Proper ventilation is not only important for a fresh and comfortable environment, but is also vital to the preparation and provisions of safe and healthy food, and through it the health of the customers.

Modes of ventilation

Windows While windows provide an inlet for fresh air, they also open the kitchen to insects, flies, and dust. They are, therefore, not sufficient as a means of ventilation. To be useful, windows need to be fitted with fly-proof shutters, which not only keep out the flies but also prevent draughts of air from affecting the kitchen work.

Ventilator hoods These are generally of two types and can be used in food service kitchens to produce negative kitchen pressure. Ventilation hoods are fitted near the ceiling in the walls. They are designed to suck out the air from the kitchen, which then gets replaced with fresh air from an inlet placed in position for the purpose. The area is wire meshed on the outside to make it fly proof. It must also be equipped with a grease filter which should be cleaned everyday (see Figure 5.1).

Nowadays canopy exhaust hoods are very common. Each ventilator hood must be connected to one large central duct receiving exhaust air from several ventilator hoods. Separate fire control units are highly recommended for these units. Ventilation systems require fans and duct openings in the ventilated rooms.

Calculation of heat generation and requirement of ventilation Computation of ventilation requirement is done depending on the amount of heat generated. The following examples will help us understand how ventilation requirement is computed.

Example one A commercial kitchen is 30 feet wide, 50 feet long, and 10 feet in height. Five appliances are in operation and are not ventilated to the outside. All appliances are electrical in nature and operate for at least 2 hours daily.

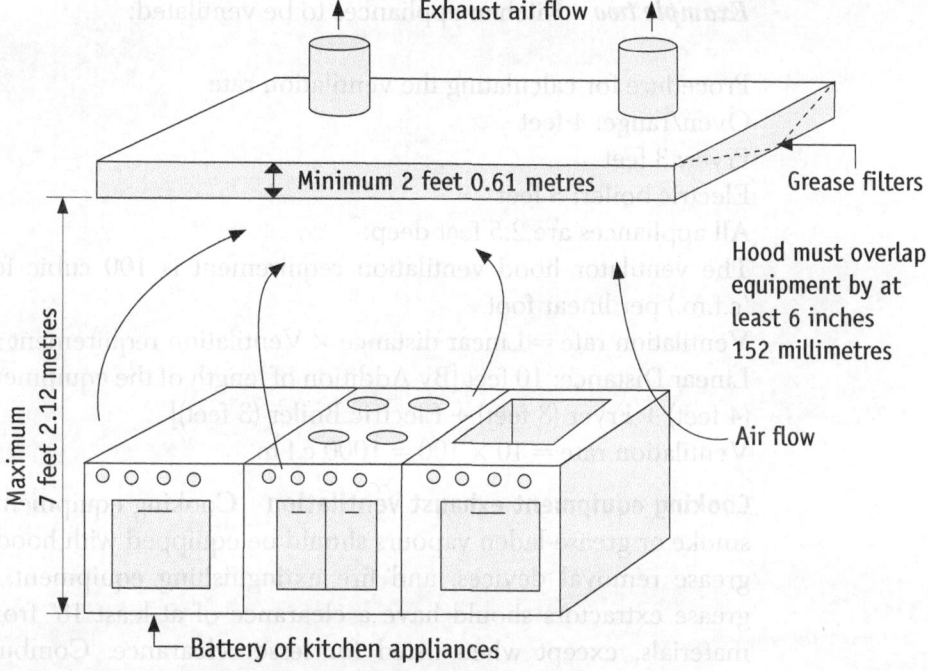

Figure 5.1   Schematic Diagram of Placement of Ventilator Hoods in a Kitchen

The appliances are

Hot Plate Dispenser: 1,000 watts
Oven: 4,000 watts
Fryer: 5,000 watts
Electric boiler: 1,000 watts
Kitchen light: 3,000 watts
Total gain of heat = 14,000 watts or 3,412 × 14 = 47,710 BTU (1,000 watt = 3,412 BTU)
The initial temperature of the kitchen is 18.3°C or 65°F

Final kitchen temperature = (Initial temperature) + Heat gain/0.018 × (Volume of kitchen)

Final kitchen temperature = 65 + 47710/0.018 × 15000 = 176.9°F
(**0.018** is a constant that reflects the density and specific heat of air)
176.9°F = 94.72°C (By applying conversion formula
9C = 5(F–32).

Example two   Kitchen appliances to be ventilated:

Procedure for calculating the ventilation rate
Oven/range: 4 feet
Fryer: 3 feet
Electric boiler: 3 feet
All appliances are 2.5 feet deep.
The ventilator hood ventilation requirement is 100 cubic feet per minute (c.f.m.) per linear foot.
Ventilation rate = Linear distance × Ventilation requirement rate
Linear Distance: 10 feet [By Addition of length of the equipment Oven Range (4 feet) + Fryer (3 feet) + Electric Boiler (3 feet)]
Ventilation rate = 10 × 100 = 1000 c.f.m.

Cooking equipment exhaust ventilation   Cooking equipment that produces smoke or grease-laden vapours should be equipped with hood, duct systems, grease removal devices, and fire extinguishing equipment. Hoods, ducts-grease extractors should have a clearance of at least 18″ from combustible materials, except when listed for lesser clearance. Combustible material should be protected to the satisfaction of authorities having the jurisdiction.

Structural features for installation of ventilation hood   The following points should be considered while going in for the installation of ventilation hoods.

1. Hoods should be constructed of and supported by metal not less than: 20 gauge stainless steel, or 18 gauge stainless steel, or other material of equivalent strength, fire and corrosion resistance. All seams and joints should have a liquid light continuous external weld.
2. Canopy hoods should completely cover equipment plus an over hang of at least 6″ on the sides of equipment not adjacent to walls.
3. Distance between floor and lower edge should not exceed 7 feet.
4. Depth from lower to upper edge should be at least 2 feet.
5. Duct systems should not be interconnected with any other ventilating system.
6. Where ducts pass through partition or walls of combustible materials, clearance to the ducts should be not less than 18″.
7. Ducts should not pass through fire walls or partitions.
8. Each duct should serve only one floor.
9. Ducts should be installed without forming dips or traps, which might collect residues, except when clean-out traps are provided for continuous removal of residue.

10. Air velocity through duct should not be less than 1,500 feet per minute.

11. Ducts should terminate as follows:

    - At least 10 feet from adjacent buildings, property lines, air intake, etc.
    - With direction of air flow exhaust away from roof surface; if not possible, a metal pan shall be provided to catch residue.
    - With discharge at least 40″ clearance from outlet of roof surface, ducts may terminate at exterior of wall provided that fire in duct cannot be transmitted to adjacent facilities.

12. Grease removal devices should be provided and consist of one of the following:

    - Extractors
    - Filters or removal devices

13. Construction of the installation should be with non-combustible materials.

Note: Exhaust air volumes should be of sufficient level to provide for capture and removal of grease vapours.

Benchmarks for determining air exhaust volume requirements

✓ Wall hoods (open to three sides), 100 c.f.m. per square feet of hood area [Figure 5.2(a)].

✓ Island hoods (open to all four sides) 150 c.f.m. per square foot of hood area [Figure 5.2(b)].

✓ Non-canopy 300 c.f.m. per linear foot of hood, if hood is pre-fabricated type and the hood manufacturer recommends otherwise.

Figure 5.2(a) Wall Hood

Figure 5.2(b) Island Hood

1. Replacement air quantity should be adequate to prevent negative air pressures from exceeding .02″ water column.
2. Dampers should not be installed in ducts or duct system except when specifically listed for such use or used as part of a listed device or system. Wiring of any type should not be installed in ducts.
3. Motors, lights, and other electrical devices should not be installed in ducts or in the path of exhaust except when specifically approved for such use.
4. Fume incinerators, thermal recovery units, air pollution control devices may be installed in ducts or hoods or path of travel of exhaust when specifically approved for such use and should not increase fire hazard.
5. Approved fire extinguishing equipment should be provided for duct systems, grease removal devices, hoods.
6. Exhaust systems should be operated during all periods of cooking time. Filter equipped exhaust systems should not be operated with filters removed.
7. Opening for replacing air exhausted through ventilating equipment should not be restricted by covers, dampers, or anything that could reduce the operating efficiency of exhaust systems.
8. Hood, grease removal devices, fans, and ducts should be cleaned at frequent intervals to avoid contamination by grease and oily sludge.
9. Depending on cooking equipment usage, the entire exhaust system including grease extractors should be inspected daily or weekly. When evidence of grease or residue deposits is sighted, the system should be cleaned.
10. Inspection of fire extinguishing system should be done every 6 months.

Benchmarks for compensating hoods These hoods are designed to supply from 60 per cent to 80 per cent of make up air requirements. Generally, 20 per cent of the air supplied should be forced through the double wall in front of the hood and directed towards the filter. The remaining 60 per cent should be forced down through the double wall at the back and out through the upward turned opening just above the cooking range. This strong upward jet flow of air draws the heat and fumes from the cooking surface by venturing (pressure) action. The remaining 20 per cent of required make up air must be supplied from the kitchen.

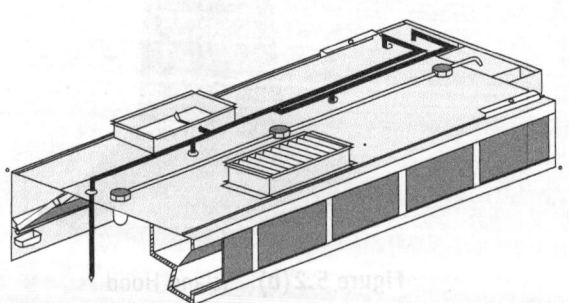

Figure 5.3 Compensating Hood

Designing for Fire Safety

While designing a kitchen it is vital to make provision for fire-fighting equipment at convenient points with reference to work areas which carry a high fire hazard potential, such as cooking areas, electrical danger zones, etc. In small establishments it may mean only one fire extinguisher; nevertheless the awareness of its need is essential. Also alarm systems must be incorporated while designing kitchens.

Accidents could result from a number of causes—physical, psychological, or environmental—leading to falls, cuts, shocks, burns, collision at work, etc. These may be classified into the following main categories:

- Structural inadequacy
- Improper equipment placement
- Improper installation
- Improper working habits
- Nature and behaviour of people
- Improper maintenance
- Improper storage

Safety practices   In all premises it is important to plan structures with safety in mind. The following are some useful tips in this regard.

- First aid facilities should be made available.
- Fire extinguishers and exits need to be asked for use in case of emergencies.
- All electric motorized equipment should be sealed.
- Pressure equipment must have safety valves.
- All switches need to be labelled and situated in a position from where they can be switched off by anyone in emergency.
- Sinks with taps should be fitted in positions from where water always splashes when used.
- Practise good working habits such that newcomers can learn by observing others who handle electricity or gas, instead of formal instructions.

Safety procedure   A safety procedure for any food service establishment may be clearly spelt out as follows:

(a) The controls for all kinds of fuel supplies must be located within easy reach.

(b) Spaces where fuel in loaded gas cylinders are stored need to be guarded and isolated from possible sources of ignition and short circuit.

(c) Mark all broken or chipped glassware to indicate that they are to be put out of use. It is wise to store them in metal containers for disposal.

A record of these may indicate certain designs that are more prone to breakage than others. They can then be discontinued for purchase.

(d) Oven pads must be provided for lifting food out of ovens or from the top of hot ranges.

(e) Regular training and retraining of staff must be planned to inculcate safety in their work methods, and develop a consciousness of the dangers that can result from a single careless act. Quite a few accidents are caused through ignorance of the perils accompanying the use of specialized equipment.

(f) Regular maintenance procedures must be set up for upkeep of premises and equipment to keep them in safe working order.

(g) Every work area should contain aids which remind people of safety, such as posters communicating right and wrong working methods, e.g., 'Now wash your hands' put up at entrances to kitchen and service areas.

(h) Provision must be made at convenient points in the establishment to install fire extinguishers and alarms in case of an emergency. It is not enough to demonstrate their use to employees once in a while, but regular fire drills must be built into the routine of every person so that the alarm is recognized and corrective measures are taken following it.

(i) It is good practice to invite experts from fire fighting departments to demonstrate the use of fire-fighting equipment, and make suggestions to improve the safety of the premises by using latest equipment in the field of safety.

(j) All accidents which have occurred should be reviewed periodically with employees so that action can be taken to avoid them in future. Records help to assess the frequency of particular types of accidents and plan remedial action.

(k) While recruiting staff, safety should be kept in mind, so that accident-prone people can be screened in the process.

(l) Provide safe tools and equipment, safety clothing, and footwear in work areas.

(m) Institute awards for departments for every accident-free month.

(n) Provision of first aid facilities in each area of work.

While a safety procedure may be available in a catering establishment, its practice is often unknown. This is because a procedure is generalized to cover all personnel and departments, and ends up in the files of managers. It needs to be translated into simple instructions to be followed in each area of activity, so that it is understood by those for whom it is meant. An example of such instructions for kitchen staff is given in Box 5.1. It would be more effective

Box 5.1   Checklist for Safety Procedure

1. Keep all areas clean and dry at all times.
2. Wash hands with soap and water before touching food and equipment.
3. Dry hands completely before touching electric plugs.
4. Keep all knives on drain boards for washing and not in the sink.
5. Keep matches covered in metal containers.
6. Light matches before turning on gas.
7. Wipe spillage, especially oil, immediately.
8. Do not overfill pans with hot liquids.
9. Store cold fat away from open sources of heat.
10. Carry cartons and equipment on trolleys, or on shoulders to prevent spinal injury.
11. If you have to walk with a knife in hand, ensure that its tip is pointed downward.
12. Stock top shelves of cupboards with light objects and those without sharp edges.
13. Walk at work, do not run.
14. Do not sit on broken stools, or use defective or unsafe tools.
15. Turn off all taps and electric switches before closing up work.
16. Do not store detergents along with food.
17. Never pour water on a 'fat or oil fire', it only gets worse. Cover with lid or blanket to cut out the air.
18. Do not rely completely on automatic controls, check equipment for over heating.

Box 5.2   Safety Checklist for Any Food Operation

- Are floor in safe condition?
- Is there a proper rack for holding garbage containers?
- Are adequate tools available for opening crates, barrels, cartons, etc. (hammer, wire cutter, card board carton openers, and pliers)?
- Is there a bypass device on the door to permit exit if an employee is locked in?
- Is adequate aisle space provided?
- Are blower fans properly guarded?
- Are portable storage racks in safe condition?
- Is the refrigerant in the refrigerator non-toxic?
- Are electrical switches located so that they can be reached readily in the event of an emergency?
- Do cutters and choppers have effective guard?

in its impact on employees if the instructions relevant to each area of activity were sorted and pasted in the respective areas within clear view of each worker. For example, Box 5.2 would be very handy for the staff involved in food preparation activity.

While it may seem a complicated or tedious task to put safety measures into practice, lack of a procedure in the establishment can lead to heavy losses. Apart from the costs of repairing damaged property or replacing equipment, there are the costs of medical expenses for employees hurt in accidents, loss of man-hours in production, plus excessive wages paid to staff. In addition, in serious cases legal costs can ruin an enterprise. The most damaging of all is the loss of reputation of an establishment which can never recover its image because lack of safety is always associated with inefficiency.

Training of safety   The training in safety should be designed for all people of an organization, irrespective of their positions or job profiles. This is vital because managers can only build safety into the establishment if their own awareness of it is aroused. All efforts to introduce safety procedures can fail if a manger walks into an area marked 'No smoking' with a cigarette in his mouth. The best method of teaching is by example, and it is, therefore, only right to expect supervisors to be trained before expecting those under their care to work safely.

Employees should be encouraged to come up with ideas for inculcating safety into work methods, and best ideas should be put into practice and awarded.

Training staff for safety may seem an unnecessary expense, but these costs are worthwhile, compared to the costs that have to be incurred when accidents take place. Training in safety can be organized under three distinct categories: safety education, enforcement of safety and inspection routine.

Safety education   Safety programmes and policies can only be effective if the staff is trained to think and act safely at work. For this, educating them in the following areas is necessary:

- Teaching safe methods, with particular emphasis on areas of potential danger, and how these can be guarded against.
- Demonstrating the use of safety equipment installed in the establishment, and location and use of first aid material.
- Inculcating in people the ability to recognize the signs of hazards around them.
- Teaching staff the legal implications of non-adherence to safety procedures.

The best time to start educating an employee in safety is during their induction into the establishment, so that every new employee is well versed in the safety procedures and policies of the establishment before they actually start their job. Teaching safe ways of performing different tasks, particularly, while on the job; making people aware of the dangers of carelessness and irresponsible behaviour at work; and the ways in which to tackle emergent situations, are all important for the safety of people at work, and the safety of the establishment. The regular practice of fire drills helps to make the staff aware of danger signals and react promptly without panic. The formation of safety committees has been found to be very effective in safety education, because of the participation of all staff in a department. The legal and financial implications of accidents should be taught to all employees.

Enforcement of safety   Safety regulations need to be enforced through the following.

- Discipline at work.
- By close supervision of all activities in vulnerable areas and at peak hours.
- Closing all switches of fuel supply and water taps when not in use.
- Immediate attention to repair of leaks and regular maintenance and servicing of equipment to ensure optimum operation.

Any discussion on 'safety' of the people and their work environment would be incomplete without a mention of the hazards caused by theft and pilferage. A food service establishment therefore, needs to be well guarded to provide security for the employees and the organization. The areas most vulnerable to theft are the stores, where daily use items are stocked in large quantities and provide temptation to the staff. While small pilferage is accepted as normal where people are handling, cooking, and serving food, when these exceed 5 per cent (which is normally accounted for as natural wastage) they make the difference between profit and loss.

The following precautions are necessary to safeguard stocks and minimize thefts:

- The storage areas must always be kept locked unless stores are being issued.
- Issues must be made at fixed times only and at no time during working hours should the place be left unattended.
- Minimum staff should operate stores, depending on the size of the establishment.
- Keys must be kept securely by only one person, who is responsible for the stores.
- In case of emergency, such as a fire, the person responsible should be informed.
- It is important to provide iron doors to all stores and there should be only one door used by staff for entry and exit.
- Security guards are desirable, who can look after the security of the whole premises after working hours.

As far as security of the kitchen and service areas is concerned, a safety procedure for checking all people entering and leaving the catering department is a precaution against theft of already issued items and small equipment and tools.

Inspection routine Periodic inspection of the facilities and departments in itself serve as an important proactive safety measure. Inspections can either be

1. Quick, and cursory inspection; or
2. Detailed inspections; generally commencing at the farthest point and working back. For various work areas it could include the following:

    (a) *Refuse storage areas* This should include checking the general condition of bins and area, evidence of rodents, frequency of collection, etc.

    (b) *Outside drainage* In this leakage and blockage, evidence of overflowing cistern, yard gullies, etc. can be checked.

    (c) *Staff sanitary accommodation* It should be checked whether staff sanitary accommodation is adequate and in a safe condition, separated from food rooms, there is proper ventilation and hand washing facilities, clothing lockers, provision of notice boards for instructions, etc. are in proper shape.

    (d) *Food storage accommodation* The things to be looked for here are ventilation, rodent and insect evidence, condition of products, codes, storage of non-food products, etc.

    (e) *Kitchen* It should include the kitchen in general, wall, floor, ceiling.

        (i) Ventilation of entire area.

        (ii) Lighting.

        (iii) *Food preparation areas* Condition of sinks—whether adequate; potato peeler, other equipment, pastry preparation, mixers, can openers, drawers for knives, etc.

        (iv) *Cooking areas* Conditions of stoves, ovens, etc. pots and pans, hoods and extracts, especially filters, lighting handling cloths.

        (v) *Storage in the kitchen* Refrigerator and freezer, check temperatures, plate and equipment storage, drawers.

        (vi) *Personal washing facilities* Toilets and change rooms; any evidence of recent use.

        (vii) *Servery areas* Storage of food, temperatures, hot plates, bain-marie, protection of open food, display of food, labeling, check ice-cream fridge, cupboards under counters, chill cabinets conditions of plates, cutlery, etc.

        (viii) *Wash-up area* Plate and crockery, use of machines, detergents, drying racks, tea cloths, sterilizer, pot wash, sinks-adequate, drainage space, waste pipes grease traps, etc.

(f) *Areas likely to create accident hazards*   These include stairs, handrails, floor surfaces, spillage, use of step ladders, electric points, guarding of dangerous machine, etc.

(g) *Personnel*   This includes overall general observation, cleanliness and tidiness, clothing, general conduct of manager, evidence of smoking, enquiry regarding illnesses, availability of first-aid kit and stock, enquiry about what training is given to food hygiene and accident prevention.

(h) *General*   Measures on this count include offering advice, stressing awareness about food poisoning, guidance on leaflets and posters, introduction of food hygiene courses, reiteration of defects, and offering of constructive suggestions for improvement.

CARE AND MAINTENANCE OF KITCHEN EQUIPMENT

All equipment large or small, heavy or light, requires care in handling, use, and storage in order to extend its life to the maximum, minimize its rate of depreciation, and maintain it in a reasonably attractive and efficient condition while in use. In small catering establishments, the care and maintenance is generally entrusted to those who operate the equipment. Where heavy duty equipment predominates, a maintenance department performs this function.

In case of small pieces like cutlery, some metals need less care than others. Stainless steel is the most non-corrosive and easy-to-care-for material, while plated cutlery tends to get scratched easily and requires re-electroplating with the passage of time.

With kitchen tools like knives, choppers, etc., care is limited to preventing the blades from rusting in the case of iron blades, by keeping them dry and covered. It is also a common practice to rub them with a little cooking oil to protect them from rusting through contact with air. With whisks and beaters, it is the rotating parts or the wiry ends that need special attention. It is a good practice to wash or soak beaters and whisks immediately after use so as to prevent food materials from drying on the rotatory parts and posing a cleaning problem.

With heavier and larger pieces of equipment, general cleanliness of the item and its environment is the guiding principle. The following schedule is a guide to general care of most kitchen equipment.

Schedule for General Cleanliness and Care of Equipment

1. Keep all equipment clean.
2. Wash all removable parts of equipment with suitable detergent and hot water after each use. In tropical summers this is not necessary

as the water in the taps is usually warm to hot, depending on the environmental temperature. After washing, wipe completely dry before replacing.

3. All small equipment like cutlery, ladles, chopping boards, kitchen tools, etc. should be washed after use and replaced in drawers and racks built for the purpose and covered to prevent them from gathering dust or dirt during storage.

4. Check that all pieces are in working order. Close supervision at work is necessary to ensure careful handling and to detect any deviations from effective operation, like an unusual sound, or fusing of warning lights, or ineffective thermostatic controls.

5. Repairs must be attended to without delay to prevent the equipment from giving way and disrupting work for any period of time.

6. A weekly, fortnightly, or monthly programme for oiling or servicing the equipment to maintain movable parts or machinery in order is important. The service instruction provided by the manufacturer along with the equipment is a good guide to the service procedure that should be followed. It is useful to prepare an instruction in as simple a form as will be understood by the operators of the equipment. This card could be kept near major pieces of equipment.

7. All electrical inputs to the equipment should be checked periodically to ensure that proper electrical load is available for efficient functioning.

8. Similarly, insulations, plumbing, and other connections need periodic checks to keep equipment running at optimum efficiency.

9. Make full use of warranty periods to help train organization staff to learn regular maintenance procedures from the manufacturer's equipment engineers.

10. Assign the care of each machine to a responsible person.

Money, time, and effort spent on care helps to maintain equipment in continuous working order, while that spent on repair can mean interruption in work causing unnecessary strain on staff, in addition to extra costs.

It is beneficial to keep records of all amounts spent on care and maintenance of every small and large equipment (see Boxes 5.3 and 5.4). This helps to estimate the depreciation every year. Excessive costs shown through records for a particular year can help to draw attention to high maintenance costs, which weighed against the cost of the equipment may result in a decision to change the model for a more efficient one. Records can also help to detect inefficiencies in operation, or defects in designs or manufacture. Every equipment must be analysed for efficiency in use.

Box 5.3 Sample Format 1. Record Format Which could be Maintained for Small Equipment

Name of Appliance ....

Purchase on ....

Manufactured by .... From ....

Cost ....

Estimated life ....

Specification .... Motor-Horse power ....

Motor-wattage, Voltage ....

Size .... Capacity ....

Estimated rate of depreciation ....

Date of Repair ....

Nature of repair ....

Cost of Repair .... Name of Engineer ....

Remarks ....
....

Box 5.4 Sample Format 2. Record Format for Large Equipment

Appliance or item .... Purchase from....................................

Style .... Date of purchase....................................

Size ....

Amount purchase .... Cost....................................

Replaced .... pieces on .... by ....

Reason for replacement ....

Balance amount .... as on ....

Thus, if equipment is cared for systematically and proper procedures followed, maintenance follows on its own to prolong the life and optimum usage of the equipment.

The cleaning schedules for some commonly used equipment in small food service establishments are given under their respective heads:

Cooking equipment (hot plates, gas stoves, or ranges)

1. Wipe the top daily while still warm, using a wet cloth or sponge.
2. Any food spilled and burnt while cooking may require the use of a mild detergent or scouring pad.
3. For open burners, a weekly boil in warm soapy water will help remove any food particles that may have been the cause of blockage leading to inefficient heating.
4. Wipe dry with a slightly oiled cloth.

Ovens

1. Wash, rinse, and dry outer surfaces daily, after every meal.
2. Use liquid wax for enamel finished parts.
3. Brush the inside to remove any sediment due to food particles charred during cooking. Any sticky areas may be wiped with a wet cloth after switching on the oven to warm it.
4. Clean all plastic knobs with wet cloth and wipe dry.

Refrigerators

1. The outside surfaces should be cleaned as for oven daily.
2. A weekly cleaning of the insides of a refrigerator is sufficient especially if the establishment is small. For this the machine should be disconnected, doors opened and the shelves removed and washed in warm water according to manufacturer's instructions.

Preparation equipment

1. All parts which are removable should be cleaned after every use with light detergent.
2. Sharp edges should be carefully handled for cleaning and dried and replaced immediately for use.

Coffee urn

1. Urns should be emptied after each meal and the insides cleaned with a hard brush using a solution of sodium bicarbonate.
2. Outer surface as for any other equipment.

In general, it is a good policy to follow the manufacturer's instructions for care and maintenance of any equipment.

Maintenance Costs

The cost of maintaining any equipment should be determined on the basis of the following factors:

(a) Cost savings in terms of fuel consumption, as compared to the fuel bill prior to the installation of the device.

(b) Cost of servicing and regular cleaning which would involve the cost of cleaning materials and detergents.

(c) Rate of depreciation calculated over the expected life of the equipment.

(d) Any savings that the installation would have resulted in, in terms of greater utilization of raw materials and prevention of waste.

(e) Any savings brought due to elimination of daily wage workers, as in the case of people being employed seasonally for peeling of vegetables for establishments which function for a limited period in the year, as for school meals, college canteens, etc.

Maintenance Schedule for a Kitchen

Table 5.2 details the maintenance schedule for a kitchen.

Table 5.2 Maintenance Schedule for a Kitchen

Area of Activity	Maintenance Schedule
Drainage	Grease traps should be properly emptied and cleaned at regular intervals before refitting.
Physical structure	
(a) Floors	Wash and mop dry daily.
(b) Walls	Those above sinks and basins should be washed daily.
(c) Ceilings	Clean ceilings and corners between walls twice a week to remove any cobwebs or prevent their formation.
(d) Work surfaces	Inspect once a week to see if laminates are lifting at places, or edges stripping off. If so, call for immediate replacement. Renew as often as necessary.
(e) Windows and doors	Dust daily, wet cleaning twice a week.
(f) Lights, fans and other fittings	Clean once a week.
(g) Equipment	Light and moveable, daily cleaning.
	Heaving, twice a week.
	Follow maintenance procedures for heavy equipment according to manufacture's instructions.

KITCHEN EQUIPMENT SPECIFICATIONS

Nowadays equipment is designed in such a manner that it fulfils most of the needs of the kitchen staff. A lot of human engineering goes into equipment manufacturing. In spite of all these facts, the following points need to be considered while designing, fabricating, or selecting the equipment.

- Use a single indicating pointer as it is the least confusing. It should not cover any numbers in its movements and should be of a colour that contrasts sharply with the scale.
- All controls and displays should be above 32 inches from the floor such that the worker does not have to bend to reach any control from normal vertical body reach.
- There should be 10 gradations between numbers and contrast between numbers or letters and the background should be stark.
- Temperature control should be on the right hand side.

As we are aware, all these pieces of equipment are expensive, and being experts it is our duty to use all of them in the most effective manner. This is possible only when they work efficiently, which depends on proper care and maintenance.

Kitchen equipment is categorized into three types:

- Large equipment
- Mechanical equipment
- Utensils and small equipment

Large Equipment

Manufacturers of large and mechanical equipment provide necessary information in the form of instructions on how to keep their apparatus in efficient working order. All types of kitchen equipment may be classified into six categories, which are as follows.

1. Receiving area equipment
2. Dry storage equipment
3. Refrigerated storage
4. Preparation equipment
5. Cooking equipment
6. Exhaust ventilation

Every equipment has its own characteristics which are reflected in the accompanying specifications lists provided by manufacturers. These specifications facilitate the process of procurement of the equipment. Specifications of equipment provide the buyer a rough idea about the equipment's features. The broad guidelines for developing specifications and selection tips for widely used equipment are given in succeeding paragraphs to facilitate the owner as well as supplier to get quality equipment.

Receiving area equipment It is commonly seen that adequate receiving areas are often neglected due to space and budget limitation. The following are some points to remember when planning receiving areas:

- Standard dock height is from 36" to 44".
- Minimum door size is 36" × 6'8".
- Provide ample space for all mobile equipment required to efficiently move merchandise received to its proper storage.
- Pest control is always a problem at receiving doors. Self-closing doors, double doors are invaluable.
- A small desk, even if wall mounted, is very useful and it is usually an excellent location for the time clock. Even in best planned restaurants and institutions a hand sink with water fountain are often overlooked. Both are very useful in receiving areas.
- Receiving areas should be well-lit and weather protected. Clear vinyl strip curtains are ideal for the purpose.

Space required for receiving areas The following charts in Tables 5.3, 5.4, 5.5, and 5.6 shows suggested sizes for various equipment and receiving areas in various establishments. It must be kept in mind that exact sizes will vary depending on frequency of deliveries and menu variations.

Typical can and drum hand trucks Hand trucks are available in many styles and capacities. The average overall height is 49". Light-duty hand trucks are available with 6", 8", and 10" wheels with a load limit of 400 lbs. Heavy duty hand trucks have usually 8" or 10" wheels with load limits of 600, 800, 900, and 1,400 lbs depending on model specified. See Table 5.6.

Table 5.3 Sizes for Receiving Areas According to the Volume of Meal Production

Meals per day	200/300	300/500	500/1000	1000/1400	1400/1600
Area in sq. ft.	50/60	60/90	90/130	130/160	160/190

Table 5.4 Specification for Hydraulic Lift/Stationary Docks

Type	Platform Size (in Feet)	Capacity (in Pounds)	Lift Speed (Feet Per Minute)	hp	Wheels (Diameter in Inches)
Portable	6 x 6	4,000	8	1.5	4
Light duty	6 x 8	5,000	12	5	10
Medium duty	6 x 8 to 8 x 11	5,000 to 6,000	12	5	10
Average duty	6 x 8 to 8 x 10	7,000 to 8,5000	8	5	12

Table 5.5 Typical Platform Truck Sizes

Platform Size (in Sq. Inches)	Wheel Diameter (in Inches)	Maximum Load (in kg)
18 × 30	5–6	100
24 × 48	6	400
24 × 48	8	600
27 × 54	6	400
27 × 54	8	600
30 × 60	6	400
30 × 60	8	600

Table 5.6 Typical Can and Drum Hand Trucks; Designed to Carry 30 gal. to 55 gal. Drums

Wheel Size (in Sq. Inches)	Load Capacity (in kg)	Inside Ring Dimension (in Inches)
3 × 13/16	125	14.25
3 × 13/16	125	17
3 × 13/16	125	19.25
3 × 1.25	225	19.25
3 × 13/16	125	21
3′ × 1.25	225	23–5/8
3 × 1.25 (heavy duty)	400	23–5/8

Scales There are as many scales as there are things to weigh. The following scales are generally required in receiving areas.

1. Dial type counter scale
2. Dial type mobile scale
3. Beam scale
4. Digital scale
5. LED (light emitting diode) scale

Dial type counter and mobile scales These are varying in platform sizes from 11″ × 14″ – 30″ × 36″ with a capacity of 10 to 1,000 kg.

Beam scales are available in different models like counter, mobile, or floor. The average platform size for counter models is 13″ × 18″; floor model platforms average 18″ × 27″.

Standard digital scales are available from 18″ × 18″ to 28″ × 28″ platform sizes with a capacity variation from 5 to 250 kg.

LED scales are latest in electronic weighing devices and are being produced in several models and sizes. These units have tare buttons (Many scales have a *tare weight* setting, which allows the user to place an empty container on the scale and hit the *tare button* to zero the scale out) and are accurate to one hundredth of a gram. The platform sizes vary from 7″ × 7″ to 12″ × 12″ and capacity from 3.5 to 35 kg.

Storage Using valuable space properly is like putting money in a bank. Storage spaces must be carefully designed keeping in mind the operational requirements like the quantity of raw materials, stock turnover, frequency of purchase, etc. We will study it in detail in the next chapter.

Preparation equipment As with all food service equipment, a variety of sizes, options, finish, and voltages are available. The following details will help you to select the proper equipment for your production requirement.

Blenders 24, 44, 64 to 128 oz; available in glass, lean or stainless steel motors, in 115 V or 220 V. Motor sizes and blades vary with manufacturer.

Hand operated breading machine Drum type 15″ × 18″; can bread up to 20 lb; 115 V.

Breaders/sifter size 58″ wide × 28.5″ deep × 52″ high; available without shelves; capacity 10 kg or 25 pounds; flour mix and 2.5 kg raw product.

Doughnut sugaring machine 60″ × 24″ × 36″; approximately 350 dozen doughnuts per hour; Powered by single phase, 115 V, and 1/3 hp. Drums are fabricated in SS (stainless steel) or aluminum.

Crepe machine 14″ × 8″ × 9″; 115 V; controlled by thermostat; 4 crepes per minute.

Automatic cookies dropper mobile 66″ × 32″ × 56″; 1200 dozen per hour; ½ hp; 3 Phase; 220 V.

Cutter mixer 20″ × 14″ × 24″; 1 hp; 220 V; single phase; 10 amp.

Application Cookie dough, fruit filling, icing, frosting, bread crumbs, cole slaw, mashed potatoes.

Meat choppers or grinders 18″ deep and 36″ wide; 0.25 to 3 hp; 15–40 pounds per minute.

Dough divider 33″ × 24″; motor 115 V; 1/2 hp; available in 18, 36, and 48 dividing heads.

Production capabilities 500–1,300 dozen rolls per hour depending on the size and dough mix.

French fry machine Dispenses cut and ready to fry at 400 portions per hour using dehydrated potato mix and water. Machine is adjustable from 1–7 servings per cycle. It is a counter top machine 12.75″ wide, 25″ deep, and 27″ high with 115 V plug-in unit.

Mixers   The various specifications of mixers along different parameters are provided in Tables 5.7 and 5.8.

Table 5.7   Capacity of Bowls in Quarts

Product	5	10	12	20	30	60	80	140
Mashed potatoes (lbs)	3 lbs	8 lbs	10 lbs	15 lbs	23 lbs	40 lbs	60 lbs	100 lbs
Mayonnaise (qts)	1.5 qts	3 qts	4.5 qts	10 qts	12 qts	18 qts	30 qts	50 qts
Pancake batter (qts)	2q ts	4 qts	5 qts	8 qts	12 qts	24 qts	32 qts	–
Layer cake (lbs)	3 lbs	10 lbs	12 lbs	20 lbs	30 lbs	60 lbs	90 lbs	165 lbs
Sugar cookies (dz.)	8 dz.	16 dz.	820 dz.	35 dz.	50 dz.	100 dz.	125 dz.	225 dz.
Dough light (lbs)	4 lbs	11 lbs	13 lbs	25 lbs	45 lbs	80 lbs	170 lbs.	210 lbs
Dough heavy (lbs)	–	–	–	15 lbs	30 lbs	60 lbs	140 lbs	175 lbs.
Pie dough (lbs)	3 lbs	9 lbs	11 lbs	18 lbs	27 lbs	50 lbs	75 lbs	125 lbs
Pizza dough (lbs)	–	–	–	–	–	40 lbs	85 lbs	130 lbs
Eggs and sugar for sponge cake (lbs)	2 lbs	4 lbs	5 lbs	8 lbs	12 lbs	24 lbs	40 lbs	75 lbs
Icing (lbs)	2 lbs	6 lbs	7 lbs	12 lbs	18 lbs	36 lbs	65 lbs	100 lbs

Note: 1. The above table is subject to slight changes due to variation in different manufacturers' models. It should be considered as maximum production.

2. Quart is a unit of liquid capacity equal to 2 pints; 1/4 of a gallon which is equal to 1.36 l in UK.

Table 5.8   Approximate Dimensions and Horsepower

Bowl Capacity (in Quarts)	Width (in Inches)	Depth (in Inches)	Height (in Inches)	Style	hp	Hub Size (in Inches)
5	10.5	15	17	Counter model	1/6	10
10	14	16	26	-- do --	1/4	10
12	15.5	19	27	-- do --	1/4	12
20	15.5	21	30	-- do --	1/3	12
20	21	21.5	41	Floor model	1/3	12
30	21	24	45	-- do --	1/2	22
60	27.5	39	56	-- do --	1	22
80	27.5	41	56	-- do --	1.5 or 2	22
120	29.5	45.5	71.5	-- do --	5	22

Hand mixer   110 V, 16″ in length and available as beaters, cutters, blenders, and non-cutting-blending for mixing. The unit may use for mashing potatoes, whipping cream, batters or dressings, and for stirring of stews and soups.

Figure 5.4   Pasta Machine

Pasta machines   A small pasta machine capable of producing 27 to 35 pounds per hour is approximately 30″ deep × 15″ wide × 47″ high. By changing its die it will produce different types and sizes of pasta. The motor is 120 V and 1.5 hp. Refer Figure 5.4.

Peelers   It may be ordered as a counter model for use on a sink drain board or with optional mobile or enclosed base with peel trap. All require electric, water and drain. Motor range varies from 1/3 to 1 hp and maximum peeling is possible 33 lbs per minute of potato/carrots and beets.

Meat saws   The specifications for meat saws are given in Table 5.8.

Table 5.8   Specifications for Meat Saws

hp	Blade (in Sq. Inches)	Cutting Clearance (in Sq. Inches)	Movable Table (in Sq. Inches)	Travel (in Sq. Inches)	Floor Space Required (in Sq. Inches)
1	5/8 × 98	13-5/16 × 10-7/8	15 × 20	18	32 × 45
2 or 3	5/8 × 112	15-1/4 × 13-1/4	15 × 19	22	35 × 45
2 or 3	5/8 × 128	18-1/8 × 15-11/16	17.5 × 24	24	40 × 52

Note: 1 or 2 hp motors available 115 V to 460 V-1 or 3 phase.

Figure 5.5   Tenderizer

Tenderizers   12″ × 20″ × 20″ high, motor ½ hp, 115 V plug-in. It is a very versatile piece of equipment and can be used for tenderizing of steaks from beef, pork, veal, lamb or turkey. Refer Figure 5.5.

Vegetable washer–dryer   A new mobile and 115 V plug-in vegetable washer and spindryer with a 20 gallon inner liner can dry up to one case of lettuce per minute. Dimensions are 18″ × 31″. Refer Figure 5.6.

Vegetable sinks (free standing)   The most popular sink for commercial purpose is 24″ × 24″ × 14″. The backsplash is usually 2″ thick and the rolled edge on the ends and front usually measure 1.5″. Using these standards a single compartment would measure 27″ side to side × 27.5″ front to back. Other sizes are as follows:

18″ × 18″, 18″ × 21″, 18″ × 24″, 24″ × 21″, 30″ × 21″, 30″ × 24″, 30″ × 30″, 36″ × 24″, 36″ × 30″.

Figure 5.6 Vegetable Washing and Drying Machine

Drain boards These are available in standard lengths of 18″, 24″, 30″, and 36″. Any drain board exceeding 36″ should have its own support legs at the end. For sanitation purpose and ease of cleaning, sinks should be set 3″ from or sealed to the wall. Shut-off valve is recommended for the water lines. Be sure that drain lines are low enough, especially if you are installing disposers. Lastly, consider high end splashes when sinks are in corners or next to high items like refrigerator.

Ingredient bins Available in stainless steel with a maximum capacity of 250 pounds and sizes varying from 12″ × 22″ × 29″ to 23″ × 25″ × 29″.

Standard work tables All are 34″ high with standard widths from 18″ to 30″ and standard lengths from 3 to 8 feet. Prefer 14 gauge with roll-down edges and bull nose corners. Tool drawers are available with stainless steel, galvanized, or plastic bowls in 15″ × 20″ × 5″ or 20″ × 20″ × 5″ sizes. These may be open type construction with channel slides or totally enclosed with roller bearing glides. Locks may also be provided.

Pot racks Common pot racks, either table mounted or ceiling hung, usually have one perimeter bar with a centre bar approximately 1 foot lower. Wall mounted racks are available with single bar or with 2 bars, one extending out from the wall above the other. Standard lengths are 48″-60″-72″-84″ and 96″. The recommended height to the top bar of a pot rack is 7′ 6″ above the floor level.

Standard stainless steel overhead shelves Standard widths of shelves are 10″, 12″, 14″, 18″, and 24″. Standard lengths are 48″, 60″, 72″, 84″, and 96″. Standard metal gauges used are 18, 16, or 14. Normally the wider and longer the shelf, the heavier the metal should be. Standard spacing for shelving is 18″ from the tabletop to the first shelf with 12″ between shelves.

Cooking equipment Most of the cooking equipment have a lot of options, so a little legwork and brainstorming must be done before making a final selection about a particular device. Verify your power supply and venting requirements, and study the energy output of various equipment to ensure their compatibility with the available systems. Table 5.9 provides the energy output or BTU (British Thermal Units) ratings for selected cooking equipment.

Table 5.9   Average BTU Ratings for Cooking Equipment

Name of Device	Type of Equipment	BTU Ratings	Pre Heat Time (in Minutes)
Broilers	Counter or back shelf salamander	30,000–45,000	15–20
	Upright radiant or infrared	50,000–1,00,000	1
	Double oven	1,60,000–2,80,000	20–30
	Char style	70,000–96,000	20
Fryers	Small	27,000–48,000	10–12
	Medium	60,000–1,70,000	10–12
	Large	80,000–2,12,000	10–12
	Pressure	57,000–90,000	
Fry pans	Tilt	80,000–1,05,000	5–7
Grillers		24,000–2,40,000	20–30
Ranges: Heavy duty	Top burners	17,000–20,000	20–30
	Ovens range	30,000–35,000	15–30
	Total average range	92,000–1,95,000	
Ranges	Restaurant style–60″ model, 6 burners, 24″ grill, 2 ovens	190,000	15–30
Steamers	Kettles	100,000	5–8
	Compartment	40,000–2,25,000	5–15
Ovens	Convection, counter	35,000 average	10–15
	Full size	75,000–1,15,000	15–20
	Deck ovens, per deck	30,000–2,40,000	30–60
	Pizza per deck	50,000–1,40,000	15–20

Preparations and service

The chef's table   The first item after preparation and cooking will be the chef's table. The design for this can vary from a standard steam table unit with a work table placed under it, to a well planned and highly elaborate factory-constructed unit. One can plan various options according to one's requirements. Box 5.5 enlists some of the options that can be provided in a chef's table.

Box 5.5 Options Available for a Chef's Table

Plate storage cabinets	Slice space
Sliding door cabinet	Pan storage
Heat lamps	Toaster area
Over shelves	Microwave on shelf or under
Sink and pipe chase	Electrical outlets
Refrigerated base	Bread dispenser
Refrigerated drawers	Hot food drawers
Freezer base	Call systems
Hot food wells	Order holders
Roll warmers	Drain
Soup warmers	Tile base at site
Ice bins	Open base
Dish shelves	Closed base
Tray rails	Compressor
Tray storage	Tool drawers
Carving board	Shut off valves

Pantry area   All pantry area should be carefully designed with the intention of reducing kitchen traffic, relieving the chef of unnecessary work, and improving customer service while controlling portions and quality.

The following equipment and items are a common feature of every efficient pantry area and space for these should be thought of in the planning stage itself.

- Soup warmers
- Salad preparations
- Desserts
- Refrigerators
- Milk, cereal, juices
- Microwave ovens, ice cream cabinet
- Coffee equipment
- Linen basket, dry storage, sinks, waste basket
- China and glass storage space
- Toasters
- Water and ice
- Sinks

A pantry area often extends into waitress stations, or combines as one unit in the dining area. When kitchen space limitations make this necessary, serious consideration should be given to shielding the area with partitions or stub walls approximately 5′ high. Some of the equipment can be located against the stub wall with an ample aisle between it and the remaining equipment against the back wall. This design will reduce noise and visual distraction in the dining room, and conceal the untidy mess that a pantry can easily become during rush periods.

Do not forget to provide a space for spare chairs. An isolated spot for off-duty waitresses is a must too. Checklists for back bar equipment, bakery shop, and bar service equipment are provided in Tables 5.10, 5.11, and 5.12 respectively.

Table 5.10 Back Bar Equipment

Soda fountain	Refrigerators	Grill stands
Dipper wells	Refrigerated display cases	Dish washer stands
Ice cream cabinets	Wall display cases	Compressor stands
Beverage stations	Urn stands	Ice chests
Freezers	Shelving units	Water stations

Table 5.11 Checklist of Equipment for a Bakery Shop

Items	Quantity	Production Equipment	Quantity	Production Equipment	Quantity
Egg beater	1	Coffee making equipment	1–2	Pairing knife	6
Measuring spoon	1 set	Decanters	6–12	Pot fork	2
Oven/Freezer	2	Silver compartment storage box	3	Slicer	4–6
Pastry brushes (flat and round)	4	Sauce pans	6	Box grater	1
Rolling pin	1	Sauce pots	2	Broiler	1
Whip, piano 10″, 12″,14″ and 16″	4	Stock pots	3	Cartons opener	1
Whip French 14″	1	Double boilers	2	Lobster cracker	2–4
Cake covers/stands	2	Bake pans	6	Parers and corers	6

(contd)

Table 5.11 *(contd)*

Items	Quantity	Production Equipment	Quantity	Production Equipment	Quantity
Display cases	1	Roast pans	2	Poultry shears	6
Pie markers	1	China cups	1	Clam/Oyster knife	3
Bread pans	12	Colander	1	Sharpening stone	1
Cake/sheet pans	6/12	Strainer	4	Storage container	10–12
Jelly moulds	36	Service pan	24	Chopping bowls	1
Muffin tin	6	Lids assorted	12	Cutting boards	2
Pie tin	12	Fry pans	6	Dish cloth	24
Dredges	2	Butter spreader	1	Towels, linens	36
Funnels	3	Eggs poacher	1	S/S pails	1-2
Measures	3	Steak weight	1	Liquid grill cleaner	1 gal
Scoops	3	Thermometer:		S/S cleaner	1 case
Pastry bags	6	Oven	1	Aluminium foil	3 units
Pastry tips	6	pocket	1	Grill bricks	12
Scrappers	2	Roast	1	Neoprene gloves	6
Food storage boxes	6	Deep fat	1	Plastic aprons	6
Ingredients bins	3	Beating spoon	6	Bags for garbage	1 unit
Utility/dish pans	2	Ladles	6	Scouring pads	12
Mixing bowls	12	Paddles	6	Floor squeegee	1
Scale, portion control	1	Tongs	6	Mops/heads	6
Scale, bakery	1	Turner	2	Brooms	2
Storage containers	12	Can opener	1	Pick up brush	1
Insulated coffee tank	1	Cheese cutter	1	Vacuum cleaner	1
Multi purpose rubber	1 roll	Egg slicer	2	Storage container for flour, sugar	3
Measuring glass	2	Knife	2	Waste receptacles	6–12
Spatula	12	Food mill	1	Glass washing brush	1
Safety mats	3–6	Tomato tamer	1	Oven brush	2
Ice cream scoops	6	Scrappers	1	Urn brush	1
Juice dispenser	1–2	Boning knife	2	Scrubbers	12
Juice extractor	1	Cleaver	1	Lemon squeezer	2

Table 5.12 Checklist for Bar Service Equipment (Small Wares) for 100 People

Equipment	Bar and Lounges	Restaurant
Blender	2	1
Ice scoop	2	1
Cocktail shakers	6	3
Jiggers	2	2
Pourers	12	5
Cutting board	2	1
Strainer	1	1
Wire bar strainer	2	1
Fruit knife	2	1
Fruit peeler	4	1
Muddler	2	1
Sugar caddy	2	1
Cork removers	3	2
Speed racks	3	1
Stirrers	120	100
Ice buckets	2	2
Water pitchers	3	2
Beer pitchers	3	2
Mixing spoon	3	2
Squeezers	2	2

Suggestive Detail Specifications of Kitchen Equipment

Figure 5.7 Working Tables

Work table

Size 850 mm wide × 750 mm deep × 850 mm high to work top on legs (Figure 5.7).

Top 18 GA SS secured to 38 mm × 38 mm × 12 mm GA SS welded angle framework with bull-nosed front down by 50 mm.

Legs frame 38 mm four tubular legs with adjustable bullet feet.

Under shelf 2 no. 18 GA SS, intermediate and bottom shelves rolled down 40 mm and underside reinforced with SS hat channels, starting at 150 mm.

Splash Fully welded 150 mm high on rear (optional).

Chapati plate with puffers

Size 1650 mm wide × 750 mm deep × 850 mm high to worktop 16 GA SS top with 150 mm high raised splash on rear, returned 25 mm and down 12 mm with body cladding. Front of work top with bull nosed front turned down by 50 mm worktop to over hang the base body by 50 mm at front and by 75 mm at rear. Cooking top shall comprise a chapati plate top on left hand side with puffer grates on the right hand side for all the units.

Plate 20 mm thick polished MS (mild steel). Plate measuring 850 mm wide × full depth. Plate should be free from any imperfection and should gently be slopped towards the front to a channel provided with an SS drawer for grease collection.

Heating It should be heated with two 70,000 BTUs rated 'V' type HI-PR burners of standard or approved make with control valves and pilot burner at 5.0 psi (pounds per square inch) pressure. Control valve to be mounted on the front recessed panel cladding.

Puffe grates Two in number on right hand side of chapati plate. Removable CI perforated chapati puffer grate top should be provided with suitable burners below, with control valves and pilots. Provide SS slide out drip tray in three pieces with formed handles, with all sides turned up 12 mm and hemmed on the outside and located below the burners.

Construction 18 GA SS on all sides with fully welded mild steel with angle framework.

Legs frame 38 mm four tubular legs with adjustable bullet feet.

Under shelf 25 mm diameter SS pipe shelf at 150 mm.

Splash 150 mm fully welded returned 25 mm and down 12 mm, raised at rear side and high on rear.

Mobile ingredient bin

Size Each bin size (internal) 400 mm wide × 600 mm deep × overall 750 mm high inclusive of castors (small wheels) and lid with handle.

Body 18 GA SS all welded SS construction with 25 mm radius covered corners. Top of bin to be rolled out on all sides of 40 mm diameter. Underside of base to be reinforced with no. 16 GA SS inverted channels.

Castors Four in number 5″ diameter rubber-tyred castors swivel type two with brakes, fitted with channel framework.

Lid Half opening centre hinged, no. 18 GA SS snug fitting removable with 12 mm diameter × 25 mm high × 100 mm wide SS rod handle welded to the lid. Base corners to be provided with rubber corner bumpers, non-marking 1″ thick, and four in number.

Work table with sink

Size 2100 mm wide × 675 mm deep × 850 mm high to work top on legs.

Top 16 GA SS secured to 38 mm × 38 mm × 12 mm GA SS welded angle framework with bull nosed front down by 50 mm.

Sink size 500 mm × 500 mm × 225 mm deep; die pressed; 16 GA SS integral with top towards right with 38 mm diameter waste outlet, rear connected over flow, hot and cold water faucet, deck mounted.

Legs frame 38 mm four tubular legs with adjustable SS bullet feet.

Splash Fully welded 150 mm and high on rear.

Cross bracing 25 mm rear and both sides, entire front open to accommodate ingredients bins.

Work table with sink and overhead shelf

Size 1800 mm wide × 675 mm deep × 850 mm high to work top on legs.

Top 16 GA SS secured to 38 mm × 38 mm × 12 mm GA SS welded angle framework with bull nosed front down by 50 mm.

Sink size 450 mm × 450 mm × 225 mm deep; die pressed; 16 GA SS integral with top towards right with 38 mm diameter waste outlet; rear connected over flow, hot and cold water faucet; deck mounted.

Overhead shelf Provide full width 18 GA SS single deck over shelf located at rear and mounted at 535 mm above tabletop and mounted on two SS 25 mm × 25 mm tubular pipe uprights, with upright taken through rear splash to tabletop and bolted to table framework. Over shelf with rear and both sides turned up 50 mm and hemmed as in wall shelf. Over shelf should be assembled at site.

Legs frame 38 mm four tubular legs with adjustable SS bullet feet.

Splash Fully welded 150 mm high on rear and left side.

Cross bracing 25 mm rear and both sides, entire front open to accommodate ingredients bins.

Work table with overhead shelf

Size 1800 mm wide × 675 mm deep × 850 mm high to worktop on legs.

Top 16 GA SS secured to 38 mm × 38 mm × 12 mm GA SS welded angle framework with bull-nosed front down by 50 mm.

Overhead shelf Provide full width 18 GA SS single deck over shelf located at rear and mounted at 535 mm above tabletop and mounted on two SS 25 mm × 25 mm tubular pipe uprights, with upright taken through rear splash to tabletop and bolted to table framework. Over shelf with rear and both sides turned up 50 mm and hemmed as in wall shelf. Over shelf should be assembled at site.

Legs frame 38 mm four tubular legs with adjustable SS bullet feet.

Splash Fully welded 150 mm and high on rear side only.

Under shelf 2 no. 18 GA SS, intermediate and bottom shelves rolled down 40 mm and underside reinforced with SS hat channels, starting at 150 mm.

Idli steamer

Body Body to be of 18 GA SS double wall, 25 mm thick insulation with perforated shelves of six nos.

Capacity Each unit to have a capacity of approximately 50 idlies at one time.

Heating Water tank fitted with electric heater to generate steam, thermostatic control, and insulated door in front, electrically heated at 2.0 kW, to operate on 220–250V-1 phase.

Tilting braising pan

Size 850 mm wide × 900 mm deep × 900 mm high to lid top on closed lid position.

Internal pan size 750 mm wide × 675 mm deep × 225 mm high, of approximately 90 litres capacity.

Pan material Inside base of cooking pan of no. 12 GA SS with all four sides of pan of no. 14 GA SS, fully welded, rounded corners, underside of cooking pan base cladded with 12 mm thick polished MS, front of pan top developed into a pouring lip.

Lid No. 16 GA SS lid with full size isolated handle, rear of lid provided with counter weight balanced or spring balance to hold lid in open position.

Heating LPG-heated rated at 1,40,000 BTU, suitably positioned for uniform heat distribution throughout base, power cord thermostat control and pilot light enclosed in SS cladded frame box on left side, total rating at .5 kW each, wired for operation on 440 V-50 Cycles -1phase.

Legs frame All welded open tubular SS heavy duty legs frame, cross-braced at rear, with SS adjustable flanged feet.

Filler faucet Rear of right side boxed SS frame of tilting control provided with SS bracket and fitted with swing out swivel cold water filler faucet with control valve.

Exhaust hood

Size To be finalized later, on stage.

Body 18 GA SS; all welded body construction.

Framework 38 × 38 mm thick, and fully welded boxed SS angle.

Light 100 watts, approximately 6 nos, and wiring in heat proof conduits.

Make up air plenum Double plenum chamber. One plenum on conventional exhaust and other for fresh air make up.

Exhaust 14,000 cfm total.

Single burner range with spreader

Size 1200 mm wide × 900 mm deep × 750 mm high on work top.

Framework 38 mm × 38 mm × 12 mm thick fully welded boxed SS angle framework with bull-nosed front down by 50 mm.

Body 18 GA SS cladding from top till drop tray.

Top 16 GA SS top with bull-nosed front. Top cut out to receive one grating. Verify corner from layout.

Burners 1, rated at 70,000 BTU/hour with pilot and controls; operated on LPG at 5.0 psi.

Gratings 350 mm × 350 mm cast iron removable heavy duty to set inside top.

Under shelf 25 mm diameter legs with SS adjustable bullet feet.

Legs frame SS legs with adjustable bullet feet.

Mainfold 1/50 mm diameter towards left.

Splash 250 fully welded, raised at rear.

Drip tray   1 no. 22 GA SS drip tray to be provided.

Spice bin drawer   Below the spreader top on right hand side, unit should be provided with an SS slide out spice bin drawer, with 16 GA SS collar top with cutouts, to support condiment GN 1/6 pans 100 mm high, total four nos removable pans to be provided. One row at front and four deep.

Three burner range

Size   2100 mm wide × 900 mm deep × 750 mm high on cooking surface.

Framework   50 mm × 50 mm × 3 mm thick fully welded boxed SS angle framework with bull-nosed front down by 50 mm.

Body   18 GA SS cladding from top till drop tray.

Top   16 GA SS front rolled down 50 mm bull-nosed front. Top cut out to receive three grating verify corner from layout.

Burners   3, rated at 70,000 BTU/hour with pilot and controls. Operated on LPG at 5.0 psi.

Gratings   16″ × 16″ cast iron removable heavy duty to set inside top.

Under shelf   25 mm diameter SS pipe shelf at 150 mm.

Legs frame   6 nos SS legs with adjustable bullet feet.

Manifold   1″ diameter towards left.

Splash   250 fully welded, raised at rear.

Drip tray   3 nos 22 GA SS drip tray to be provided.

Water filler   Wall-mounted cold water filler faucet swivel type.

Two burner range

Size   1950 mm wide × 900 mm deep × 750 mm high on cooking surface.

Framework   38 mm × 38 mm × 1/8″ thick fully welded boxed SS angle framework with bull-nosed front down by 50 mm.

Body   18 GA SS cladding from top till drop tray.

Top   16 GA SS front rolled down 50 mm bull-nosed front. Top cut out to receive three grating verify corner from layout.

Burners   2, rated at 70,000 BTU/hour with pilot and controls; operated on LPG at 5.0 psi.

Gratings   350 × 350 cast iron removable heavy duty to set inside top.

Under shelf 25 mm diameter SS pipe shelf at 150 mm.

Legs frame 4 nos SS legs with adjustable bullet feet.

Manifold 1/50 mm diameter common for all burners.

Splash 250 fully welded, raised at rear.

Drip tray 2 nos 22 GA SS drip tray to be provided.

Water filler Wall mounted cold water filler faucet swivel type.

Mobile work table

Size 1250 mm wide × 600 mm deep × 850 mm high to work top on castors.

Top 16 GA SS secured to SS angle framework.

Splash None, worktop with marine edges on all four sides, turned down 50 mm and in 12 mm.

Legs frame 4 nos SS tubular legs with 100 mm diameter rubber-tyered swivel castors, two nos with brakes.

Under shelf 2 nos 18 GA SS, intermediate and bottom shelves with all four sides of shelves provided with raised with marine edges and rolled 40 mm.

Hand wash sink unit

Size 600 mm wide × 600 mm deep × 200 mm high to worktop.

Top 16 GA SS secured to SS welded angle framework.

Sink 2 nos size 450 mm × 450 mm × 225 mm deep; dye pressed; 16 GA SS integral with top towards right with 50 mm diameter waste outlet, rear connected over flow, hot and cold water faucet, deck mounted.

Splash 150 mm high fully welded at rear and both sides.

Brackets 14 GA SS secured to underside with acorn nuts and to wall with anchor fasteners.

Attachment holding rack with hooks

Size 750 mm wide × 300 mm deep; mounted to wall.

Shelf 50 mm wide × 1/4″ thick SS bar with corners rounded on 25 mm radius. Ends of unit welded to 100 mm height × 50 mm × 6mm thick SS flange for securing to wall with anchor fasteners. Total of six sliding SS pot hooks should be furnished for each rack.

Wall shelves

Size   2,100 mm wide × 300 mm deep mounted to wall.

Shelf no   18 GA SS W/rear and sides turned up 50 mm and edges hemmed on the outside. Front rolled down 40 mm.

Brackets   14 GA SS secured to underside with acorn nuts and to wall with anchor fasteners

Mounting height   1400 mm and 1700 mm. Clear 25 mm away from the wall unit to be mounted.

Masala grinder

Size   750 mm wide × 600 mm deep × 1200 mm high.

Capacity   15 litres.

Miscellaneous   Tilting type grinder with SS body and provision of coconut scrapper attachment. Motor should be rated 1.5 HP.

Wall shelves

Size   1800 mm wide × 300 mm deep mounted to wall.

Shelf   18 GA SS with rear and sides turned up 50 mm and edges hemmed on the outside. Front rolled down 40 mm.

Brackets   14 GA SS secured to underside with acorn nuts and to wall with anchor fasteners.

Mounting height   1,400 mm and 1,700 mm; clear 25 mm away from the wall unit to be mounted.

Potato peeler

Size   650 mm diameter.

Capacity   12–15 kg of potatoes per minute.

Miscellaneous   Motor should be at the bottom of the unit. Outlet for peeled vegetable should be about 30″ above finished floor. The unit should operate on 1.0 hp motor, 220 V-50 A-1 phase.

Double sink unit

Size   1,350 mm wide × 675 mm deep × 850 mm high to work top.

Top   16 GA SS secured to 38 mm × 38 mm × 12 mm SS welded angle framework with bull-nosed front.

Sink 2 nos size 450 mm × 450 mm × 225 mm deep; dye pressed, 16 GA SS integral with top towards right with 38 mm diameter waste outlet, rear connected over flow, and provision of pre-rinse spray unit on the deck.

Splash 250 mm high fully welded at rear.

Legs frame 38 mm 4 nos SS legs with adjustable bullet feet.

Under shelf One no. SS pipe shelf at 150 mm.

Hot display cabinet

Size 1,200 mm wide × 750 mm deep × 12,000 mm high inclusive of 150 mm high feet.

Make Body to be made of 20 GA SS with curved vacuum glass at front. All interiors to be of SS with two nos infrared food warmer heater inside.

Doors To be of sliding type towards the inside, with vacuum glass on 18 GA SS frame.

Shelves 2 nos full length glass shelf.

Pot wash unit with sink

Size 2400 mm wide × 800 mm deep × 865 mm high to worktop.

Top 14 GA SS with 75 mm raised front and left side, turned out 40 mm, down 50 mm and in 12 mm. SS welded angle framework with bull-nosed front.

Sink 1 no. size 610 mm × 610 mm × 300 mm deep; die pressed on right side, complete with lever handle, 14 GA SS integral with top towards right with 50 mm diameter waste outlet, rear connected over flow, and provision of dye punch hole on rear splash behind sink with SS flat reinforcement behind and provided with 12″ long goose neck type splash mounted swivel mixer faucet behind sink.

Splash 250 mm high; fully welded at rear; sloping type against wall.

Legs frame 38 mm 6 nos SS tubular legs with adjustable feet.

Framework 40 mm × 40 mm × 12 GA SS welded angles.

Strainer basket 1 no. 50 mm high 20 GA SS removable perforated with handle for trough at front.

Cross bracing Rear and both sides, front open below the washing platform section, legs below the sink, cross braced front and right side, rear kept open.

Faucet Wall mounted type; one no. 12″ long; gooseneck spout, swivel type to be furnished of the table and should be mounted to rear wall above the washing drain board.

Mobile pot rack

Size 900 mm length × 610 mm deep × 1,900 mm high, and on castors.

Shelves 5 shelves should be provided.

Castors 150 mm diameter rubber-tyred; swivel type; 2 with brakes.

Uprights 40 mm diameter top; ends closed and rounded; smooth, cross tubing welded to uprights.

Pick up counter

Size 2,250 mm wide × 750 mm deep × 850 mm high to work top.

Top 16 GA SS secured to 38 mm × 38 mm × 12 mm GA SS welded angle framework with bull-nosed front down by 50 mm.

Overhead shelf 2 nos 18 GA SS provide full width 7 feet wide × 150 mm deep turned down 38 mm and in 6 mm with SS hat channel reinforced, mounted at 1500 mm, and with SS uprights.

Legs frame 38 mm four tubular legs with adjustable SS bullet feet.

Miscellaneous Rear of worktop suitable to accept the turned up edge of top of adjoining dish storage cabinet.

Under shelf 2 nos 18 GA SS intermediate and bottom shelves turned down 38 mm and in 50 mm and underside reinforced with SS hat channels.

Four doors reach in refrigerator

Size 1,350 mm × 750 mm × 2,100 mm high inclusive of 150 mm high feet.

Make 20 GA SS rear cladding with 20 GA SS sheet. All insides to be of SS.

Doors 4, exterior cladded with 18 GA SS sheet; locking arrangements and gaskets; doors to be flushed with exterior; handle to be part of the door and should not protrude out.

Temperature Capable to maintain zero to 4°C at ambient temperature of around 45°C, assuming that doors will be opened 20 times per hour for a duration of 10–12 seconds.

Cooling Air cooling with fans.

Accessories Door activated lights at 220 V-50 A-1 phase.

Shelves   6 nos full length SS wire shelf with a provision of expanding the number of 8 shelves.

Refrigeration   1.0 hp normal temperature type. Kirloskar make compressor. Digital thermometer with time delay auto start.

Condense   Bottom provided with 25 mm diameter waste outlet and removable SS perforated false bottom and slide-out drip tray below waste outlet. All sides to be tilted towards waste outlet to remove excess water.

Insulation   50 mm thick insulation.

Bain marie counter

Internal size   750 mm wide × 750 mm deep × 250 mm high.

Material   16 GA SS integral with top.

Insulation and cladding   50 mm thick tightly packed glass wool; sheathed with 20 GA SS sheets on exterior.

Waste   Bottom sloped to 1″ diameter with angle valve.

Faucet   Deck mounted 1/2″ diameter HW filler faucet.

Miscellaneous   Provide 3 kW electric immersion type heating elements clamped 25 mm off the bottom; complete with thermostat, on-off switch, red indicator light and controls.

Electrical rating   220V- 50 A -1 phase, full complement of 200 mm diameter and 300 mm deep round pans. 4 nos of pans with lids to be furnished. No. 18 GA SS perforated. Removable false bottom with all sides turned down 50 mm and in 12 mm to be provided with 1″ diameter lift-out finger holes.

SUMMARY

A good kitchen layout plan is totally dependent on the positioning of equipment, drainage, ventilation, working area for staff, lighting levels, safety, and scope of maintenance of the equipment. The chapter covers all these points in detail. Computation of requirement of ventilation is given in illustrations and requirement of level of light varies from kitchen to kitchen depending on various factors such as colour scheme, floor finishes, positioning of equipment and so on. Requirement of equipment of various sub areas of a kitchen is briefly summarized and specifications are detailed for the convenience of students. By and large, the equipment is generally tailor-made depending on volume of production, skills of the kitchen staff, space available, etc. Maintenance of kitchen equipment and safety precautions are very important to follow and practise in day-to-day life.

CONCEPT REVIEW QUESTIONS

1. Prepare a checklist of equipment required in kitchen for 120-cover Indian specialty restaurant and recommend specifications for the following equipment:
   (a) Four burner gas range
   (b) Deep fat fryer
   (c) Bain marie
   (d) Chef's table
2. Discuss various modes of ventilation of a food production unit with their characteristics.
3. Enlist features of a good kitchen layout plan and what points you will consider to ensure all these features.
4. Recommend the area ratio between the following:
   (a) Dining area: kitchen area
   (b) Dining area: pantry area
   (c) Kitchen area: storage area
   (d) Storage area: pantry area
   (e) Kitchen area: pantry area
5. Prepare a write up on kitchen safety.

PROJECT ASSIGNMENTS

1. Collect some catalogues of equipment suppliers and prepare a report on specifications of kitchen equipment.
2. Visit some kitchen equipment manufacturing units and collect detailed information about latest equipment developed by them.
3. Compare the equipment specifications given in the topic with the existing equipment in the kitchen of your institution.
4. Prepare a complete handbook of the kitchens of your institution with emphasis on features of the kitchen.

REFERENCES

Anthony M. Rey, Ferdinand Wieland EI Publication Manser (Jose) and Manser (Michael) (1976), *Planning Your Kitchen, Managing Service in Food and Beverage Operation*, Design Council, London.

Dana, Arthur W. (1988), *Kitchen Planning for Quantity Food Service*, Harper and Bros, New York.

Kinton and Ceserani (1980), *Theory of Catering*, Fourth edition, Edward Arnold Publishers Ltd, London.

Morel, J.J. (1957), *Scientific Catering in Hotel Operations*, Isaac Pitman, London.

Scriven Carl and James Stevens (1989), *Food Equipment Facts*, Van Nostrand Reinhold, New York.

Sethi, Mohini and Surjeet Malhan (1984), *Catering Management*, Wiley Eastern Limited, New Delhi.

West-Wood and V.F. Harger (1977), *Food Service in Institutions*, Fifth edition, John Wiley and Sons, New York.

West-Wood and V.F. Harger (1996), *Food Service in Institutions*, Fourth edition, John Wiley and Sons, New York.

CHAPTER 6

Storage Facilities, Layout, and Design

Chapter Outline:

The following topics are covered in this chapter
- Features of a good store
- Types of stores
- Scenario of stores equipment used in Indian hotels
- Guidelines and planning for storage facilities
- Cellar
- Flow process of store
- Kitchen stewarding

Learning Objectives:

This chapter will enable you to understand
- The definition of a store
- The points to be considered while planning and designing storeroom facilities
- Computation of space, lighting and ventilation requirement
- The ideal storage temperature of frozen foods, fish, meat, fruits, vegetables and general groceries
- How to maintain security of the cellar and storeroom
- The concept of kitchen stewarding

INTRODUCTION

An owner or the manager of a hotel has to store commodities for several reasons. When prices are low, it may necessitate buying more than the normal requirement. If chances of shortages loom large, they might buy more to tide over the period of shortage. Moreover, there are several kinds of commodities and beverages such as rice, flours, wines, and liqueurs, which gain their qualities and values when stored for a longer time period. Storing of all items is the basic responsibility of a storekeeper and the person must be well aware about the nature of materials to be stored. In a good class of hotel there are approximately more than 700 items, which require storage. As students of facility planning, it becomes our responsibility to design a facility in a perfect manner so that every item can be stored under its optimum and desired storing condition. Size and type of store facilities vary from hotel to hotel according to their size, nature of business, traffic flow, volume of business, and type of clientele, etc. A small hotel may have a general store for storing all its requirements, while a large hotel may have different storage areas/sections but the basic fundamental of storage facilities will be the same as per the nature of commodities. We should not forget that a good amount of fund is always tied up with the store for smooth operations of a hotel.

Before we begin the discussion on storage and related facilities, let us have a general understanding on the various terms that we are likely to come across during the course of our study.

Hygiene   The word hygiene is derived from the Greek word *hygia*, which means goodness of health. It is essential to form a clear conception of the importance of kitchen hygiene at the very outset. The aim of ensuring satisfactory hygienic conditions is to prevent any food being served from becoming a source of infection to the consumer.

Sterilization   It is the destruction of all pathogenic or disease causing microorganisms including their spores.

Surfactants   Formed by a blend of three words, *surface, active,* and *agent,* surfactants are wetting agents that lower the surface tension of a liquid, allowing easier spreading, and lowering the interfacial tension between two liquids. They are usually organic compounds that are amphiphilic, meaning they contain both hydrophobic (water repelling) and hydrophilic (water dissolving) groups. Therefore, they are soluble in both organic solvents and water. Surfactants have wide commercial use, such as cleansing agents, paints, adhesives, etc.

Detergents   These are chemical compounds that are used for cleaning purposes. They contain significant quantities of surfactants. In the hotel industry, they may be used singly, or in combination with other cleansing agents to produce a detergent suitable for specific use.

Soap It is a compound of fat and soda which is used in washing and cleansing.

Tarnish It is a discolouration caused by chemical reaction between a metal and other substances, such as cloth, furniture, etc.

Polivit It is a perforated aluminum sheet, which is best used in an aluminum or galvanized iron bowl.

Par stock It is minimum cutlery, crockery, hollowware required to meet the daily demands of a kitchen facility so as to ensure smooth operation.

Inventory It is a detailed list of goods, which are used in operations.

FOOD STORE: DEFINITION AND TYPES

A food store is a clean, well-ventilated, properly illuminated, easy to operate, and efficient place used by a catering establishment according to its catering policy. A well-controlled storeroom and cellar provides a daily check on all issues and costs, and helps to lower the cost of raw materials (food/beverage cost), by controlling pilferage, wastage, and reducing the possibility of frauds by user department.

Necessity to Have a Store

There are a lot of myths about the store facilities in the Indian catering industry. If we were to exclude large hotel or restaurant chains, then there would be a lot of entrepreneurs in this sector, who are not in favour of having a separate or a dedicated store in their catering organizations or food and beverage outlets. A very simple question they ask is: 'Why is it necessary when we can purchase commodities as per our requirement on a daily basis? Why should we keep a storekeeper and waste space and capital in equipment and furnishing of a store?' But they are wrong. It is very necessary to have a store in a catering facility for the following reasons:

- Successful and smooth operations
- A storekeeper can save double the amount of his salary by controlling theft, waste, and spoilage by
  - o keeping a track on receiving and issuing control.
  - o maintaining records of shortages/spoilage.
  - o maintaining reasonable par stock as per business volume and popularity of menu items.

- Psychological impact on various user departments created by a storeroom.

Types of Stores

According to the nature of food and beverage commodities, stores may categorized in the following types:

Perishable food store   These are used to store perishable food items such as meat, poultry, game, fish, dairy products, fats, vegetables, and fruits.

Frozen store   These are used for storing of frozen foods, which must be placed immediately in a deep freeze.

Non-perishable items or dry store (groceries store)   These are used for storing pulses, cereals, sugar, flour, jams, pickles, bottled foods, canned foods, breads, cakes, etc.

Cellar   It is a dark and silent room in the purchase department, hidden from public view. It is run jointly by the purchase and food and beverage department. It is an ideal place to store alcoholic beverages as it is dark, airy, and quiet, with a constant temperature, and protected from unpleasant smells. If a true cellar is not available in a catering organization, a dark quiet place where temperature remains constant can be fitted with wine bins and, if necessary, with a humidifier.

A large hotel may have additional storage facilities other than for food and beverages. They are:

Linen store for storing of all types of linen used in a hotel.

Stationery store for storing of all types of stationery used in a hotel.

Maintenance store for storing of all types of equipment, tools, fixtures, devices, etc. used in a hotel.

Audio-video store for storing of all types of audio video facilities used in a hotel.

Food and beverage store for storage of chinaware, glassware, tableware, etc.

LAYOUT OF A GOOD FOOD STORE

Size

Size and shape of a storeroom varies from establishment to establishment and depends on individual requirement, availability of sources of supply, volume of business, and inventory turnover. Inventory turnover of 3 to 4 times a month is ideal and can be calculated by the following formula:

$$\text{Rate of stock turnover} = \text{Cost of food consumed/Average value of stock at cost price}$$

Illustration In 28 days trading period the cost of food consumed was Rs 30,000 and opening stock on day 1 was Rs 10,000 and closing stock on day 28 was Rs 5,000.

$$\text{Rate of stock turnover} = 30,000 \div [(10,000+5,000) \div 2]$$
$$= 30,000 \div 7,500$$
$$= 4.0 \text{ times}$$

This means that in the 28-day trading period the total value of stock turnover is four times and that an average of one week's stock was held during the period.

Average Space Required for Dry Storages

Storing food can be a great way to lower down your food costs and also prepare for the possibility that food shortages could occur. Beyond the essentials, exactly how much room do you need for storing food and for how long? Well, there are several factors to take into consideration including the size of catering units, amount of space available for storage, and length of time for storing; for example you want to store for two/three months.

The most important point that determines the space requirement for storage facility is the number of meals served per day in restaurants and clubs, or number of employees being served at a particular facility. A rough idea of the space required for storage of dry rations can be made on the basis of these points. Tables 6.1 and 6.2 provide an estimate of the space required for dry storage in various establishments.

Restaurants and clubs

Table 6.1 Estimated Area Required for Dry Storage Space Areas in Restaurants and Clubs Based on Number of Meals

Meals per day	100–200	200–350	350–500	500–1000
Square Feet Required	120/200	200/250	250/400	300/650

Employees feeding or staff cafeteria

Table 6.2 Estimated Dry Storage Space Area for Employee Cafeteria

Meals Per Day	400	800	1200	1500
Square Feet Required	350/450	550/650	700/850	950/1050

Location

Location of the store should ideally be near the receiving zone where goods are delivered by various vendors, and should be easily approachable by the person of any section authorized to receive issues. Facing north is right direction for a store so as to maintain a cool temperature and avoid sunshine.

Structural Features, Cleanliness, and Shelving

The following points with respect to the structural features, cleanliness, and shelving may be borne in mind while designing the layout of a store.

- Store should be airy and free from moisture (dampness).
- The maintenance of a standard of hygiene requires that the walls and ceilings be free of cracks.
- Floors of the store should be tough enough to hold heavy traffic, and easy to clean and wash.
- There should be no right angle corner in between floor and wall to prevent accumulation of dirt.
- There should be sufficient lighting—natural and artificial—in all the areas (recommended level 30 foot candle) and storekeeper's desk should be well illuminated (recommended level 70 FCL).
- A store should have a separate issuing counter/window.
- The ceiling of store should not be less than 12 feet from floor level.
- The height of issuing counter (reception platform) should not be less than 30″ from floor level and length should not be less than 36″. It should be well illuminated.
- A make up counter is an essential feature and should be located at the centre of the store for holding commodities before issuing to the user department.
- The recommended height of the racks is 8 feet from floor level and space between shelves may vary from 50–90 cms, and for stacking of small cans or jars it should not be less than 15″.
- Racks should be arranged with a minimum distance from wall not less than 3″ and the same gap should be maintained between two racks.
- Follow a minimum aisle space of approximately 36″ for gangway.
- Space required for turning an average truck is 72″.
- Storekeeper should be provided with a suitable working table along with space to keep documents.
- Shelving:

    For perishable foods Shelving should be slatted to permit maximum circulation of air in refrigerated facilities.

    For non-perishable food items Solid steel shelving is usually preferred.

Flow of Work at the Store Facility

The basic aim of a food store is to maintain an adequate supply of foods for the immediate needs of the business with the very minimum loss through spoilage and pilferage. This entails establishing standards and standard procedures for storing. In general, the standards established for storing food should address the following principal concerns:

1. Location of storage facilities
2. Layout of storage facilities
3. Condition of facilities and equipment
4. Arrangement of foods
5. Security of storage areas

The sequence of activities encountered during store operations may be depicted through the following flow diagram (Figure 6.1).

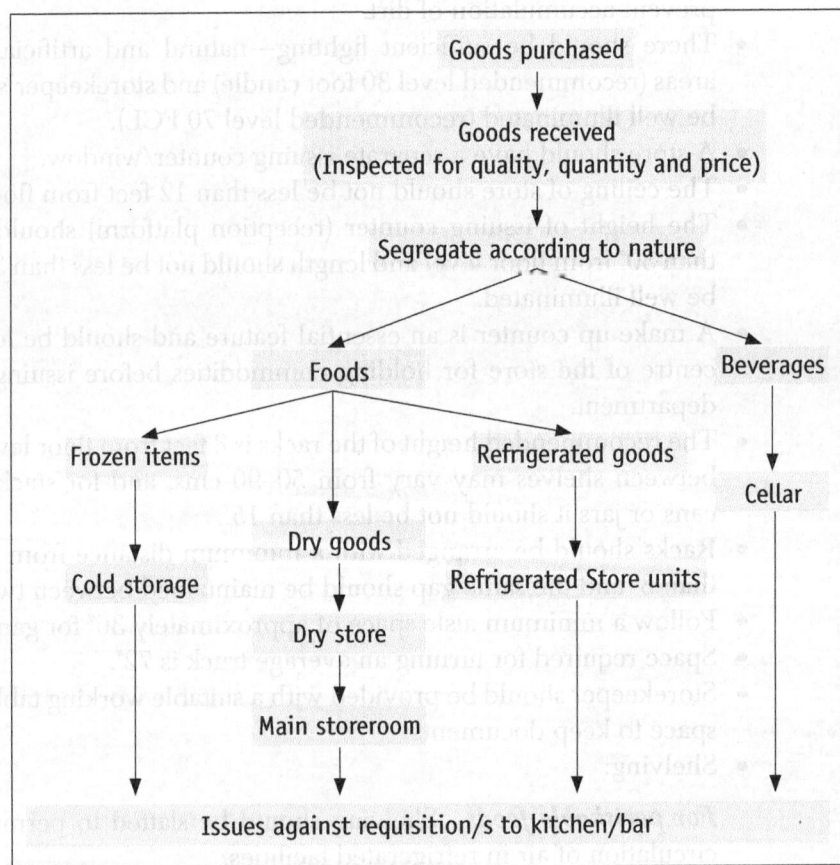

Figure 6.1   Flow of Work at a Store Facility

Recommended Storage Temperatures

Foods must be stored at correct temperatures. The optimum storage temperature varies depending on the nature of the item. The generally accepted storage temperatures and periods for storing foods are indicated in Tables 6.3, 6.4, and 6.5 respectively.

Table 6.3 Storage Temperatures for Frozen Food Items

Meat	-20°C to -16°C (- 4 to 3°F)
Fish	-20°C to -16°C (- 4 to 3°F)
Frozen foods	-20°C to -16°C (- 4 to 3°F)
Ice-cream	-22°C to -18°C (- 8 to 0°F)

Table 6.4 Storage Period at 0°F

Frozen Food	Maximum Storage Period at 0°F
Meat	
Beef	6–12 months
Lamb and veal	6–9 months
Pork	3–6 months
Sausages and ground meat	1–3 month
Cooked meat not covered with gravy	1 month
Meat sandwiches	1 month
Poultry	
Chickens	6–12 months
Turkeys	6–9 months
Giblets	3 months
Cooked poultry meat	1 month
Cooked poultry dishes	1 month
Eggs	6–12 months
Vegetables	8–12 months
French-fried potatoes, par fried	2–6 months
Fruit	8–12 months
Cookies	6–12 months
Cakes—pre-baked	4–9 months
Batters	3–4 months
Fruit pies—baked and unbaked	3–4 months

Table 6.5 Storage Temperatures and Period for Refrigerated Items of Foods

Food	Maximum Storage Temperature °F	Maximum Storage Period
Dairy products		
Milk (fluid)	40	3 days
Butter	40	2 weeks in waxed cartons
Cheese (hard)	40	6 months tightly covered
Cheese (soft)	40	7 days
Ice cream	10	3 months in original container covered
Eggs	36	7 days
Fish		
Fresh	36	20 days
Shellfish	36	5 days
Fruits		
Peaches, plums, berries	50	7 days unwashed
Apples, pears, citrus	50–70	2 weeks
Leftovers	36	7 days
Poultry	36	7 days
Vegetables		
Leafy	45	7 days
Root vegetables, onions, potatoes, etc.	50–70	7–30 days
Meat		
Ground	38	2 days
Fresh meat cuts	38	6 days
Liver	38	2 days
Cold cuts (sliced)	38	6 days
Cured bacon	38	1–4 weeks
Ham (tender cured)	38	1–6 weeks
Ham (canned)	38	6 weeks
Dried beef	38	6 weeks

Best Practices and Storage Procedures

The following points comprise best practices in storage procedures and should be followed scrupulously.

1. Foods should be generally divided into three categories: perishable, frozen, and dry items from the receiving dock and inspected with respect to quality, quantity, and delivery performance. If any discrepancies are there, they should be reported to the higher authorities for necessary action/documentation.

2. Most frequently used items should be stacked near the entrance area of the store.

3. There should be a definite place for each commodity.

4. Food items like spices, herbs, etc. delivered in unsealed containers such as paper bags, and boxes should be transferred to suitable airtight containers.

5. Stock rotation should be on FIFO (first in and first out) basis.

6. Items should be grouped if they are similar commodities such as bottled or canned items.

7. Items must be stacked by a coding system of numerical bin sequence or alphabetical index.

8. Meat items should be hung on hooks with drip trays underneath to collect any blood.

9. Humidity level should be approximately 90 per cent.

10. Meat and poultry should be stored separately.

11. Cuts of meat may be brushed with oil or wrapped in oiled greaseproof paper.

12. Decayed or spoiled vegetables should not be stored.

13. Vegetables should be stored separately on racks in a cool and dry place.

14. Hard fruits and stone fruits should be stored in cold store.

15. Eggs have a tendency to absorb smells. So store them away from other foods at 1–4°C in refrigerated equipment and use in rotation.

16. Cut pieces of cheese should be wrapped and refrigerated at a temperature below 5°C.

17. Flour bags should be piled off the floor on skids to enable free circulation of air all around the piles. The storage area should be well ventilated and should be kept away from direct sunlight. Temperature of storage area should be 65–75°F and relative humidity 55–65 per cent. Quality of flour may deteriorate if too low or too high humidity is maintained. Flour has tendency to pick up foreign odours and should be kept away from such ingredients, which may impart odours. While storing, it must be ensured that the flour is free from insect infestation.

18. Rotation of dry goods should be on the basis of last in last out.
19. Storeroom should never be left open and unattended.
20. Proper key control should be implemented.
21. Employees' access should be restricted and there should be a time schedule for delivery of goods according to user departments/sections.
22. Check date of packing/expiry before issue.
23. Discard stores of expired date or found unit for consumption.
24. Protect from insects/rodents approach.
25. Store properly and protect items from chances of contamination.
26. Keep storage floor clear.
27. Never use floor for storing food commodities or empties.

Equipment and Utensils Used in a Store with Their Sizes/Dimensions

Shelves   Shelves are integral to a storeroom, more so in the modern age when space has become an extremely rare and expensive commodity. They come in various designs and sizes depending upon the nature of the item to be stored and the available space. The standard sizes of various kinds of shelves that are available in the market are stated in Table 6.6.

Table 6.6   Standard Sizes of Shelves in the Market

Shelf Width (in Inches)	Lengths Available (in Inches)
12–14	24, 30, 36, 42, 48, 60
18, 21, or 24	24, 30, 36, 42, 48, 60, 72

The above units are manufactured as flat or louvered metal shelves and open welded wire shelves. The open wire shelving is recommended where ventilation is important.

All are available in aluminum, galvanized, coated galvanized and stainless steel. Stainless steel (SS) is of course the ultimate finish for both wet and dry storage. Uncoated zinc plated units should be used for dry storage only. The average shelf load limit is 1000 lbs. The height of upright shelves varies from 26″ to 86″.

Mobile ingredient bins for dry storage   Mobile ingredient bins nowadays are available either in plastic or metal and may have sliding or hinged covers. Clear and see-through covers are also available in most models of mobile ingredient bin.

Table 6.7 provides an insight into the standard sizes of ingredient bins generally available in the market and their capacities with respect to various ingredients.

Table 6.7 Sizes and Capacities of Various Ingredients

Sizes (in Inches)	Capacities			
	Cu Ft	**Gals**	**Lbs Sugar**	**Lbs Flour**
12 × 29 × 28	3.4	26	175	125
21 × 23 × 28	3.9	34	195	140
15 × 29 × 28	4.4	34.5	220	155
21 × 23 × 23	5.1	43	260	185
18 × 29 × 28	5.7	44	285	205

Chinaware and glassware carton sizes   Chinaware and glassware are among the most important service equipment used in a catering facility and need to be stacked and preserved with great care and caution. They need to be protected from chipping and discolouration, as even minor flaws in their handling can be damaging. Table 6.8 provides the standard carton sizes with respect to various crockery items so as to help in planning storage shelf space sizes of the most commonly used Chinaware and glassware.

Table 6.8 Standard Carton Sizes with Respect to Crockery Items

Item	Carton Size (in Inches)
6.25″ plates	9.5 × 13 × 6.75 high
9″ plates	9.5 × 13.5 × 6.75 high
Cups	13 × 16 × 9.5 high
Saucers	10.5 × 12.75 × 6.75 high
Bowls	9.5 × 16 × 10 high
Monkey dishes	9.25 × 10.25 × 5.5 high
8 oz. bulge glasses	16.5 × 16.75 × 8.5 high
8 oz. stemware	19 × 18.5 × 6.25 high

Note: To determine square feet when inches are given, multiply length x width and divide by 144.

Example: 12″ × 42″ shelf = 504 square inches or 504/144 = 3.5 square feet.

Table 6.9 provides an insight into the space required for various storage items with respect to their size and capacities.

Table 6.9 Sizes, Weights, and Shelf Space Required in Terms of Square Feet

Item	Size (in Inches)	Approx. wt. (Lbs)	Approx. sq. ft.
Flour or sugar sack	18 × 13 × 11	100	4.0
Shortening can	16 diameter × 17	50	1.8
Cooking oil	9.5 × 9.5 × 13	40	0.7
Case 6 oz cans (96)	11.25 × 22.5 × 7.25	37	1.7
Case 8 oz cans (72)	11 × 16.5 × 10	28	1.2
Case #2 cans (24)	14 × 10 × 9.25	28	1.0
Case #10 cans (6)	19 × 12.75 × 7.25	37	1.5

Refrigerated storage   Various options are available for refrigeration systems—both indoor and outdoor installations. Indoor units are available in various finishes and with colour panels. Outdoor units require weathercaps for the roof and rainhoods for the doors. Walk-in coolers may be set directly on existing concrete or tiled floors. Audio and visual alarm systems are available for both coolers and freezers. Plastic air curtains hung at door openings can cut down running time of the compressor and save money. Tables 6.10 and 6.11 provide useful information of standard refrigeration equipment available nowadays.

Table 6.10 Specialized Walk-ins

Overall Size without Floor			Compressor Rating	
Height	Width	Depth	Cooler (hp)	Freezer (hp)
7'6"	6'	8'	0.75	1.5
7'6"	8'	8'	0.75	1.5
7'6"	8'	10'	1	2
7'6"	6'	10'	0.75	1.5
7'6"	10'	10'	1	2
7'6"	6'	12'	1	2
7'6"	8'	12'	1	2

Table 6.11   Standard Blast Freezer Sizes

Size W × l × h (in Feet)	Area Occupied (Cubic Feet)	Ice Cream Storage (Gallons)	Frozen Food Storage (Cases)
8 × 8 × 8.5	318	1400	270
8 × 10 × 8.5	416	1800	400
8 × 12 × 8.5	514	2000	480
8 × 14 × 8.5	612	2500	570
8 × 16 × 8.5	710	2900	680
8 × 20 × 8.5	906	3700	870
8 × 22 × 8.5	1004	4100	920
8 × 26 × 8.5	1200	4800	1150
8 × 28 × 8.5	1298	5000	1300

Note:

• Ice cream: Figured in rectangular 0.5 gallon packages (per unit)
• Frozen food case (size per unit) size: 12″W × 17″ L × 5″H

All storage capacity for blast freezers allows for working aisles and air space over stored product.

Figure 6.2   Blast Freezer
Source: rjspanel.com.au

Blast freezer   Under ideal conditions, harmful food based bacteria can multiply once every 20 minutes or so. In a span of 12 hours, over 69 million bacteria are capable of growing on food surfaces. Every time you freeze a cooked food product, it must pass through the 'danger zone' as it cools from 150°F to below 41°F. It is crucial that food passes through this stage of freezing as quickly as possible. Blast freezing and chilling is the method of rapid heat removal, typically by means of convection in which cold air is circulated over the product. This method quickly seals the outer layer of food products prohibiting bacteria growth and preventing product dehydration. The process must happen quickly enough to prevent ice crystals from forming (commonly referred to as freezer burn) and also preserves food texture and consistency. A blast freezer is depicted in Figure 6.2.

The advantages of blast freezing/chilling are as follows:

1. Damaging bacteria rendered dormant.
2. Food colour, texture and nutritional value sealed in.
3. Prevention of large ice crystals, which can damage food.
4. Reduced kitchen waste, as unused portions can safely be stored for later use.

5. Increased kitchen efficiency lets you prepare large batches and use some portions later.
6. Cost effective operation and maintenance.

Thumb rule for space requirement for walk-in refrigeration A general rule for estimating space for walk-in refrigeration is to allow 0.5 cubic feet of usable space per meal served. Small walk-ins with only one door and a single aisle can have from 50 to 60 per cent of usable space. Larger walk-ins with multiple aisles and doors can have 35 to 45 per cent usable space. Table 6.12 provides information on estimate storage space requirement of various feeding facilities based on the number of meals served per day.

Table 6.12 Refrigerated Storage for Various Operations

In plant feeding	Meals/day	400	800	1200	1600
	Space (sq. ft.) required	75–120	115–135	140–175	170–210
Schools	Meals/day	200	400	500	1000
	Space (sq. ft.) required	35–35	35–50	50–75	75–100
Central hospitals	Number of beds	50	100	150–200	400
	Space (sq. ft.) required	40–50	80–100	200	400

Glass door display units The capacity of various kinds of glass door display units is given in Table 6.13.

Table 6.13 Capacity of Glass Door Display Units

Doors	Width	Cubit Feet	No. of Shelves	Total sq. ft. of Shelving	1/2 gal. Milk Capacity	1/2 gal. Ice Cream Capacity
3	98″	78	15	78	720	792
4	128″	103	20	104	960	1056
5	159″	128	25	130	1200	1320

Note: All glass display units are 37′6″ deep 78′6″ high.

ROLE OF STOREKEEPER

The primary role of a storekeeper is to store and to maintain adequate stocks of materials with minimum loss through theft and spoilage. A storekeeper must make follow-up checks of the storage facilities and checks of the articles, the storage methods, and the storage temperatures. Immediate corrective action should be taken whenever there is a deviation from the established standard operating procedures. Key functions of a storekeeper are as follows:

Stock Control

Establishing standards and standard procedures for stock control should address the following concerns:

1. Stock taking
2. Determining the value of stock held in stores
3. Comparing actual physical stock value with the book value of the stock
4. Determining rate of stock turnover
5. Establishing stock levels
6. Maintaining stock records

Stock Taking

Stock taking is an important task and should be undertaken by the staff from the control or accounts department together with the members of the food and beverage management team. It is generally undertaken by the following two methods.

Monthly inventory method The process of taking a physical inventory of products on hand in all storage areas at the end of the month or the trading period is called a monthly inventory. The physical inventory would involve physically counting or weighing the goods held in stock and recording the information accurately in the stock taking sheet for management reporting.

Perpetual inventory method The process of maintaining a continuous record of all purchases and issues is called a perpetual inventory. The perpetual inventory may be maintained on cards or in books, usually in the control office for each commodity of item held in stock. The perpetual inventory provides the 'book value' of stock for comparison with the physical inventory.

Book value of the stock is calculated by the formula:
Value of opening stock + purchases during the period – Requisitions made in the same period = Value of closing stock

Rate of stock turnover is calculated by the formula:

$$\frac{\text{Cost of food consumed}}{\text{Average value of stock at cost price}} = \text{Rate of stock turnover in a given period}$$

Maintain Stock Levels

The level at which an item of stock is to be held in stores/cellars at any point in time of the business in a particular trading period is called stock level. The following are determinants of stock levels.

1. The forecasted usage figures for the trading period
2. The Economic Ordering Quantity (EOQ)
3. The reordering time for the item (lead time)
4. The rate of stock turnover
5. The budget available
6. The market trends
7. The storage space available
8. The shelf life of the item

Minimum stock level   It indicates the minimum figure of inventory quantity held in stock at any time.

Minimum level = ROL (Reorder level) – (Average usage × Average reorder period)

Maximum stock level   It indicates the maximum figure of inventory quantity held in stock at any time.

Maximum level = ROL + EOQ – (Minimum usage × Minimum reorder period)

Reorder level   It indicates the level at which fresh orders should be placed for replenishment of stock.

Reorder level = Maximum usage × Maximum reorder period

Note:

Average stock level = (Minimum stock level + Maximum stock level)/2

Average reorder period = (Minimum reorder period + Maximum reorder period)/2

Issuing control

Establishing standards and standard procedures for issuing control should address the following concerns:

1. Setting up a requisition system
2. Pricing the requisition

Setting up a requisition system   A requisition system is a highly structured method for controlling issues. All storeroom issues should be made against a written requisition signed by an authorized person, often the chef. Whenever practical, it is advisable that requisitions be submitted in advance to enable the storeroom clerk to prepare the order without haste.

The items listed on requisitions fall into two categories:

Directs   The food category charged to food cost as received, e.g., perishable food items.

Stores The food category charged to food cost as issued; e.g., staples and tagged items.

Pricing the requisitions (pricing of commodities) The various methods of pricing the requisitions are as follows:

Actual purchase price This method involves pricing of commodities at purchased price.

Simple average price This method involves pricing of commodities at a simple average price.

Weighted average price This method involves pricing of commodities taking into account both quantities as well as prices, thus giving a more accurate average price.

FIFO method This method involves pricing of commodities at the earliest purchased price. This may be applied to items, which have a fluctuating market price.

LIFO method This method involves pricing of commodities at the latest purchased price. This also may be applied to items, which have a fluctuating market price.

Standard price This method involves pricing of commodities at a standard price for a specified time period, usually 3–6 months.

Inflated price This method involves pricing of commodities at an inflated price, i.e., cost plus, say 10 per cent or 15 per cent to recover the cost of handling and storage charges.

Summary of Duties and Responsibilities of Storekeeper

The duties and responsibilities of a storekeeper are summarized in the following points, while Figure 6.3 provides the hierarchy of a stores department in a large hotel.

1. Maintenance of instructions and duty chart register.
2. Safe custody of store materials and ensuring safety of the storing area.
3. Receipt of the store material.
4. Responsibility of arranging the stores layout.
5. Accounting for the materials in, and those that have been issued to the outlets.
6. Maintenance of relevant papers such as stores credit and bin cards.
7. Documentation of relevant papers such as stores credit report daily perishables and presentations and all resuscitations.

8. Maintenance and preservation of material in stores.
9. Giving out necessary information and dates to the departments closely associated with the stores operation.
10. Maintenance of a high standard of hygiene of stores.

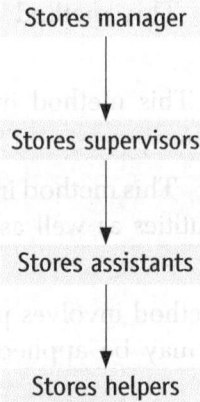

Figure 6.3   Hierarchy of Store Department

Documentation and Procedures in Store

Many different approaches have been taken over the years in an effort to control food and beverage costs. However, the objective has always been the same: to keep costs in line without sacrificing the quality or quantity of the food which goes to the customer.

To control and to maintain highest level of service standards, a storekeeper has to follow certain procedures and document or record all the transactions of the day. The following documents serve as essential tools to keep a check on the storage procedure.

Daily perishable order   This is one of the most important documents handled by the stores. All the perishables that are purchased by the hotel are ordered through this format. The Executive Chef of the hotel does the ordering a day ahead of the receipt of the perishables. While ordering the items, the chef takes into account any social functions due to be hosted and the stock level in the stores. The stores department is consulted to know the stock in hand. While ordering fruits, an excess stock is necessary as this would help in the following day issues. When ordering fruits, it is done in numbers of the item.

An adequate stock of perishables helps to give a speedy issue to the outlets. If there is a remainder for the items, then those are issued once the new supplies arrive. The order form is made in four copies. The original and second copy goes to the Purchase Department, the third copy is sent to the stores, and the fourth is the book copy. The Purchase Department in turn places the order with the suppliers, and the original is sent to the Receiving Department to receive the items. If an item is short supplied then it is notified to the Purchase Department, Executive Chef, and the store through a shortage report.

The ordering of the perishables by the Executive Chef means that the chef takes responsibility of the items including those that fall short. But in the same way, if the items are short supplied, the chef can hold the Purchase Department responsible for that lapse.

The purchase requisition   Ordering of the storeroom provision on a daily basis is done through the requisition. Reordering of grocery items is done twice a month—normally on the first and the fifteenth of every month. But this may vary as per the consumption. Although ordering is done on two days, the store can send a requisition that it needs the stocks.

At any given time the store should have a grocery stock adequate for 25 days for consumption.

The requisition is made in three copies, of which two copies are sent to the Purchase Department and the third copy is the book copy.

In case of the grocery items, the Purchase Department retains the copy and sends out a purchase order to the supplier of which one copy is sent to the stores for its reference.

The purchase has to be sanctioned by the F&B Controls before it is sent to the Purchase Department. In case of the short supply of items ordered, the store in turn prepares a shortage report and sends it to the Purchase Department for them to rectify the matter.

Store's credit report   When food and beverage items are received by the stores from the receiving department, the items are either weighted or counted as per the requirements and the quantity of the items, date of receipt, serial and the remarks are entered in the receiving tag which is sent to the stores with the items. Generally the items weigh more than what is weighed at the receiving end as there is a margin for shrinkage.

In the mean time these details are entered in the store's credit report that has a receiving Report No., Date, Item, Quantity and Unit, Unit Price and Extension, and the Bin Card No. At the end of the day the original copy of this report is sent to the F&B Controls for their references. The F&B Controls department reconciles the receiving report and the store's Credit Report to look for any kind of discrepancy. In case of one, the tags from both the stores and the receiving department can be tallied to trace the folly.

Store receiving procedures The receiving procedures in the store can be summarized in the following points.

1. When the items are received at the stores, the items are weighed or counted as per the requirements and entered in the store credit report.
2. In case of groceries, they are counted or weighed and entered in the store credit report and in the bin card.
3. In case of perishables, they are stored at the appropriate temperature as per the requirements.
4. Groceries and beverage items are entered into the cards after consulting the stores credit report.
5. In case of smokes (cigarettes/cigars) and liquor, two entries are made in the card.

BEVERAGE STORAGE FACILITIES (CELLAR)

Alcoholic beverages are among the major revenue grossers of any hospitality property. Little wonder, cellars or rooms where beverages are stored form an important feature of any big hotel or restaurant and bar. Like food items, various beverages require different optimum conditions for their storage, which makes the organization and planning of cellars an arduous task that must be executed carefully and meticulously. The security aspect of the cellar is an equally important task.

Guidelines for Planning and Operations of a Beverage Storage Facility

Some useful tips or guidelines that have evolved in the industry pertaining to the operations of beverage storage facilities are as under.

1. **Ensuring safety and security of the beverage facility** This includes assigning responsibility for the security of stored items to a single person, and keeping the facility locked when required.
2. **Organizing the beverage storage facility** In general, the physical arrangement of a cellar comprises the following:

   - The main storage area held at 13–16°C for the storage of red wines and spirits. This area is also used for general collections and preparations of orders for the various bars.
   - A refrigerated area held at 10°C for storage of white wines and sparkling wines.
   - Another refrigerated area held at 6–8°C for the storage of keg beers only if necessary.
   - An area held at 13°C for the storage of bottle beers and soft drinks.
   - A totally separated area for the stacking empty bottles, crates, etc.

3. **Maintaining appropriate conditions** It includes maintaining the temperature, humidity, and light in the beverage storage facility to maximize shelf life of the stored beverages.
4. **Maintaining cellar records** This is necessary for the purpose of control.
5. **Ensuring par stock for bars** Par stock is the precise quantity stated in numbers of bottles or other containers that must be on hand at all times for each beverage in the bar.
6. **Beverage store** This should have only one access and it must be locked and sealed with a print on a tape with time of entry and code of key used to open the door.
7. **Ideal location** This is necessary to provide direct and easy access to bars.
8. **Maximum height of shelves** This should be 7′6″ from floor level as it reduces the chances of breakages.
9. **Size of the shelves** This should be according to the size of bins which are approximately 22″ wide, 14″ high, and 18″ deep.
10. **Space for cleaning** Leave 4″ space between the lower shelf and floor to facilitate cleaning and to keep goods dry in case of flooding or spillage.

List of Documents Used in the Cellar of a Five Star Hotel

The following is the list of documents that are generally used in five star hotel beverage storage facilities.

- Cellar control
- Cellar control ledger
- Bin card
- Cellar perpetual inventory control ledger
- Daily beverage inventory sheet
- Beverage requisition book
- Empties outward book
  Ullage (word used to describe sub-standard quality/weeping wine bottles due to loose cork and the air space above the wine and under the cork or screw cap) and breakages book

Checklist of Cellar Tools

A good cellar should have all essentials tools and equipment, which should be stored in one part of the cellar over a workbench. It is a simple task that entails building a rack for taps, mallets, and other larger items.

The minimum cellar tools and equipment are:

- Adequate number of taps
- Vent pegs

- Scotches
- Shivers
- Spiels
- Corks
- Tapping plugs
- Hard wood or rubber mallet
- Gimlet for boring shivers
- Punch for knocking the holes
- Spanners for beer pipes, engines, and unions
- Washers
- Filtering equipment and filtering papers
- Jugs
- Brushes for taps cleaning
- Brooms and scrubbing brushes
- Swabs and glass cloths
- Glasses for sampling and tasting
- Thermometer
- Torch and spare battery
- Vice on bench
- Dipstick
- Washing soda and salt
- Disinfectant (outside the cellar)

Standard Practices and Procedures: Dos and Don'ts of Cellar Management

Dos

- Location: between bar and receiving area.
- Follow FIFO.
- Wines should be laid down.
- Spirits and liqueurs should not be laid down but keep straight.
- Port and sherry should keep upright.
- Crusted and vintage port must be binned or moved with the whitewash mark on the top.
- Keep separate bin cards for all wines and liquers.
- Keep a record of breakage with appropriate evidence.
- Unwrap all bottles and destroy the packing.
- Make sure that access to the cellar is controlled.
- Priority should be given to the security of keys.
- Keep your beer at even temperature between 56–60°F.
- Keep everything clean in the cellar: walls, ceilings, drains, pipes, draining boards, and floor.

- Keep the cellar free from smell.
- Keep the cellar free from small and unnecessary gadgets.
- Keep your beer engines free from traces of dirt and yeast.
- Deal with returned beer promptly.
- Wash glasses well.
- Cork and peg the casks as soon as they are empty.
- Turn off taps of casks in use and tighten spiles at each session.
- Sample for all beers for brightness, condition, and flavour at the beginning of each day.
- Learn about the product you are selling.
- Keep your utensils spotless.

Don'ts

- Overstock.
- Return stale beer to casks.
- Hang a thermometer on the wall.
- Permit warm or cold draughts in the cellar.
- Be afraid of consulting your brewer.
- Clutter up the cellar with lots of rubbish, odds and ends, or anything with a strong smell.

Useful measures   Some useful measures used in connection with beverages along with equivalent quantities in popular unit measures is given in Table 6.14.

Table 6.14   Popular Measures Used in a Bar/Cellar

Measures	Quantity
1 Barrel	36 Gallons (288 Pints)
1 Kilderkin	18 Gallons (144 Pints)
1 Firkin	9 Gallons (72 Pints)
1 Pin	4.5 Gallons (36 Pints)
1 Gallon	8 Pints (160 Fluid Ounces)
1 Quart	2 Pints (40 Fluid Ounces)
1 pint	20 Fluid Ounces
1 Gill	0. 25 Pints (5 Fluid Ounces)
1 Magnum	2 Bottles (53.33 Fluid Ounces)

KITCHEN STEWARDING

The kitchen stewarding department has a very important role to perform in the hotel and catering industry. It is primarily responsible for maintaining cleanliness and hygienic conditions in the kitchen. They provide all the important backup services of the food and beverage department by maintaining and cleaning all the utensils and equipment used, ensuring proper garbage disposal. Figure 6.4 depicts the organization of the kitchen stewarding department of a large hotel, while the duties of the various staff of the department are detailed in Table 6.15.

Duties and Responsibilities of the Kitchen Stewarding Staff

Executive kitchen stewards are responsible for all silver, dish, and glass washing and the maintenance of high standards of kitchen cleanliness. They report

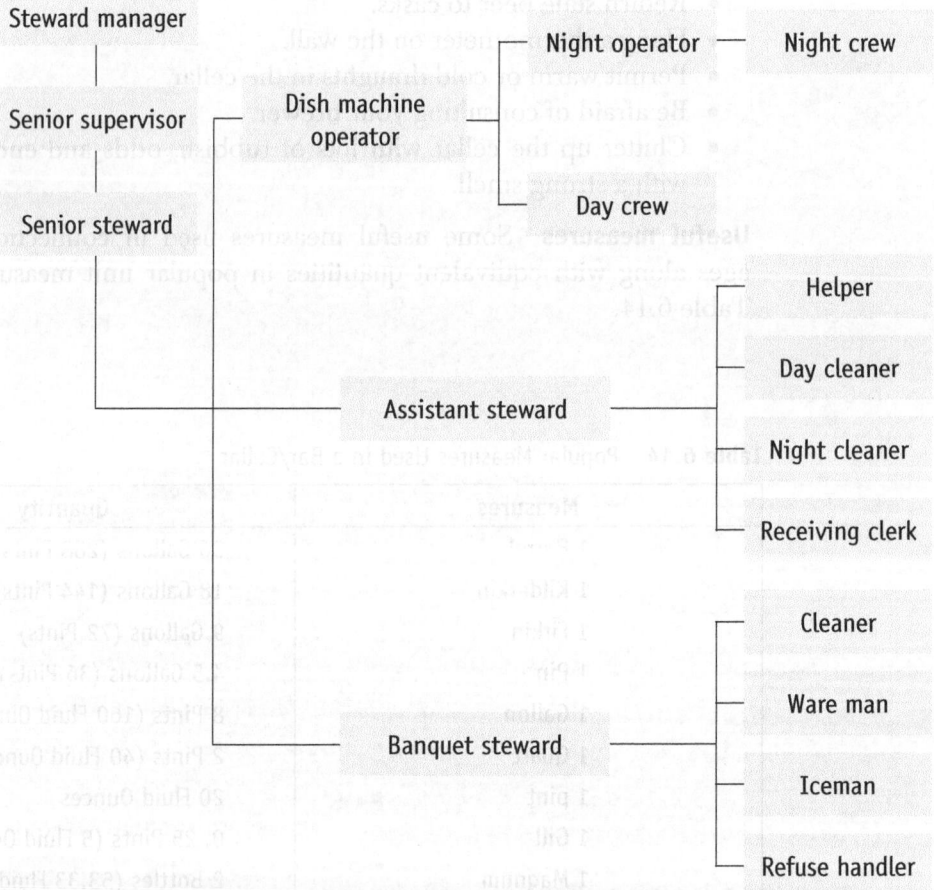

Figure 6.4 Model Organization Structure of Kitchen Stewarding Department of a Large Hotel

Table 6.15   Duties and Responsibilities of the Kitchen Stewarding Department

Section	Activities
Main range	• To clean thoroughly all grilled plates, troughs, grease traps, edges and corners. • To clean all oven and salamanders with oven cleaner. • To clean steam tables, steam table stands, and shelves below steam tables. • Clean dust strong below steam tables. • Clean shelves above steam table. • Scrub down duckboard and scrub below them.
Soup kitchen	• To clean all pots steam kettles, large steamers, and electric pots. • To clean all fixtures and exposed pipes. • To clean all shelves and wipe all boxes and cans and arrange neatly. • To remove items from shelves below all work table and remove and scrub all grill shelves. • To wipe and polish sinks and pots of all work tables. • To scrub floors. • To thoroughly clean can openers.
Butcher shop	• To dismantle and clean thoroughly the meat saw. • To clean and protect with light coating and grease the food choppers. • To remove and clean drawers of fish box steam inside and below the fish boxes. • To scrub all other working surfaces with soap and very hot water. • To scrape and cleanse thoroughly the chopping blocks and wood tables. • To remove items kept below the table and scrub the lower shelves thoroughly. • To wash wall shelves and work sink thoroughly. • To wipe refrigerator doors. • To scrub floors.
Pantry	• To remove and scrub duck boards. • To scrub top of all working tables. • To scrub all wall shelves and shelves in all front areas. • To wipe down coffee urns. • To remove items kept below the work tables and scrub the shelves below the table. • To wipe down drinks and stainless steel edgings. • To scrub floors.
Front of kitchen	• To scrub all stainless steel areas including shelves and egg machines. • To thoroughly scrub floors.
Garbage	• To empty and steam out all garbage cans and scrub them both inside and out. • Garbage rooms to be cleaned and floor to be thoroughly scrubbed.

(contd)

Table 6.15   *(contd)*

Section	Activities
Bakery shop	• To clean sinks and all work areas under the work tables. • To clean stove and ovens, inside and out. • To scrub floor. • To clean and polish stainless steel surfaces.
Ice	• Ice to be racked in the morning. • All the ice troughs to be filled in the morning.

directly to the executive chef. They must be familiar with all kitchen and service equipment, their usage procurement, and maintenance and storage, and government laws enforced by the health and sanitation department.

Assistant managers   They assist the executive kitchen steward and supervise the utility personnel in the absence of the chief steward. He/she is a working supervisor and normally collects the carts, room service trays, and cafeteria dishes. He/she scraps and stacks dishes and racks up glasses. They also make the coffee, fill up ice trucks, rack ice, and mop up spilled fluids. They distribute clean silverware in their proper storage area.

Dishwashers   They are responsible for cleaning and feeding the stacked dishes into the dish machine, to pull out the washed and dried dishes from the machine and stack them into carts, and to run the glasses and silver utensils through the glass machine.

Potmen   They clean all pots used by kitchen and soup kettles. During slack periods, they empty the kitchen garbage.

Ware men   They clear, polish, and burnish all silver flatware and hollow ware. During slack periods they clear all copperware.

Scullery men   They are responsible for the wash up of metal kitchen vessels and implements. The kitchen scullery is known as plonge, and the scullery man as the plongeur.

Night duty stewards   The peak workload occurs at different sections at different times during the work shift; therefore, the related stewards in each section pitch in and help each other under the directions of the supervisor on duty.

Benefits of Kitchen Stewarding

The management of any catering operations cannot be complete without the function of cleaning, rearranging the utensils for next operations, and proper inventory of the stock. Earlier all these activities were either performed by the food production staff, or by food and beverage service staff. In the wake of increasing pressure on maintaining quality of food or quality of service, and low prestige associated with dish washing as a task, there was a demand for setting up a new department for all cleaning task, inventory control of all equipment, garbage disposal, etc. The kitchen stewarding department thus came into existence. Its inception has helped the hotel and catering industry in the following ways:

Meeting the requirements of the food and beverage department The kitchen stewarding play a vital role in maintaining the highest levels of hygiene and sanitation standards, which spells success for the hotel and catering property.

Conserving input material and energy or cost reduction The installation of large efficient cleaning equipment operated by technically skilled people of the department contributes in great measure to saving cost inputs that go into maintenance of equipment as also the presentation of items.

Enhancing image and market share of the hotel property and competitive advantage The presence of a dedicated skilled staff for maintaining the best standards of cleanliness and hygiene contribute towards enhancing the brand image of a property, and also provides a competitive edge to it.

Checklist of Key Heavy Duty Equipment

Keeping the equipment spick and span and clean not only contributes towards cleanliness and hygiene, which in turn contributes to ensuring the making of good and healthy food. Maintenance of equipment results in its efficient working as also lower consumption of energy. But all this heavy physical activity is largely mechanized and done with the help of huge machines, and a range of chemical agents and cleansers (See Table 6.16).

Table 6.16 Common Cleansing Products (Agents) Used in the Hotel Industry

Products	Nature/Purpose
Champ	General purpose detergent
R-klin	Liquid detergent for dishwashing machine
Dry master	Rinse or drying aid for dishwashing machine
Superklin	Heavy duty floor cleaner
Sheqa	Stain remover
Runner	Oven cleaner
Ed	Bio free agent degreaser for pipes
Olive	Silver detarnisher
Shine	Descaler
Mp 8	Hood cleaner and filter degreaser
Chase	Insect repellent
Kool	Hand wash

Box 6.1 Heavy-duty Equipment—Useful Tips

- Temperature of water for washing 40–160°F.
- To kill bacteria, rinse water is to be heated to 180°F.
- Temperature for sterilization of cutlery, crockery is 170–180°F.
- Door type dishwasher can handle 810 to 1875 dishes per hour.
- A single-tank conveyer can handle from 4500–5650 dishes per hour.

- A double-tank conveyer can handle from 8,500–12,000 dishes per hour.
- A flight type dish washer can handle from 6,750–34,000 dishes per hour.
- Most flight units contain pre-wash, power wash, power rinse, and final rinse cycles.
- ph value of water should be below 10.2.

A list of some heavy duty equipment that are generally found in a large hotel include the following. Box 6.1 gives useful tips on the use of some common heavy-duty equipment.

1. Automatic dish washing machine
2. Ice cube machine
3. Glass cleaning machine
4. High pressure spray cleaner
5. Floor scrubbing machine
6. Conveyer belt
7. Mobile Bain Marie
8. Auto lift
9. Mobile tray master
10. Racks
11. Loaders (all sizes)
12. Reject trolley
13. Warming cabinet
14. Three sinks dish washing
15. Silver polishing machine
16. Dish landing table
17. Garbage container

Other detergents/cleaning agents/chemicals

- Liquid shop
- Caustic soda
- Suma grill d 9
- Suma scale d 5
- Suma nova
- Suma bright

- Suma rinse
- Suma onex
- Liquid bleach
- Tepol
- Silver dip
- Cleaning powder

Coordination with Kitchen and Other Departments/Sections

Coordination is of great importance not only between the various service staff members but also between them and the kitchen staff. It requires proper layout of the kitchen that would facilitate systematic and easy pickup of food by the waiter/waitress. Pickup areas should be clearly defined; and entrance and exits should be laid out to establish a standard format for traffic flow. In many hotels, a buffer zone is provided between the service and preparation staff by having a side man, mostly the chef, who remits all orders to the cooks.

SUMMARY

Storeroom, cellar, and kitchen stewarding department are very essential to a catering organization and there is a vital link between receiving, storing, and issuing of stocks. More often than not these activities are found neglected. If properly and professionally managed, these departments can go a long way in helping a facility build its name while contributing towards cost reduction in more ways than one. The staff responsible for functioning of a store must be qualified and have excellent knowledge about food and beverage commodities and he/she should be carefully selected and trained for the job. Physical facilities must be such that they contribute to efficiency and ensure efficacy in the performance of these functions. The functions of a storeroom and cellar are not only to store food or beverage items but also to control the department in coordination with the kitchen stewarding department. Various types of food commodities and beverages require special handling to maintain quality. Good storeroom practices and procedures help in generating revenue.

CONCEPT REVIEW QUESTIONS

1. Define a store and justify the need of a storeroom in a hotel.
2. Differentiate between a perishable food store and a cellar.
3. Discuss the architectural features of a good store.
4. Illustrate the flow of work diagram of a storeroom.

5. Enlist points to be considered while planning a cellar.
6. Prepare a checklist of equipment required in a food store and cellar.
7. Do you think that a store helps in reducing cost, and control pilferage and wastage? Express your views with suitable examples.
8. Explain the functions of kitchen stewarding department.
9. Propose the organizational structure of the kitchen stewarding department of a 500-room hotel property.
10. Make a checklist of equipment required and list of detergents/chemicals to be used by the kitchen stewarding department.

NUMERICAL PROBLEMS

1. Compute the area required for an 80-cover specialty having a seat turnover of 3.
2. A three star hotel has 50 rooms, a coffee shop of 50 covers, and 45 cover bar with banquet facilities of 300 covers. Determine the space and equipment requirement for food and beverage stores. (Assume necessary information).
3. The Institute of Hotel Management has an annual intake of 300 students in a three years BSc course. Workout the storage facilities for the hostel of the institute.

PROJECT ASSIGNMENTS

1. Visit a five star hotel in your city and prepare a report on the various stores in the hotel and enlist their special features.
2. Conduct an interview with the storekeeper of the same property and confirm the standard practices and procedures adopted by them.
3. Visit a local retail store in your city and compare the functioning of that store with that of a dry store of a five star hotel.
4. Visit the store of your organization and confirm its strengths and weaknesses. Interview the storekeeper and ask about problems faced by him/her due to poor planning and designing (if any).
5. Collect the documents used in a storeroom and cellar.

REFERENCES

Borsenik, Frank D. and Alan T. Stuffs (1996), *The Management of Maintenance and Engineering Systems in the Hospitality Industry,* John Wiley and Sons, Inc. New York.

Dana, Arthur W. (1986), *Kitchen Planning for Quantity Food Service,* Harper and Bros, New York.

Kinton and Ceserani (1980), *Theory of Catering,* Fourth edition, Edward Arnold Publishers Ltd, London.

Scriven, Carl and James Stevens (1989), *Food Equipment Facts,* Van Nostrand Reinhold, New York.

Sethi, Mohini and Surjieet Malhan (1984), *Catering Management,* Willey Eastern Limited, New Delhi.

West-Wood and V.F. Harger (1977), *Food Service in Institutions,* Fifth edition, John Wiley and Sons, New York.

CHAPTER 7

Project Management

Chapter Outline:

The following topics are covered in this chapter
- Network models
- Network analysis
- CPM and PERT
- Comparison between CPM and PERT
- Basic rules and procedures for network analysis
- Network crashing
- Determining crash and normal cost

Learning Objectives:

This chapter will enable you to understand
- The definition of CPM and PERT
- The difference between CPM and PERT
- The development of a network diagram
- The rules and procedures for network analysis
- Designing of network models
- The computation of crash and normal cost
- How to apply the concept of network analysis in project management

INTRODUCTION

In the previous chapters, we have discussed various activities pertaining to the operations in the hotel business right from scratch; that is, setting up of a new property to making it an operational success. During the course of our discussions, we often came across terms such as project planning, facility designing, activities, etc. being used in various contexts. So far, the focus was on the various activities or tasks that went into each and every aspect of planning a hotel facility as also the kind of resources required for those activities. An important aspect of these tasks is their accomplishment within the desired time frame and within the budget or finances at hand. This is because apart from good planning, what is required is careful and scrupulous implementation of those plans to ensure the success of the business activity undertaken.

The process of planning and executing a project by synchronizing various constituent activities to achieve its accomplishment within the desired timelines and available resources is called project management. Experts have defined project management in various ways. According to the UK Association of Project Management, 'it is a process of planning, organizing, monitoring, and controlling of all aspects of a project and the motivation involved to achieve the project objectives safely and within the agreed time, cost and performance criteria.' As a future manager of the hospitality and service industry, you are likely to come across scores of projects, such as planning a new hotel/restaurant/bar, or may be renovating an old property, or even a research project, during the course of your career. It is, therefore, necessary to not only have an idea of the contours of planning but also a good grasp of the tools or instruments that aid in efficient project management.

Planning a new project requires identification of various activities involved in the project and the sequence in which these activities have to be performed. A well planned project leads to completion within the scheduled time, thus avoiding unnecessary delays and extra cost. In this chapter, we shall focus on various aspects of project management, particularly on the tools and models that are widely used to ensure the completion of projects within the specified time and within the limitation of all resources.

THE NETWORK MODELS (CPM/PERT)

The key to successful implementation of the objectives and policies in any organization is to clearly delineate and execute various projects that would lead to the achievement of the organizational goals. Simply put, a project is a group of tasks aimed towards the achievement of an objective within stipulated time and cost. Thus, the first step in project management would be determination of the constituent activities and their interrelationships, estimation of the resources required, and a realistic projection of the time needed to accomplish these activities. This detailed analysis of the project has to be followed up with execution of the activities under complete monitoring and control to meet the time lines and avoid cost escalation of the projects.

Network Analysis

An important aspect of project management is cost control and time management. The project managers would always aim to accomplish activities in the shortest possible time without compromising on the quality of work and the costs involved. A technique helping them achieve this is network analysis. It is a technique for sequencing problems interested in minimizing the total time required to complete the project, as well as minimizing the overall project costs. It is particularly suitable for projects which are not routine or repetitive, and which are conducted only once or a few times. For example, construction of building, dams, research and development, marketing of new products, building a ship, construction of factories, missile production, etc.

Modern management uses two forms of network analysis or techniques in most scheduling projects as sequencing models:

- Critical Path Method (CPM) and
- Programme Evaluation and Review Technique (PERT)

Both these are planning techniques and tools of management control that can meet multiple demands of the modern business. These are by far the most popular techniques used in the world today.

History of PERT and CPM   The development of PERT began in the US navy around 1958 when the navy was faced with the task of production of Polaris Missile system under severe time constraints. The major challenge was the timeframe and the cost performance of the project. It took a longer time period to complete and cost a lot more than was estimated. A research team was assembled to tackle the problem and that in effect resulted in the development of PERT.

Critical Path Method (CPM), on the other hand, was the result of an industrial effort which was jointly initiated by DuPont Company and Remington Rand Univac. The objective of the CPM research team was to determine how best to reduce the time required to perform routine plant overhead, maintenance, and construction work. In essence, they were interested in determining the optimum tradeoff of the project duration and the total project cost.

PERT/CPM (Planning and Control Tools) PERT/CPM are widely accepted network tools for planning and controlling all the events and activities in a complex and dynamic project or programme. A project is a combination of various activities. For example, construction of a fast food restaurant involves a series of activities such as searching for a site, purchasing land, construction of the building, floor planning for fast food as well as kitchen, procurement of equipment, etc. Similarly, a banquet function would comprise many activities. In planning and scheduling the activities of large sized projects, PERT and CPM are used most commonly. They enable the management to plan and implement a project, and to achieve the desired goals of timely completion with optimum use of available human, material, and financial resources.

In PERT and CPM the milestones are represented as events. Event or node is either the beginning of an activity or its conclusion. Activity consumes various resources such as time, money, materials, etc. When all activities and events in a project are connected logically and sequentially, they form a network, which is the basic record in network management. In network records, events or nodes are denoted by numerals such as 1, 2, 3, etc. while activities are denoted by alphabets such as A, B, C, etc.

Difference between PERT and CPM Although PERT and CPM are both planning tools meant for keeping a project on track, there are some basic differences between the two. PERT is *event oriented* and CPM is *activity oriented*. This is to say that while discussing a project as per PERT network, we say activity 1-2, activity 2-3, and so on. Or event 2 occurs after event 1, event 5 occurs after event 3, and so on. However, while discussing CPM network, we say activity A follows activity B, activity C follows activity B, and so on. In PERT network, it is easy to write a network diagram, because successor and predecessor event relationships can easily be identified.

PERT activities are *probabilistic* in nature. The time required to complete a PERT activity cannot be specified accurately because of uncertainties involved while carrying out the activity. PERT network is used when the activity times are probabilistic; hence three time estimations are considered: *optimistic time, most likely time and pessimistic time.*

Optimistic time estimate This is the shortest possible time estimate of an activity and is based upon the premise that everything will go right for the earliest completion of the activity.

Pessimistic time estimate It is the longest possible time estimate of an activity and is based on the premise that there are chances of interruptions in the completion of the activity.

Most likely time   This estimate has the highest probability of occurrence. It is the feeling of the project manager.

From these three time estimates a weighted mean or average is calculated and termed as expected time of the activity.

CPM does not take into account the uncertainties in the estimation of time for an activity. The time required is deterministic; only one time is considered as activity time or duration is related to cost. By decreasing the activity duration, direct cost can be increased (crashing of activity duration is possible). In PERT, as there is no certainty of time, activity duration cannot be reduced. Hence, cost cannot be expressed correctly. So we can say that expected cost of completion of activity (crashing of activity duration) is not possible. Table 7.1 summarizes the comparison between PERT and CPM network tools.

Table 7.1   A Brief Comparison between PERT and CPM Network Tools

Key Words	PERT	CPM
Devised by	US Navy	DuPont Company
Model	Probabilistic model	Deterministic model
Orientation	Event oriented	Activity oriented
Dummy activities	Use of dummy activities required for representing the proper sequencing	Use of dummy activities is not required
Repetition	Used for repetitive jobs	Used for non-repetitive jobs
Purpose	Mainly used for planning and scheduling research programmes	Used for constructions and business programmes
Control	Used as an important control device	Cannot be used as a control device

PERT/Cost   Developed in 1962, PERT/cost is an extension of PERT for planning. It has now added to the managerial effectiveness in planning/control. PERT/cost is a very useful tool for planning, monitoring, and controlling the cost progress as well as time progress of a project. The combination of PERT/time and PERT/cost can indicate the extent to which the managers have met time schedules, cost estimates, and technical performance standards. If there are shortfalls or deviations, the managers can re-plan and re-combine the resources to minimize costs and meet time schedule.

Advantages of PERT/CPM to Management   The following are the advantages of adapting PERT and CPM models while executing projects.

1. PERT is the least mathematical device. It is very simple. It has considerable practical utility in project management. It covers all the phases of project management such as:

(a) Project planning,
(b) Time and resource estimation,
(c) Basic scheduling,
(d) Time-cost tradeoffs,
(e) Resources allocation, and
(f) Project control

2. CPM and PERT force managers to plan projects as time-event analysis cannot be made without planning.
3. PERT is an excellent tool for control. The critical path method (CPM) offers an effective tool for management control. PERT cost tradeoff acts as a means of cost control also.
4. PERT cost system is useful as a tool for budgetary control.
5. PERT is also an effective means of communication. Network methods (CPM/PERT) provide a clear and unambiguous way of documenting the plans and schedules and communicating the time and cost performance of the projects to the project team and higher management.
6. PERT can be used for projects of any size. It is simple, easy to understand, and it can be easily sold to the users.
7. PERT/CPM methods, if properly developed by the project team, can encourage team spirit and build project confidence in completing projects within the required time span. The clear delineation of activities can aid in allocating responsibility to achieve project objectives. Lower management is motivated as the people are involved in project execution.

Limitations of CPM/PERT

1. CPM assumes that there is a certain time for the activity performance. In real life the assumed time interval may not be realized.
2. CPM does not offer statistical analysis in determination of estimates of time.
3. CPM is a static planning model and not a dynamic controlling device. Any change in the network leads to repetition of the entire evaluation.
4. PERT is not suitable for routine planning or recurrent events.
5. PERT emphasizes only on time and not on costs.
6. PERT is not a complete system of cure for all devices. For instance, it forces planning, it does not do planning. It creates an environment for effective control, but it cannot provide automatic control.

Note: 1. Budgeting is primarily directed towards control of cost. It is a traditional device of control.

2. PERT/CPM are system-oriented planning and control devices. They emphasize upon the control of time, which are in addition to the usual control devices.

3. PERT/Cost is very useful in project management. It is an instrument of cost control.

DRAWING OF A NETWORK DIAGRAM

As discussed earlier, in PERT and CPM the milestones are represented as events. Event or node is either the beginning of an activity or its conclusion. Activity is represented by means of an arrow, which is resource consuming. The resources could be time, money, materials, etc. Event does not consume any resource, but it signifies either the start or the end of an activity. In a network diagram, an event is represented by a circle, rectangle, or a triangle. When all activities and events in a project are connected, logically and sequentially they form a network, which is the basic record in network management.

Basic Steps

The basic steps for drawing a network diagram are the following:

Listing List out all the activities involved in the project.

Arranging Once the activities are listed, they are arranged in a sequential manner and logical order.

Estimation of time After arranging the activities in a logical sequence, their time is estimated and written against each activity. For example: foundation digging, 7 days or a week

Beginning of activities Some of the activities do not have logical relationship; in such cases, they can be started simultaneously. For example, preparation of food items and decoration of *mandap* (stage for marriage rituals) for organizing a marriage function do not have a logical relationship, hence both of them can be started simultaneously. Here by logical it is meant that one activity is not dependent on the occurrence of the other activity.

Activity addition Activities are added to the network, depending upon their logical relationship towards completion of the project network.

Basic rules In network drawing there are some basic conventions that are followed universally. These help in easy understanding of the network drawing. Some of the points to be remembered while drawing the network are as follows:

(a) There must be only one beginning and one end for the network as shown in Figure 7.1.

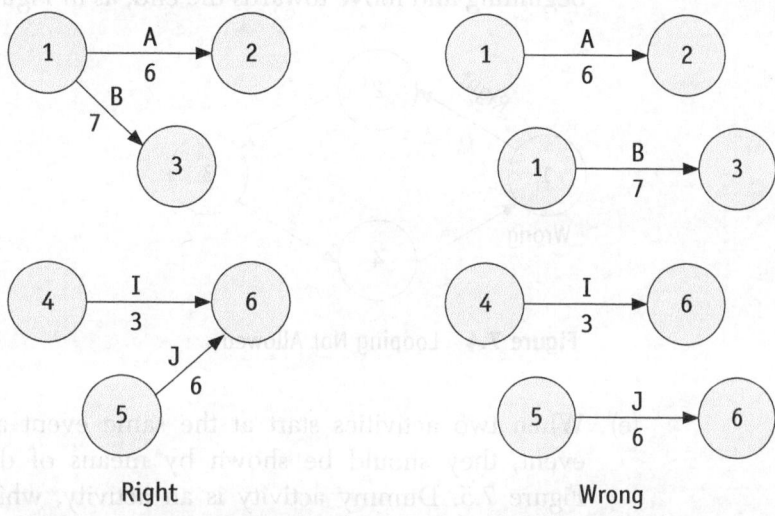

Right   **Wrong**

Figure 7.1 Writing the Network

(b) Event number should be written inside the circle or node (or triangle/ square/rectangle, etc.). Activity name must be represented by capital alphabetical letters and written above the arrow. The time required for the activity should be written below the arrow as in Figure 7.2.

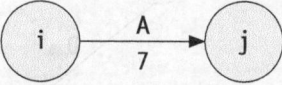

Figure 7.2 Numbering and Naming the Activities

(c) While writing the network, ensure that activities do not cross each other. Also, arcs or loops as in Figure 7.3 should not join activities.

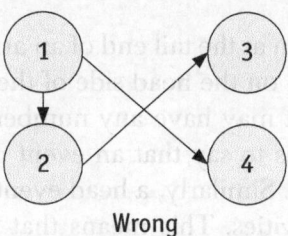

Wrong

Figure 7.3 Crossing of Activities Not Allowed

(d) While writing a network, looping should be avoided. This is to say that the network arrows should move in one direction, that is start from the beginning and move towards the end, as in Figure 7.4.

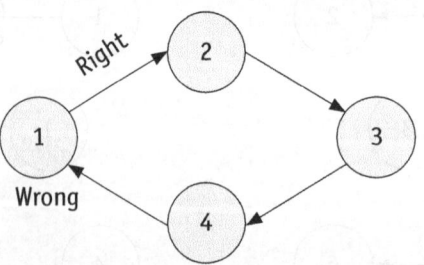

Figure 7.4   Looping Not Allowed

(e) When two activities start at the same event and end at the same event, they should be shown by means of dummy activity as in Figure 7.5. Dummy activity is an activity, which simply shows the logical relationship and does not consume any resource. It should be represented by a dotted line as shown. In Figure 7.5, activities C and D start at event 3 and end at event 4. C and D are shown in the full lines, whereas dummy activity is shown in dotted line.

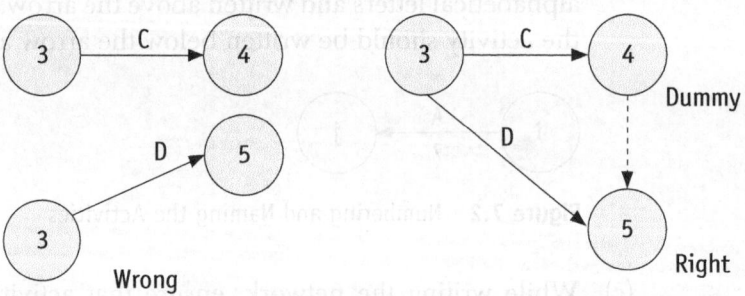

Figure 7.5   Depiction of Dummy Activity

(f) When the event is written at the tail end of an arrow, it is known as tail event. If event is written on the head side of the arrow, it is known as head event. A tail event may have any number of arrows (activities) emerging from it. This is to say that an event may be a tail event to any number of activities. Similarly, a head event may be a head event for any number of activities. This means that several activities may conclude at one event. This is shown in Figure 7.6.

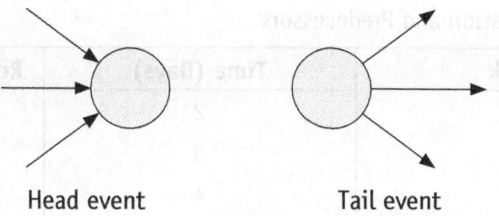

Figure 7.6 Head Event and Tail Event

Time Estimation in PERT

There are three kinds of time estimates in PERT, namely optimistic time, pessimistic time, and likely time.

Optimistic time It is represented by 't*o*'; here the estimator presumes that everything goes on well and he or she will not come across any kind of uncertainties. Thus, the shortest possible time is estimated for project completion.

Pessimistic time It is represented by 't*p*'. In this case, the estimator presumes the worst case scenario that everything goes wrong. Expecting all sorts of uncertainties to crop up, the longest possible duration is estimated for project accomplishment.

Likely time It is represented by 't*l*'. In this case, the estimator expects that he or she may come across some sort of uncertainties and many a time things will go right.

Critical path The critical path is defined as the longest duration between the first and the last nodes of a project. While tracing the path from the first node to the last node, one should always move along the direction of the arrows. The duration of a path is simply the sum of the duration of all activities on the path.

Writing the CPM Network

The first step in writing the CPM network is to establish the logical—predecessor and successor—relationship between the various constituent activities. That is, which activity is to be taken up after a specific task. Let us see how it is done by means of the following problem.

Illustration 1 Prepare a network diagram and identify the critical path of various tasks for a hotel project. Duration and predecessors are given in Table 7.2.

Table 7.2   Duration and Predecessors

Task	Time (Days)	Required Predecessor(s)
A	2	---------
B	3	---------
C	4	---------
D	1	A
E	2	B
F	5	B
G	7	C
H	2	D,E
I	3	F,G
J	1	H,I

Solution   As first three tasks A, B, and C do not require any predecessor, that is, no other tasks need to be completed for these to get started. Therefore, these become the starting tasks of the project. Make a small circle to represent the starting event or node of the project. Mark this node as 1. Then draw three arrows starting from this node to represent the activities A, B, and C [Figure 7. 2(a)].

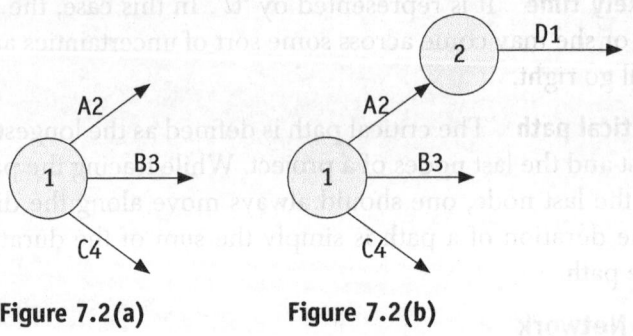

Figure 7.2(a)   **Figure 7.2(b)**

We show these along with the names of the three activities in the network diagram. Activity D needs A as its preceding activity, which means that D can be started only when A gets over. Make a small circle at the end of the arrow for activity A to represent event 2, which marks the completion of activity A. Then draw an arrow from node 2 to represent activity D [Figure 7.2(b)].

Table 7.2 shows that the predecessor for activities E and F is B. Activity B gets completed in event 3. Therefore, draw two arrows from node 3 to represent activities E and F [Figure 7.2(c)].

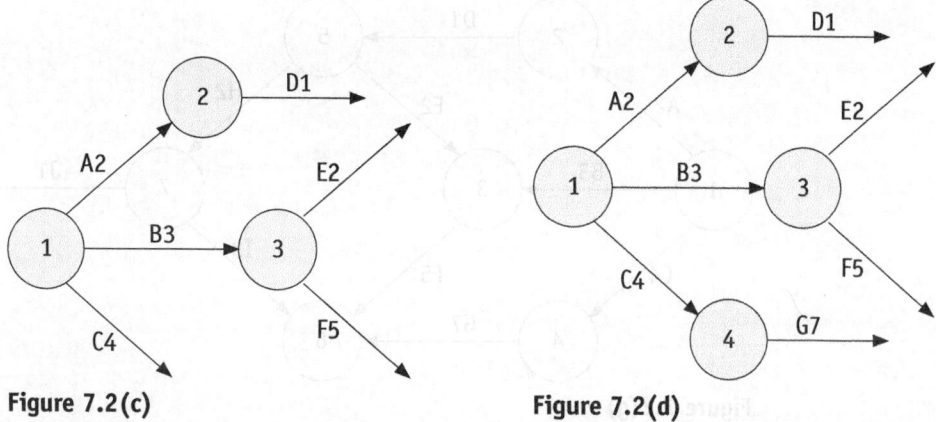

Figure 7.2(c)   Figure 7.2(d)

Activity G can be started at event 4 as its required predecessor is C, which ends at node 4 [Figure7.2(d)].

Activity H requires both D and E to be over before it starts. Therefore, join arrows D and E to end at a common node 5. From this new event 5, draw an arrow to represent activity H [Figure 7.2(e)]. Similarly, activity I requires both F and G to end before it starts. Therefore, join arrows F and G to end at a common node 6. From this new event 6, draw an arrow to represent activity I [Figure 7.2(f).].

Activity J requires both H and I to be over before its start. Therefore, join arrows H and I to end at a common node 7. From this new event 7, draw an arrow to represent activities H and I. From event 7, draw an arrow to represent activity J. Activity J ends at node 8, which becomes the last node of the project [Figure7.2(g)].

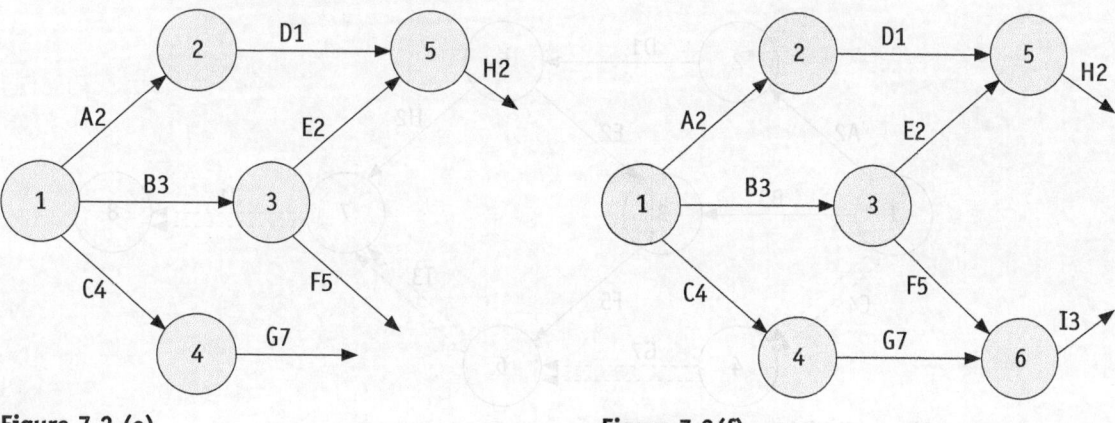

Figure 7.2.(e)   Figure 7.2(f)

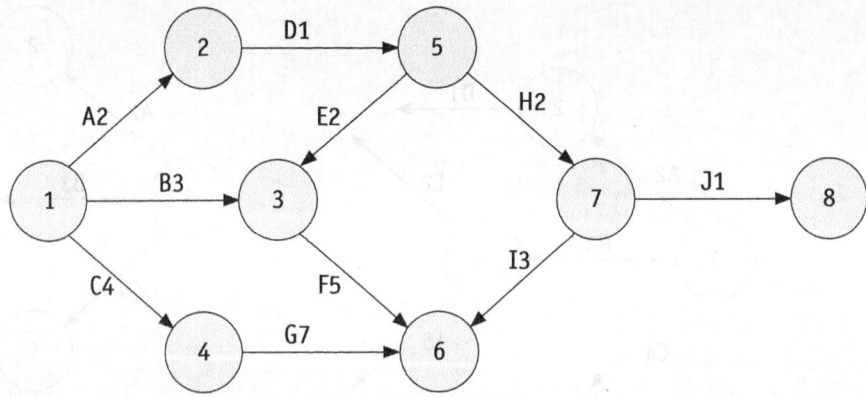

Figure 7.2(g)

From Table 7.2, we find that among all the possible paths, the longest duration is 15 days for the path 1-4-6-7-8 (CGIJ) as computed in Table 7.3. Therefore, this is the critical path. Always mark the critical path with double (dotted) arrows in a network diagram as shown in Figure [7.2.(h)]. The duration of a project is always the same as the duration of its critical path.

Table 7.3 Duration of Various Activity Paths

Paths	Duration
1-2-5-7-8 (ADHJ)	2+1+2+1=6
1-3-5-7-8 (BEHJ)	3+2+2+1=8
1-3-6-7-8 (BFIJ)	3+5+3+1=12
1-4-6-7-8 (CGIJ)	4+7+3+1=15 (Critical path)

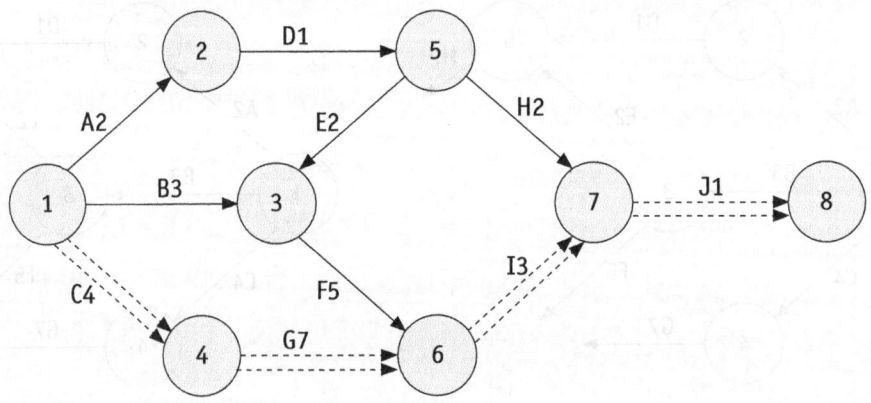

Figure 7.2(h)

Table 7.4

Activity	Duration in Days
A	6
B	8
C	3
D	4
E	6
F	10
G	3

Table 7.5

Activity	Immediate Predecessor	Time in Days
A	---	6
B	---	8
C	A	3
D	A	4
E	B,D	6
F	B,C and D	10
G	E	3

Illustration 2 A small project has 7 activities and the time in days for each activity is given in Table 7.4.

Given that activities A and B can start at the beginning of the project. When A is completed, C and D can start. E can start only when B and D are finished. F can start when B, C, and D are completed and is the final activity. G can start when E is finished and is the final activity. Draw the network and find the project completion time.

Solution: Based on the data provided, establish the logical relationship between the activities (Table 7.5).

Draw the network and enter the times and find Te. Refer Figure 7.3.

Time Estimation in CPM

Once the network is drawn, that is the activities and nodes are completed, the next step is to number the events (nodes) and enter the time distribution of each activity. Thereafter, calculate the project completion time. As we know, the CPM activities have single time estimates, and no uncertainties are presumed,

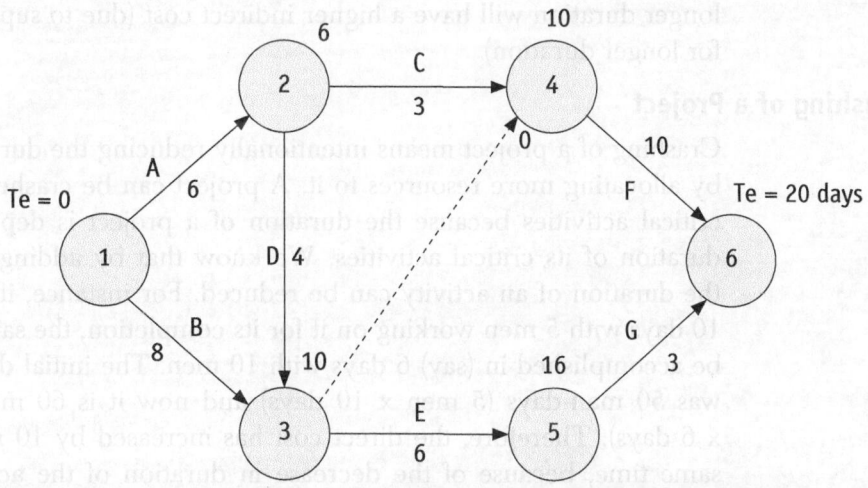

Figure 7.3 Project Completion Time=20 Days and Critical Path is A-D-F

the system is deterministic in nature. While dealing with CPM networks, we come across the following kinds of time estimates.

Earliest start time   This is the earliest occurrence time for the event from which the activity arrow originates.

Earliest finish time   This is the earliest occurrence time for the event from which the activity arrow originates plus the duration of the activity.

Latest start time   This is the latest occurrence time for the node at which the activity arrow terminates minus the duration of the activity.

Latest finish time   This is the latest occurrence time for the node at which the activity arrow terminates.

Free float   Free float for an activity is based on the possibility that all events occur at their earliest times that means all activities start as early as possible.

PROJECT COST ANALYSIS

All projects have two types of costs: *direct* and *indirect*. *Project direct cost* is the cost involved in all the activities of the project. *Activity direct cost* is the cost of materials, labour (salaries, wages, overtime cost, hiring and firing cost, etc.), and machines and equipment.

Project indirect cost is mainly the cost of supervision during the implementation of the project. The salaries paid to the project manager/supervisor, etc., miscellaneous costs due to delays in the project, and rewards to the project team members for its early completion are indirect costs. Project indirect cost is dependant upon the length of duration of the project. A project having a longer duration will have a higher indirect cost (due to supervision required for longer duration)

Crashing of a Project

Crashing of a project means intentionally reducing the duration of a project by allocating more resources to it. A project can be crashed by crashing its critical activities because the duration of a project is dependent upon the duration of its critical activities. We know that by adding more resources, the duration of an activity can be reduced. For instance, if an activity takes 10 days with 5 men working on it for its completion, the same activity could be accomplished in (say) 6 days with 10 men. The initial direct activity cost was 50 man-days (5 men x 10 days) and now it is 60 man-days (10 men x 6 days). Therefore, the direct cost has increased by 10 man-days. At the same time, because of the decrease in duration of the activity by 4 days, the indirect cost (cost of supervision) decreases. Hence, it is observed that the direct and indirect costs are inversely proportional to each other, that is when one increases, the other decreases.

An activity can crash by adding more resources only up to a definite limit. Beyond that limit, the duration of the activity does not decrease because it results in reduction of labour efficiency following increasing confusion due to a large number of resources. In the above-mentioned example, if we increase the number of workers to 15, the same activity could be accomplished within 5 days; but by adding five more men (so that 20 men work on this activity), the activity time may not decrease. The limit beyond which the duration of the activity does not decrease by adding any amount of resources is called the *crash time* and the corresponding direct cost is called the *crash cost*. The normal time mentioned in the example (10 days) can be defined as the duration of an activity when just the adequate resources required for its performance are deployed. The corresponding minimum direct cost is called the *normal cost*.

In the actual time-cost curve (refer Figure 7.4), note that for crashing the activity from 10 days to 9 days, the incremental direct cost involved is approximately Rs 2. On other hand, for crashing the activity from 6 to 5 days, the incremental cost is Rs 20. This means that the cost of crashing keeps on increasing as the crash time is approached. For the sake of simplicity, in problems of crashing, assume that the linear approximation of the actual curve (shown by a dotted straight line in the graph (Figure 7.4) is followed. The linear approximation curve has a constant slope representing a constant incremental cost of crashing.

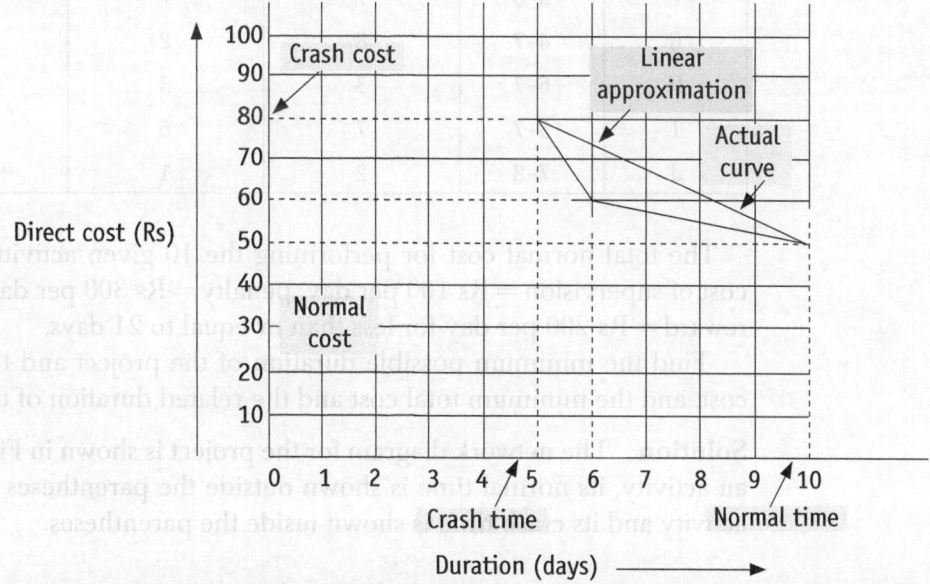

Figure 7.4   Direct Cost with Respect to Duration of an Activity

$$\text{Incremental cost of crashing} = \text{(Crash cost} - \text{normal cost)} \div \text{(normal time} - \text{crash time)}$$

$$= \frac{\text{Rs } (80 - 50)}{(10 - 5) \text{ days}} = \frac{\text{Rs } 30}{5 \text{ days}} = \text{Rs 6 per day}$$

During the process of crashing of a project, the critical path may get changed. At some stage of crashing, there may even be two or more critical paths (having the same duration) simultaneously. In such situations, one activity is chosen from each of the critical paths and these activities are crashed by unit time to reduce the duration of the project.

To understand the concept better, consider Table 7.6.

Table 7.5

Activity	Nodes	Normal Time (Days)	Crash Time (Days)	Incremental Cost of Crashing (Rs/Day)
A	1–2	6	5	50
B	1–3	8	7	100
C	2–5	9	8	80
D	2–4	11	7	60
E	3–4	5	1	90
F	3–6	7	7	–
G	4–7	8	2	40
H	6–7	3	3	–
I	5–7	7	6	100
J	7–8	2	1	50

The total normal cost for performing the 10 given activities = Rs 2,000, cost of supervision = Rs 100 per day, penalty = Rs 300 per day over 25 days, reward = Rs 200 per day for less than or equal to 21 days.

Find the minimum possible duration of the project and the related total cost, and the minimum total cost and the related duration of the project.

Solution   The network diagram for the project is shown in Figure 7.5(a). For an activity, its normal time is shown outside the parentheses adjacent to the activity and its crash time is shown inside the parentheses.

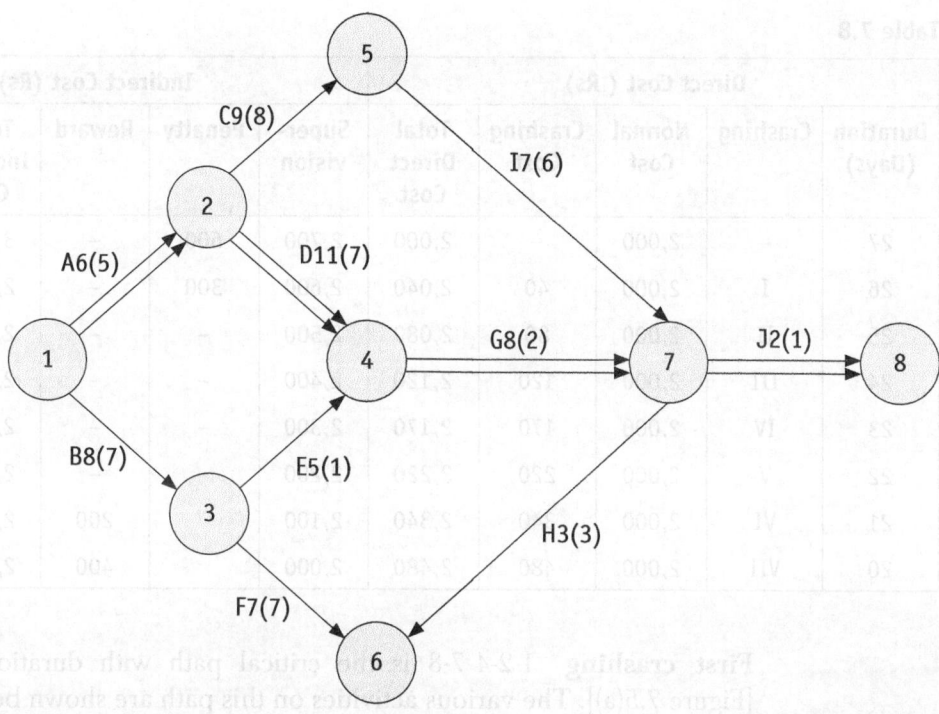

Figure 7. 5 (a)

Table 7.7

Path	Normal Time	Crash Time
1-2-5-7-8	24	20
1-2-4-7-8	27	15
1-3-4-7-8	23	11
1-3-6-7-8	20	18

Let us find the duration of the different paths possible between nodes 1 and 8 (Table 7.7).

Thus the critical path is 1-2-4-7-8, as its normal time is the highest at 27 days. In Table 7.5, for the project duration of 27 days, the normal cost is Rs 2,000, which is also the total direct cost. The cost of supervision at the rate of Rs 100 per day will be Rs 2,700 for 27 days. The penalty is Rs 300 per day over 25 days. With duration of 27 days, we are exceeding the 25 days duration by 2 days. Thus the penalty will be Rs 600. The total indirect cost is Rs 2,700 + Rs 600 = Rs 3,300.

The total cost is the sum of the total direct cost and the total indirect cost. Hence for 27 days, the total is Rs 2,000 + Rs 3,300 = Rs 5,300. At the end of each crashing, the table is updated according to the duration of the project. Remember that the cost of crashing given in Table 7.6 is the cumulative cost of crashing, i.e., as we proceed with the process of crashing, we add the cost of crashing to the value in the previous duration of the project (refer Table 7.8).

Table 7.8

Duration (Days)	Direct Cost (Rs)				Indirect Cost (Rs)				Total Cost
	Crashing	Normal Cost	Crashing Cost	Total Direct Cost	Super-vision	Penalty	Reward	Total Indirect Cost	
27	–	2,000	–	2,000	2,700	600	–	3,300	5,300
26	I	2,000	40	2,040	2,600	300	–	2,900	4,940
25	II	2,000	80	2,080	2,500	–	–	2,500	4,580
24	III	2,000	120	2,120	2,400	–	–	2,400	4,520
23	IV	2,000	170	2,170	2,300	–	–	2,300	4,470
22	V	2,000	220	2,220	2,200	–	–	2,200	4,420
21	VI	2,000	340	2,340	2,100		200	2,300	4,640
20	VII	2,000	480	2,480	2,000		400	2,400	4,880

First crashing 1-2-4-7-8 is the critical path with duration of 27 days [Figure 7.5(a)]. The various activities on this path are shown below.

Activity	Node	Crashing cost (Rs/days)
A	1-2	50
D	2-4	60
G	4-7	40
J	7-8	50

Crash G (4-7) by one day, as its cost of crashing is the lowest [(Figure 7.5(b)]. In Table 7.6 the cost of crashing shows Rs 40. The total cost now becomes Rs 4,940 (Table 7.8).

Second crashing 1-2-4-7-8 is still the critical path with duration of 26 days. The duration of various paths are revised as shown below. Again crash G (4-7) by one day [Figure 7.5.(c)] as its crash cost is lowest. The total cost is now Rs 4,580 (refer Table 7.8).

Path	Normal time	Crash time
1-2-5-7-8	24	20
1-2-4-7-8	26	15
1-3-4-7-8	22	11
1-3-6-7-8	20	18

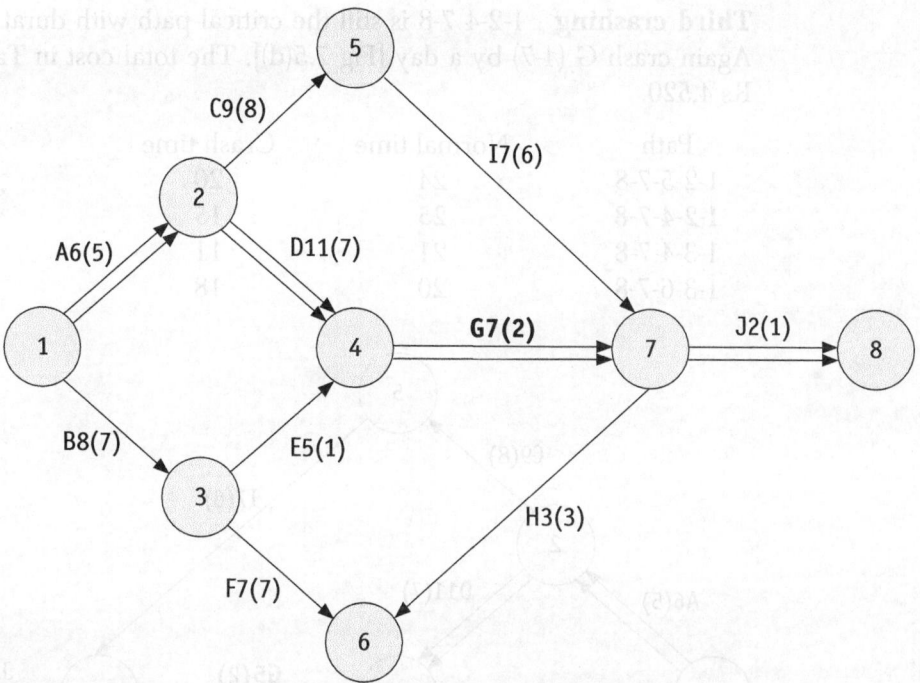

Figure 7.5(b)

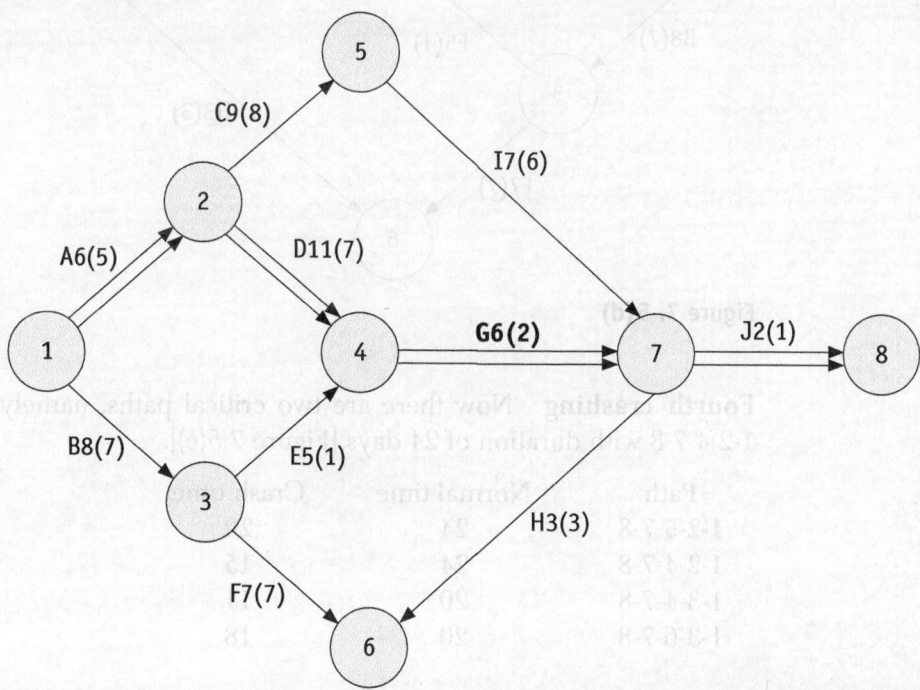

Figure 7.5(c)

Fourth crashing   Now there are two critical paths, namely, 1-2-5-7-8 and 1-2-4-7-8 with duration of 24 days (Fig. 7.5(c)).

Third crashing   1-2-4 7-8 is still the critical path with duration of 25 days. Again crash G (4-7) by a day [Fig 7.5(d)]. The total cost in Table 7.8 is now Rs 4,520.

Path	Normal time	Crash time
1-2-5-7-8	24	20
1-2-4-7-8	**25**	**15**
1-3-4-7-8	21	11
1-3-6-7-8	20	18

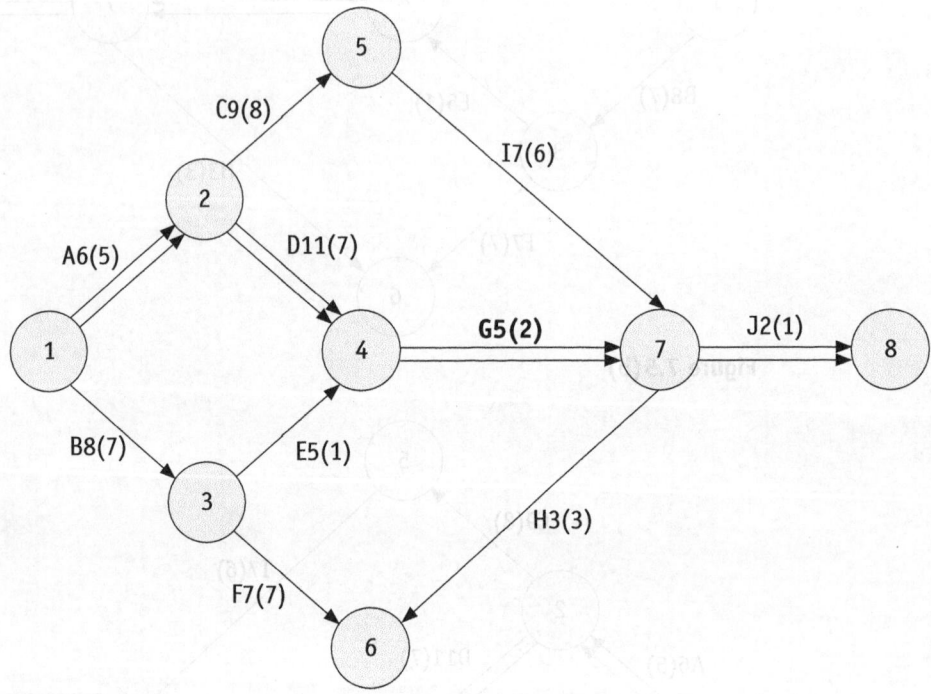

Figure 7. 5(d)

Fourth crashing   Now there are two critical paths, namely 1-2-5-7-8 and 1-2-4-7-8 with duration of 24 days [Figure 7.5(e)].

Path	Normal time	Crash time
1-2-5-7-8	**24**	**20**
1-2-4-7-8	**24**	**15**
1-3-4-7-8	20	11
1-3-6-7-8	20	18

Let us crash J (7-8) for Rs 50 (due to minimum combination costs). The total cost in Table 7.8 now becomes Rs 4,470. The costs of crashing various combinations are given as follows:

Combination	Crashing cost (Rs)
2-2	50
7-8	**50**
2-5, 2-4	$80 + 60 = 140$
2-5, 4-7	$80 + 40 = 120$
5-7, 2-4	$100 + 60 = 160$
5-7, 4-7	$100 + 40 = 140$

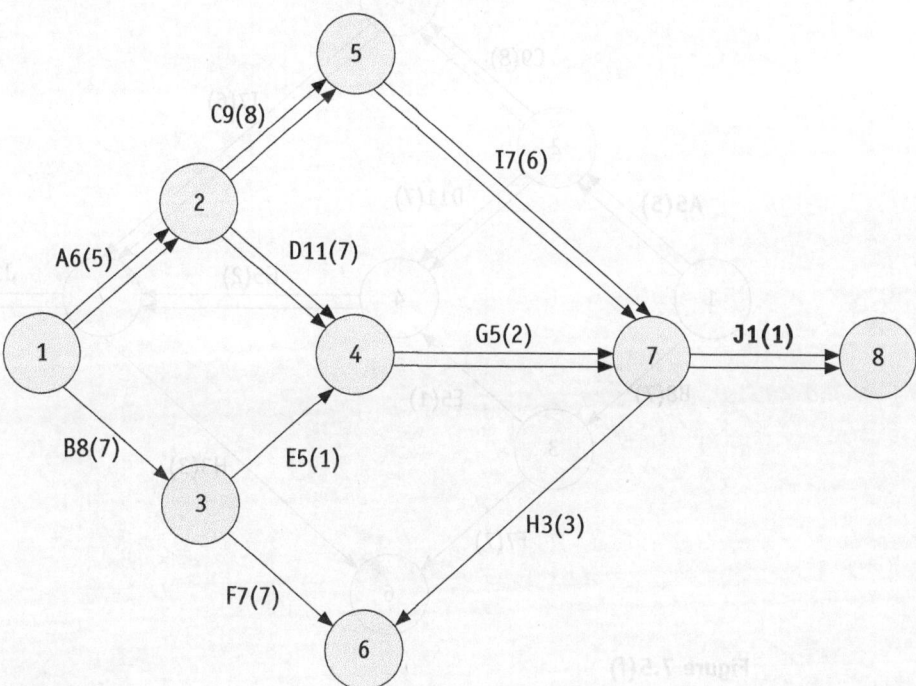

Figure 7.5(e)

Fifth crashing We still have the same two critical paths, namely 1-2-5-7-8 and 1-2-4-7-8 with duration of 23 days. Activity J (7-8) cannot be crashed further, as it has attained its crash time of one day.

Path	Normal time	Crash time
1-2-5-7-8	23	20
1-2-4-7-8	23	15
1-3-4-7-8	19	11
1-3-6-7-8	19	18

Therefore, crash A (1-2) for Rs 50 (Fig. 7.5 (f). The total cost in Table 7.8 is now Rs 4,420.

Combinations	Crashing cost (Rs)
1-2	**50**
2-5, 2-4	80, 60 =140
2-5, 4-7	80, 40 = 120
5-7, 2-4	100, 60 =160
5-7, 4-7	100, 40 =140

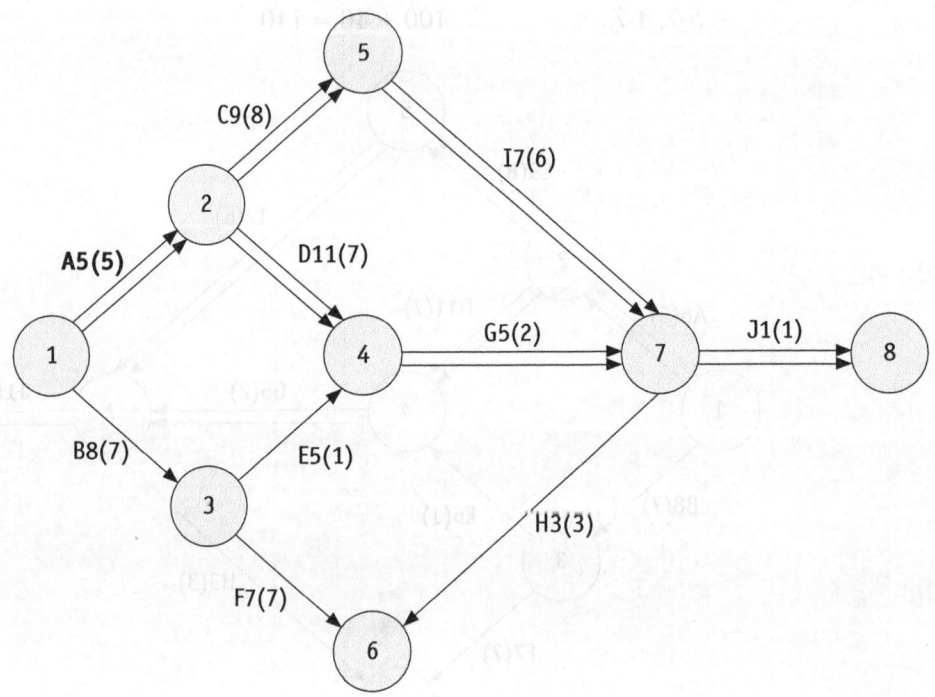

Figure 7.5(f)

Sixth crashing　Again we have the same two critical paths, namely 1-2-5-7-8 and 1-2-4-7-8 with duration of 22 days.

Path	Normal time	Crash time
1-2-5-7-8	**22**	**20**
1-2-4-7-8	**22**	**15**
1-3-4-7-8	19	11
1-3-6-7-8	19	18

Activity A (1-2) cannot be crashed further, as it has attained its crash time of five days [(Fig 7.5(g)]. Hence choose the combination 2-5, 4-7 for crashing at Rs 120 (due to minimum cost). The total cost in Table 7.8 is now Rs 4,640.

Combination	Crashing cost (Rs/day)
2-5, 2-4	80 + 60 = 140
2-5, 4-7	**80 + 40 = 120**
5-7, 2-4	100 + 60 = 160
5-7, 4-7	100 + 40 = 140

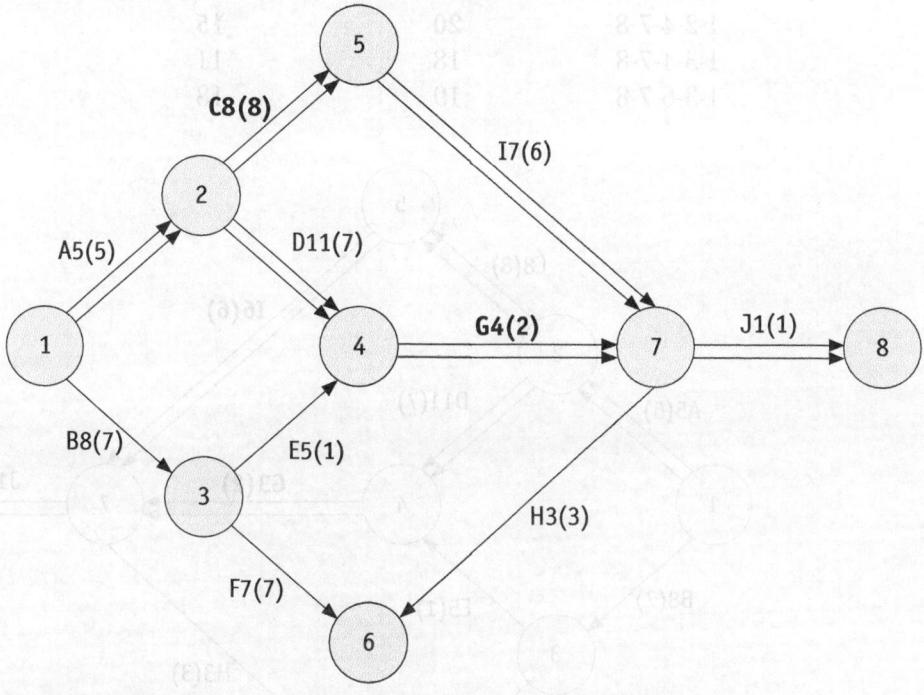

Figure 7.5(g)

Seventh crashing   Again we have the same two critical paths, namely 1-2-5-7-8 and 1-2-4-7-8 with duration of 21days. Activity C (2-5) cannot be crashed further, as it has attained its crash time of eight days.

Path	Normal time	Crash time
1-2-5-7-8	**21**	**20**
1-2-4-7-8	**21**	**15**
1-3-4-7-8	18	11
1-3-6-7-8	19	18

Choose the combination 5-7, 4-7 for crashing at Rs 140. The total direct cost in table is now Rs 4,880.

5-7, 2-4   100 + 60 = 160
5-7, 4-7   100 + 40 = 140

Again we have the same two critical paths, namely, 1-2-5-7-8 and 1-2-4-7-8 with duration of 20days. Refer [Figure 7.5(h)].

Path	Normal time	Crash time
1-2-5-7-8	**20**	**20**
1-2-4-7-8	**20**	**15**
1-3-4-7-8	18	11
1-3-6-7-8	19	18

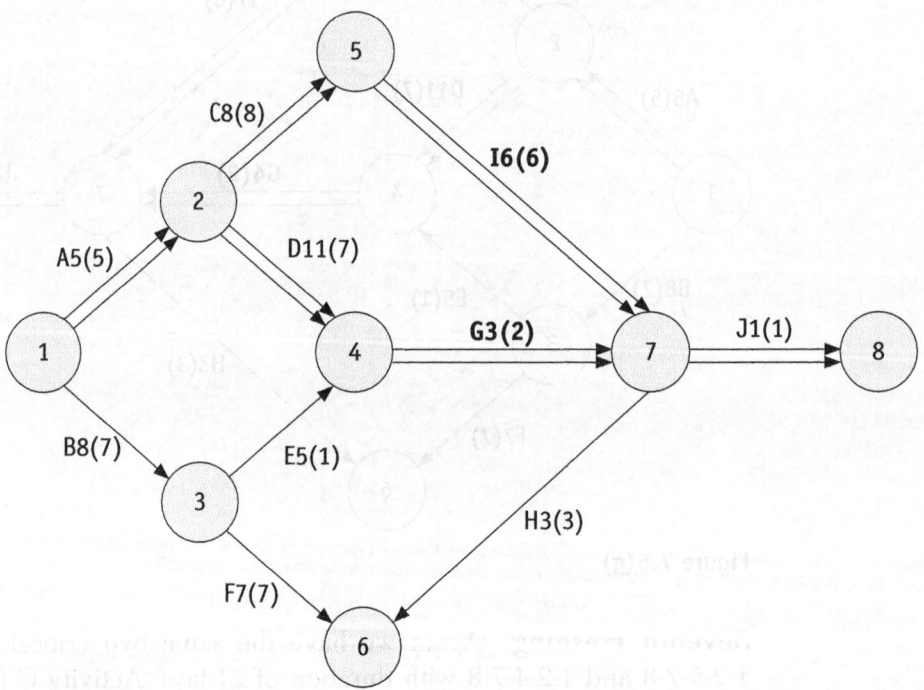

Figure 7.5(h)

Note that the minimum total cost is Rs 4,420 for 22 days duration. The minimum possible duration of the project is 20 days with a cost of Rs 4,880.

SUMMARY

Project management is the hallmark of success in any business situation. A timely completion of the project not only motivates the manpower engaged in project planning and development, but helps in keeping the costs under control by avoiding project over-runs and consequent losses. PERT/CPM are widely accepted network tools for planning and controlling all the events and activities in a complex and dynamic project or programme. In planning and scheduling the activities of large sized projects, PERT and CPM are used most commonly. They enable the management to plan and implement a project, and to achieve the desired goals of timely completion with optimum use of available human, materials, and financial resources. Although PERT and CPM are both planning tools meant for keeping a project on track, there are some basic differences between the two. PERT is event oriented and CPM is activity oriented. PERT activities are probabilistic in nature. CPM does not take into account the uncertainties in the estimation of time for an activity. The time required is deterministic; only one time is considered as activity time or duration is related to cost.

In PERT and CPM the milestones are represented as events. Event or node is either the beginning of an activity or its conclusion. Activity is represented by means of an arrow, which is resource consuming. The resources could be time, money, materials, etc. Event does not consume any resource, but it signifies either the start or the end of an activity. In a network diagram, an event is represented by a circle, rectangle, or a triangle. When all activities and events in a project are connected logically and sequentially they form a network, which is the basic record in network management.

All projects have two types of costs: *direct* and *indirect cost. Project direct cost* is the direct cost involved in all the activities of the project. *Activity direct cost* is the cost of materials, labour (salaries, wages, overtime cost, hiring and firing cost, etc.), and machines and equipment. *Project indirect cost* is mainly the cost of supervision during the implementation of the project. The salaries paid to the project manager/supervisor, etc., miscellaneous costs due to delays in the project, and rewards to the project team members for its early completion are indirect costs. Crashing of a project means intentionally reducing the duration of a project by allocating more resources to it. A project can be crashed by crashing its critical activities because the duration of a project is dependent upon the duration of its critical activities.

CONCEPT REVIEW QUESTIONS

1. Discuss the role of project management techniques in the hospitality industry with suitable examples.
2. What do you understand by the term 'network diagram'? Enlist the points to be considered while developing a network diagram.

3. Differentiate between CPM and PERT.
4. Discuss the limitations of CPM and PERT.
5. What do you mean by crashing of a project and how will you compute incremental cost of crashing?
6. An activity can be crashed by adding more resources only up to a definite limit. Beyond this limit, the duration of activity does not decrease by adding more resources. Justify the statement with suitable illustrations.
7. Enumerate the importance of dummy activities and dummy events in network diagrams of projects.
8. CPM and PERT become similar in application after a certain time. Discuss this statement.
9. Define the following terms:
   (a) Project
   (b) Dummy activity
   (c) Optimistic time estimate
   (d) Crashing
   (e) Crash time
   (f) Normal cost
   (g) Project direct cost
   (h) Project indirect cost

NUMERICAL PROBLEMS

1. A project comprises the activities shown in Table 7.9. Draw the network diagram and find the duration of the project.

Table 7.9

Activity	Predecessor/s	Time (Weeks)
A	–	7
B	A	10
C	A	12
D	B	3
E	B	8
F	B	7
G	F	2
H	D,E	5
I	C	13
J	C	6
K	H	14
L	E,F	5

2. A project has activities with duration and precedence requirements as shown in Table 7.10. Draw the corresponding network diagram.

Table 7.10

Activity	Predecessor/s	Time (Weeks)
A	–	6
B	A	4
C	A	5
D	A	12
E	A	10
F	B,C	5
G	F,D,E	8
H	E	7
I	F	5
J	I,J,H	3

3. For the construction of a restaurant project, the normal cost, crash time, and incremental cost of crashing is given in Table 7.11:

Table 7.11

Activity	Nodes	Normal Duration (Days)	Crash Duration (Days)	Incremental Cost of Crashing (Rs/day)
A	1–2	5	3	40
B	1–3	4	2	10
C	1–4	7	5	20
D	2–3	4	2	30
E	4–3	3	2	50
F	2–5	2	2	–
G	3–5	7	5	20
H	3–6	3	1	10
I	4–6	4	3	30
J	5–6	6	5	40

The total normal cost is Rs 500, cost of supervision Rs 20 per day and penalty Rs 10 per day over (beyond) 20 days, and rewards Rs 10 per day below or equal to 18 days. Crash the duration of the project, and find the duration of the project with the minimum total cost and the minimum possible duration of the project.

PROJECT ASSIGNMENTS

1. Prepare a network model for a 100-room five star hotel. Discuss it with a project manager and ask him to evaluate the model (assume necessary information).
2. Find a live construction project in your city. It may be a hotel/multiplex/factory/township/plant under construction. Interact with the project manager and ask him about the techniques that have been adapted in planning the project.

REFERENCES

Bedi, Kanishka (2004), *Production and Operations Management*, Oxford University Press, New Delhi.

Rama Murthy, P. (2007), *Operations Research*, New Age International Pvt. Ltd, New Delhi.

Sherlekar and Sherlekar (1984), *Principles of Business Management*, Himalaya Publishing House, New Delhi.

CHAPTER 8

Energy Conservation Programme in the Hotel Industry

INTRODUCTION

Exponential consumption owing to rising demands has brought fossil fuels—the drivers of industrial revolution—on the brink of exhaustion. Faced with the grim scenario of depleting these energy resources, human beings have turned to several non-conventional sources such as sun, water, wind, tides, and biomass to produce electricity. Notwithstanding these discoveries, fossil fuels still remain the main sources of power generation. This has also led to an increase in the prices of power as a result of the huge demand supply gap. As a result, the consumers are forced to change consumption patterns if power has to be used at all. World over the call for decreasing consumption patterns of power, and switching over to non-polluting natural resources is gaining ground.

The hospitality industry, which is among the biggest power or energy consumers, has responded positively with more and more major players making serious efforts at adopting energy conservation techniques and practices. There are a lot of factors such as class and type of categorization, building material, location, etc., on which consumption of energy depends to a great extent. For example, the energy needs of a hotel located in the mountains (such as Jammu and Kashmir, Uttarakhand, etc.) will be different from one in the southern and western parts of India, where state-of-the-art heating as well as cooling systems would be required. In the hilly regions, the energy requirement of heating could suffice with solar heating systems as has been done in many government-owned tourist hotels in Uttarakhand.

In this chapter, we shall focus on the various energy needs of a hotel property, the benchmarks for optimum energy consumption, how an energy audit is conducted prior to the formulation of a detailed energy conservation programme, tips for power saving and the costs of energy conservation, and the benefits of saving energy.

MAJOR RESOURCES OF ENERGY

The main primary sources of energy used in the hotel industry are fossil fuels such as coal, petroleum, wood, etc. Apart from these, water or steam energy is also used for producing energy.

Fuel is defined as a substance which can be combined chemically with oxygen to produce heat and light, and is used for burning or production of heat energy for general, domestic, and industry needs. Fuels such as wood, which were once thought of as renewable sources of energy, as they could be replenished, are now considered as non-renewables as their rate of consumption has far exceeded their rate of replenishment. Fossil fuels, which were formed millions of years ago from fossils or the remains of vegetation and living organisms in the belly of earth, are also considered non-renewable due to their massive consumption rate that is far too much than the time taken for their formation.

Fossil fuels are available in three forms, namely solid: coal, peat, lignite, etc.; liquid: petroleum products; and gas: methane, natural gas, etc. and higher gases. These fuels are taken out of the earth through mines and serve as major energy generating materials in the world.

The hotel industry mainly uses natural gas, coal, and biogas as fuel sources for heat energy. However, over the years fossil fuels have been replaced by electrical energy for the purposes of lighting as well as heating and operating sophisticated equipment in kitchens. This power is either obtained from the grid (municipal supply) or captive power plants comprising huge generators powered by diesel. Box 8.1 provides information regarding the amount of heat energy produced by various sources.

Box 8.1   Know Your Fuels

- One litre of LPG produces 11,850 Kcal.
- One kWh of electricity produces 850 Kcal.
- One litre of light diesel oil produces 5,946 Kcal.

Electrical energy is also referred to as 'artificial' or 'manufactured' fuel in the hotel industry. Electrical energy is produced from other energy sources such as thermal energy (burning of fossil fuels), hydro power (kinetic energy), etc. Conventional generation of electric energy utilizes coal, gas, oil, or nuclear reactors to heat water, producing high temperature pressure steam. The steam flows through an electric turbine generator, which converts steam power into electric power that is supplied though the grid for domestic and industrial consumption. As the steam leaves the turbine generator, it contains energy adequate to heat or cool buildings. This steam is also called *city steam* or *street steam*. The development of city steam systems could be very important to the hospitality industry.

ENERGY CONSERVATION

What is energy conservation?

Let's go through the following situation. You are the manager of a 100-room three star hotel property located in Agra, which is operating at 100 per cent occupancy. Every room is carrying a total connected load of 5.0 kWh including all types of fixtures, fittings, building systems, etc. The power tariff paid to the municipal authorities is @ Rs 5.00 per kWh. How would you compute the annual energy cost (bill) incurred by you for the rooms?

Solution:

Total annual cost or amount of bill = No. of rooms × Connected load × Operating hrs of a day × Tariff rate × 365 days of a year

$$= 100 \times 5 \times 24 \times 5 \times 365 = \text{Rs } 2,19,00,000$$
$$= \text{Rs } 219 \text{ lakh or } 2.19 \text{ crore}$$

This is a massive cost. Now you initiate an energy conservation programme and ask your staff to switch off all the lights of the guest rooms, when the guests are not in the room. Assuming that a guest generally spends 2/3 of the time (16 hours) in the room and 1/3 of the time outside the room, and the staff follows your instructions, then

The total amount of bill = $100 \times 5 \times 16 \times 5 \times 365 = \text{Rs } 1,46,00,000$

Rs 146 lakh or 1.46 crore

The savings made by small efforts is equal to

$$2,19,00,000 - 1,46,00,000 = \text{Rs } 73,00,000$$

Thus, we see that savings or conservation made is an effort to conserve or extend the availability of our energy resources for a longer period of time for future generations. At the same time no compromises have been made in maintaining the standard of services provided by the hotel, plus you are getting monetary benefits by cutting down the energy expenses and prudently using your energy resources. The savings made also help soar your profit per cent directly without putting stress on the marketing and sales team, or the food and beverage service brigade.

Energy Cost: An Overview

There are various forms of energy that are consumed in various sections of a hotel property; for example, electricity, water, kitchen gas, district heating, boiler gas, and other fuels. Energy costs of a hotel vary according to its type, size, location, etc. However, the total energy cost generally ranges from 9 to 13 per cent of the total operating cost of a hotel, or 2 to 3 per cent of the total turnover of the hotel business.

Indian hotels consume approximately 70 per cent of electricity, 12 per cent water, 4 per cent kitchen gas (LPG), 4 per cent district heating, 4 per cent boiler gas, and 6 per cent other fuels.

Major energy usage department of hotels Some of the major energy consuming areas/departments of a hotel are the following.

- Guest rooms
- Food production

- Laundry
- Food and beverage service
- Elevators/escalators
- Swimming pool
- Hotel engineering especially in heating, ventilation, and air conditioning system which is the biggest user of energy.

How to conserve energy in key discipline areas of a hotel

Energy conservation is a team job, and the contribution of every single staff makes a difference. Therefore, it is important that all employees be appropriately counselled and apprised of small habits that go a long way in conserving energy. Some useful tips on power saving for some energy consuming majors in the industry are enlisted as under.

Food and beverage department

- Switch on only that equipment which is required.
- Prepare a schedule clearly indicating additional equipment requirement during peak season.
- Check the capacity of heavy duty equipment like ovens, deep fat fryers, dough kneaders, etc., and plan for optimum capacity utilizations.
- Time required for preheating the oven should be known and notified to all staff concerned.
- Do not open oven doors for longer than necessary for loading and unloading.
- Opening doors frequently reduces efficiency and results in energy loss.
- Switch off ovens, and gas ranges that are not necessary/not in use.
- Limit the general use of hot water to 106 °F.
- Cook on the largest volume possible.
- Turn down heat as soon as food begins to boil.
- Keep all cooking surfaces clean.
- Bring the frosted meat/vegetable/fruit items to room temperature before you start cooking.
- Soaking of lentils and rice helps in energy conservation.
- Place foil under range and griddle burners.
- Do not turn on the gas burners until you are ready to cook.
- Timers should be installed on the kitchen equipment.
- Burners should always be at minimum before placing the pot or kettle on them.
- Use flat-bottom pans and pots to maximize heat transfer.
- Regularly check all gas units for uneven or yellow flames.
- Replace the outdated equipment with more energy efficient ones.
- Follow scheduled maintenance of equipment.

- Check proper insulation and earthing of equipment on a routine basis.
- Proper cleaning and maintenance of equipment reduce fuel consumption.
- Install chandeliers and other decorative light fixtures in restaurants, coffee shops, banquets, night clubs, discotheques, etc.
- Banquet is a major section of energy consumption. So control the functioning of air conditioning according to the time of function; for example: if function starts at 1,500 hrs, then switch on the AC system at 1,430 hrs, and if it is states closing at 2,100 hrs, then switch off the AC half an hour before the closing time.
- Timely defrosting in case of refrigerated equipment helps in energy conservation.
- Replace incandescent bulbs with CFL lamps.

Room division

- Make use of natural light when designing the rooms. A saving of half an hour per day results in energy conservation of almost 180 hrs per room per year.
- Use light finishes for walls and ceilings for better reflection.
- Reduce wattage of lamps with the help of light savers.
- Switch off light in corridors bearing in mind safety and security.
- Switch off TV or music in an unused room.
- Keep draperies closed in guest rooms.
- Ensure that leakage in water taps is promptly attended.
- Laundry is a major section of energy consumption in the housekeeping department, so develop a regular preventive maintenance and cleaning programme of the heavy duty equipment.
- Control neon fixtures and other floodlights and spot fixtures used for illuminating building exteriors on present automatic time switches.
- Place alternate lights in passages, corridors, staircases, backyards, and compounds on separate circuits.
- Practise preventive maintenance.
- Turn off all the lights of all the public areas when not required.
- Turn off the corridor lights during the day when natural light is adequate.
- Install master switch controls in all lights of the guest rooms and which can be synchronized with looking arrangements from outside the entrance door to turn off and turn on supply of electricity.
- Follow manufacturer's instructions for maximum output of an equipment.

Engineering

- Do not deploy reheating for comfort applications; under perfect conditions reheating units are not desirable.
- Check the quality of water and provide necessary water treatment solutions to prevent scaling and fouling of heat exchangers.
- Switch off HVAC equipment in unoccupied areas paying attention to the humidity condition.
- Ensure that the heat exchangers, cooling towers, cooling coils are thoroughly cleaned and maintained periodically.
- Check air handling unit for air quantities.
- Check ventilation and exhaust systems and limit the number of air changes to the minimum that is acceptable.
- Implement regular cleaning programmes for HVAC system filters.
- All electrical distribution system should be checked and all the phases balanced.
- Implement an effective preventive maintenance programme for the boiler house.
- Hot water supply and return pipes should be adequately insulated to minimize heat losses.

Beneficiaries of Energy Conservation

The benefits of energy conservation are several. There is not a single stakeholder, be it the owner, staff member, or even the guest, who does not benefit from the exercise of energy conservation. The manner in which various stakeholders stand to benefit from saving energy is discussed as under:

Owners   The foremost benefits of energy conservation are the monetary ones that accrue as a result of reduced cost of operations and consequent increase in the net profits of the property. The benefits of energy conservation generally go to the owners and senior management of the hotels. For instance, if a hotel earned Rs 5,00,000 by reducing the energy cost per annum, then to save the same amount, they would have to increase the sales of their property by Rs 25,00,000 per year to achieve same net profit, if the profit percentage is 20.

Guests   They may not be getting direct benefits in terms of money, but tremendous energy conservation is directly related to environment friendly practices and judicious use of natural resources. This intangible benefit in terms of enhanced well-being results in guest satisfaction that translates into repeat business to the hotel.

Staff   The employees stand to gain in terms of a higher level of morale as also a sense of pride and achievement that comes from an increase in the level of effectiveness and efficiency. Maintenance of high level of service standards, better output, and productivity are other benefits derived from energy conservation.

Environment   The biggest gainer of the energy conservation exercise happens to be the environment. As 'energy saved is energy generated,' this means that the rate of depletion of energy resources is slowed down, and they could be available for the consumption of future generations. An idea of the scale of saving natural resources can be drawn from the following statement: One ton of lost steam each day is equivalent to 80 litres of light fuel oil commonly termed as light diesel oil (LDO) or approximately 30,000 litres/year.

Energy Audit

An energy audit is an essential step of energy management. Its objective is to analyse and evaluate collected data to determine the energy performance of an entire property and its major consumers. In simple words, energy audit means comparison of the actual performance with the standard benchmark of a particular equipment to find out the variance in terms of the actual and desirable performance.

Tips for energy audit
Some useful tips while conducting an energy audit are as follows:

- Carry out a departmental energy audit to get a fair idea of major energy consumers.
- Compare the result to determine potential savings from a section/department.
- Energy audit should be done on a regular basis.
- Convert energy units to kWh.
- Establish a monitoring and targeting system.
- Install sub meters for each utility.
- Calculate on monthly basis energy consumption per kg for laundry.
- Compare the result with benchmarks and calculate the difference in percentage and money to see how much could be saved.

Benchmarks
Benchmarks are yardsticks against which assessment or evaluation is done. The first significant move towards sustainable tourism by conserving environment and energy was made in the early 1990s by the International Hotel Environment Initiative, launched by some leading corporate players in the industry. The move, backed by the Prince of Wales, evolved into the

International Tourist Partnership, in 2004. This forum is credited with several ground-breaking firsts on environmental management in the tourism industry. It is also reported to have outlined guidelines for the hotel and catering industry to conserve energy and save the earth. The following tables provide information regarding benchmarks for some commonly used equipment in various sections of the hospitality sector.

Table 8.1   Benchmark for Large Hotels (More Than 150 Rooms) with Air-conditioning, Laundry, and Indoor Pool but Without Garden

Efficiency Rating	Good	Fair	Poor	Very Poor
Electricity (kWh/metre square per year)	<165	165-200	200-250	>250
Fuel/ gas (kWh/metre square per year)	<200	200-240	240-300	>300
Total (kWh/metre square per year)	<365	365-440	440-550	>550
Water (cubic metre per guest staying) (Overnight per year- average daily guest)	<220	230-280	280-320	>320

Source: Liz (1993)

Table 8.2   Benchmark for Small Hotels (4 to 50 Rooms) with Minor Air-conditioning, Without Laundry, or Indoor Pool

Efficiency Rating	Good	Fair	Poor	Very Poor
Electricity (kWh/metre square per year)	<60	60-80	80-100	>100
Fuel/ gas (kWh/metre square per year)	<180	180-210	210-240	>240
Total (kWh/metre square per year)	<240	240-290	290-340	>340
Water (cubic metre per guest staying) (Overnight per year-average daily guest)	<120	120-140	140-160	>160

Source: Liz (1993)

Table 8.3   Benchmark for Medium (4 to 50 Rooms) with Minor Air-conditioning, Without Laundry, or Indoor Pool

Efficiency Rating	Good	Fair	Poor	Very Poor
Electricity (kWh/metre square per year)	<70	70-90	90-120	>120
Fuel/ gas (kWh/metre square per year)	<190	190-230	230-260	>260
Total (kWh/metre square per year)	<260	260-320	320-380	>380
Water (cubic metre per guest staying) (Overnight per year-average daily guest)	<160	160-185	185-220	>220

Source: Liz (1993)

Table 8.4   Benchmarks for Kitchen Equipment

Efficiency Rating	Good	Fair	Poor
Energy for cooking, dishwashing, and cold storage (kWh)	<3	3–4.5	>4.5
Energy for lighting, ventilation, heating, and hot water	<1	1–1.5	>1.5
Water (litres)	<35	35–45	>45

Note: Figures are given per cover in kWh for energy and litres per covers for water.
Source: Liz (1993)

Table 8.5   Benchmarks for Kitchens—Multiplying Factors

Food Service For	Factor
Chinese restaurant	2.0
à la carte restaurant	1.6
Coffee shop	0.8
Banquet	0.7
Staff restaurant/cafeteria	0.5
Snack bar, tea lounge	0.2

Note: Multiplying factors are the standard benchmark/guidelines multiplied by the capacity of the food and beverage outlets. They are used to compute standard energy consumption and perform energy audits for food and beverage outlets/catering establishments.
Source: Liz (1993)

Table 8.6   Benchmarks for Laundries

Energy Efficiency Rating	Good	Fair	Poor
Electricity equipment only (kWh)	0.1–0.13	0.13–0.16	>0.16
Electricity including light, ventilation (kWh)	0.19–0.22	0.22–0.28	>0.28
Steam (kWh) 1 kg = 0.67 kWh	1.5–1.8	1.8–2.0	>2.0
Total energy requirement (kWh)	1.8–2.2	2.2–2.5	>2.5
Water (litres) without recovery	23–26	26–30	>30
Water (litres) with recovery	12–15	15–18	>18

Note: All figures are given per kg of linen.
Source: Liz (1993)

Calculations based on consumption   Calculate water consumption in cubic metres per person per year, if
  Annual consumption = 69,000 cubic metres

Number of rooms = 300

Average occupancy = 80% including 25% double occupancy

Total number of rooms occupied = 240

Total house count = 300 guests

(Hints: If 100% rooms are single occupied, then house count from single rooms = 240

If 25% rooms are double occupied, then house count from double rooms = 60)

Water consumption = 69,000/300 = 230 cubic metres per person per year.

Table 8.7 Conversion Table

Kitchens		
Natural gas cubic metre × 9.3	=	kWh
Cubic feet × 0.263	=	kWh
Therms × 29.3	=	kHz
Liquid Petroleum Gas (LPG) litres × 7.0	=	kWh
Boilers: above values × 80%		
District heating		
Hot water	GJ × 278 =	kWh (GJ gigajoule SI Unit of energy. 1 GJ = 10,000,000,000 Joule
MWh × 1,000	=	kWh
Gcal × 1,163	=	kWh
Steam	tons × 698 =	kWh
MWh × 1,000	=	kWh
Conversion factors:		
1 MWh = 1,486 tons steam		
1 MWh = 3.6 GJ		
1 MWh = 1,000 kWh		
1 ton steam = 0.6 Gcal		
1 Kcal = 3.97 BTU		
1 Gcal = 1,000,000 kcal		
1 Therm = 100,000 BTU		

Convert the annual fuel, gas, district steam, or hot water energy into kWh.

Note: Use net calorific value and not gross.

Calculations based on energy audit

The following information about the food and beverage department of a five star hotel is given. Conduct an energy audit and find out the results.

Covers sold in the month of August 2006.

- Banquet 12,000 covers
- Coffee shop 10,000 covers
- à la carte restaurant 6,000 covers
- Employee meals 4,000
- Total covers 32,000

Consumption of energy for cooking, dishwashing, and cold storage = 1,20,000 kWh

Consumption of energy for lighting, ventilation, and hot water = 30,000 kWh

Water (cold and hot) 2,000 cubic metre

Rate electricity @ Rs 5.00 kWh

Rate water @ Rs 10.00 cubic metre

Solution

Banquet	12,000 covers × 0.7	=	8,400
Coffee shop	10,000 covers × 0.8	=	8,000
à la carte restaurant	6,000 covers × 1.6	=	9,600
Employee meals	4,000 covers × 0.5	=	2,000
Total covers	32,000	=	27,600

The total equivalent covers at factor 1.0 are 27,600 covers. Now we will use this figure to calculate consumption per cover with benchmarks.

Energy for cooking, dishwashing, and cold storage = 1,20,000 kWh ÷ 27,600 = 4.034 kWh per cover

RATING: Fair, excess 40% above 3 kWh (benchmark), monthly wastes in this case is Rs 1,86,000

Energy for lighting, ventilation, and hot water = 30,000 kWh/27,600 = 1.086 kWh

RATING: fair, excess 9% above 1 kWh (benchmark), monthly waste in this case is Rs 12,000

Water (cold and hot) 2,000 cubic metres × 1000/27,600 = 72.1 litres per cover

RATING: very poor, excess 37 litres above 35 litres (benchmark), monthly waste in this case is Rs 11,340

Total monthly waste = (1, 86,000 + 12,000 + 11,340) = Rs 2,09,340.

Energy Conservation Programme

Once an energy audit is complete, the next logical step is to draw out and execute the exercise to accomplish energy consumption in sectors of the hotel where there is scope. This exercise constitutes the energy conservation programme. It must, however, be borne in mind that energy conservation is not a one man or one department programme. It requires involvement and commitment of every employee of the hotel from the General Manager to the entry level staff of any section.

Generally, an energy committee is constituted with the head of the committee being appointed from the department concerned. The committee is tasked to plan, implement, and monitor the energy conservation programme. The details of the philosophy of the programme are left to the committee. A flow chart of the steps involved in the exercise is depicted in Box 8.2. The committee must be made aware that the energy conservation programme is a three phase programme.

The first phase includes the things that can be done immediately with minimum inconvenience to the guests as well as to the organization. The

Box 8.2 Flow Chart for Developing an Energy Conservation Programme

Phase One

Step 1 Collect data on consumption of energy and convert it into the amount

Step 2 Compare the data with the benchmark by performing an energy audit

Step 3 Analyse the findings and identify a department where differences are the highest

Step 4 Call a meeting and invite the head of the department and her/his team for discussion on the results

Step 5 Seek their suggestions and ask about the problems faced by them regarding the poor performance in the energy audit

Step 6 Appoint an energy conservation committee headed by the department head and give them a target to reduce energy consumption within a set time frame.

Phase Two

Step 7 Review the results of phase one. If the results are positive after the target time, commend the efforts of the task force and seek their

suggestions to invest the savings in the second phase. Allow them to make certain changes in the existing standard operating practices/minimum investment in replacing the light equipment/accessories. Give them a target to reduce energy consumption within a set target time in the second phase.

If the results are not encouraging, then repeat the first phase till the desired results are obtained.

Phase Three

Step 8 Review the results of phase two after the target time. If the results are positive, then praise the efforts of the task force and solicit their advice. Invite the senior management/owners for a discussion on the success story of the task force. Ask for the owner's investment in making changes in the infrastructures, building systems, and inducting the latest technology, etc. to further improve energy conservation.

If the results are not encouraging, then the second phase is repeated till the time the desired results are obtained.

point to remember here is that there is no budget for an energy conservation programme, so the payoff of this phase is usually fairly large for the efforts put in.

The second phase involves readjustment of the operational practices. The savings made in these two phases should be fed back into the operations so that the third phase can be implemented.

The third phase involves changes in the physical property, which may require the owners' investment plus the savings made in the first and second phases. For instance, installing an equipment that would be instrumental in conservation.

Table 8.8 depicts the composition of an energy conservation committee in various operational areas of a five star hotel.

Table 8.8 General Composition of Energy Conservation Committees in Different Operational Areas of a Five Star Hotel

Food and Beverage	Food Production	Hotel Accommodation	Hotel Engineering	Front Office
Manager food and beverage	Executive chef	Executive housekeeper	Chief engineer	Front office manager
Restaurant manager	Chef de Partie	Assistant housekeeper	Shift in charge	Duty manager
Banquet manager	Commis I	Control desk in charge	Shift supervisor	Resident manager
Guest relation executive	Commis II	Laundry in charge	Electrician	Front office assistant
Captain	Commis III	Floor supervisor	Lift operators	Bell desk in charge
Stewards	Kitchen stewarding manager	Room attendant	Boiler operators	Bell boys
Bartender	Utility worker	Chamber's maids	Assistants	Front office assistant

Tips on energy conservation programme

1. Energy conservation programme is a three phase programme. Phase one should be completed by developing awareness and without any investment.
2. Energy conservation efforts should not create any obstacles in the operations of the hotel. There should be minimal disturbance to the guests.

3. Always choose one department at a time and continue with other departments only after achieving success in the earlier one.
4. Energy conservation is not a fly by night programme. Participation of each and every staff member contributes a lot towards it.
5. Successful completion of phase one/two should be communicated to all departments in the meeting.
6. Staff members involved in energy conservation should be appreciated for their efforts with suitable rewards and recognition, which should not necessarily mean monetary benefits.
7. Do not treat energy conservation as a cost cutting exercise. Rather, take it as an effort made to save the planet for future generations.
8. Programme success is dependent on the management. A positive attitude is the key to its success.

SUCCESS STORIES OF INDIAN HOTELS

This section comprises some of the success stories in energy conservation taken up in Indian hotels. In fact, some hotels have made conscious efforts in adopting environment-friendly techniques aimed at energy conservation and have earned the Ecotel certification making environment conservation their USP. Mumbai's Hotel Orchid pioneered this concept in the country. Some of the highlights of the energy conservation programmes of such hotel properties are described as follows.

The Orchid, Mumbai

- The hotel uses more than 90 per cent of bulbs that are energy efficient such as CFL, fluorescent.
- Solar energy is used for terrace lighting.
- Timers switch on/off street/neon lights.
- Double speed motors are installed for improved working and energy efficiency.
- Urinal sensors are used in public toilets to conserve water. This results in 30 per cent reduction in total water usage.
- Taps with aerators are installed, conserving 40 per cent of water.
- Drip irrigation method is adopted for gardening.
- Water closet flushes off 6.5 litres against normal usage of 8–10 litres flushing.
- Recycling of linen such as bed linen/towels in making dusters, face towels, swab cloths, waiter clothes, etc.
- Left over cooking oil is sold for manufacturing soap.

Orchid is a pioneer in conducting day trips to show its premises to school and college students for developing awareness, project assistance, competitions, etc. It has the credit of having assisted 45 schools and more than 12,000 students in the field of environment awareness.

The Lake Palace, Udaipur

The Lake Palace Udaipur, a Taj property, has woven the message of 'save the planet' in its energy conservation programme. Its environmental initiative programme statement proclaims that being 'eco-friendly' means working with the environment, creating a positive impact on the finite resources available on this planet so that we can conserve these for the present and future generations. The salient features of its programme are as follows:

- Energy cards are placed in the guest rooms.
- Energy conservation training programme is mandatory for all employees of the hotel.
- The hotel uses energy efficient bulbs.
- Road lights, public area, and corridor lighting have centralized on/off control, operated by photocells.
- Orifice is provided in each water outlet to monitor water usage.
- Practice of reuse, reduce, and recycle waste is adopted for food, plastic, water or any other waste material.
- Optimum utilization of handmade paper.
- Using both sides of paper for internal communication to save trees.

The Ambassador Pallava, Chennai

- Promotion of renewable energy (wind power).
- Wound dimmers and tubelight chokes have been replaced with electronic dimmers and chokes.
- Bulbs used in the hotel are energy efficient.
- Save water stickers are displayed in all rooms and toilets.
- Duration of flushing cisterns has been reduced and taps with aerators have been installed, conserving 40 per cent of the total water usage.
- A segregation system of wet and dry garbage is adopted for recycling, reusing, and recovering the waste.
- The hotel has taken initiatives to clean the city along with the local authorities by planting trees and maintaining a mini garden.
- Auto/taxi drivers are facilitated by providing them with toilet facilities in the hotel.

Leela Kempiski, Mumbai

- Usage of timers for automated cut off power.
- Solar water heating system for potable hot water and solar pool heating system.
- Economizers are used in the boiler to recover the heat from the hot exit gas, which is used for preheating the water fed to the boiler.
- Use of timers for street lights eliminates human errors.
- Drip irrigation system and sprinkler system is used in gardening.
- Infrared sensors are installed for auto flush urinals.
- Used soap cakes are utilised in laundry/housekeeping.
- Bed linens/towels are given to orphanages, and discards used for cleaning.
- Unused side of writing paper is used for photocopying, while envelopes are reused in internal office communication.
- Use of natural gas as fuel for boilers almost nullifies the air pollution.
- Maintaining massive gardens in and around the premises of the hotel to encourage greenery.

SUMMARY

The hospitality industry is one of the largest industries in the world in terms of investment, infrastructure, generating revenue and jobs, as also energy consumption. Over the last two centuries, the invention of the steam engine and the discovery of fossil fuels powered the industrial revolution, leading to massive consumption of energy resources. So much so, that what were once thought of as infinite and renewable sources stand dangerously depleted with an energy crisis looming large over the world. Even as the quest for efficient and viable energy sources such as solar, water, wind, and other non-conventional sources continues, the chorus for better energy management and conservation of conventional and finite sources is getting louder.

The hospitality industry, which is among the biggest energy consumers and power guzzlers, is also gradually shifting towards energy conservation and proper management. Having adopted conservation practices, hoteliers have found that not only is energy saved, energy generated, but it results in substantial monetary benefits also.

CONCEPT REVIEW QUESTIONS

1. What do you mean by energy conservation? List all the various energy resources and indicate how each would be used in the hospitality industry.
2. Write about the various practices of energy conservation adopted in key discipline areas of a hotel.
3. Explain the factors affecting efficiency of energy in a restaurant.
4. What are the repercussions if planning and operation of a laundry are faulty?
5. Justify the statement that energy conservation exercise is not a fly by night programme.
6. Enlist the points you will consider while designing an energy conservation programme.
7. Plan and develop an energy conservation programme of a hotel.
8. What do you mean by an energy audit? Explain the points to be considered while conducting the energy audit of a three star hotel property.
9. Define benchmark and explain the role of benchmarks in energy auditing.
10. State whether the following are true or false:
    (i)   Improving reflection of lighting fixtures helps in reducing wattage.
    (ii)   You can track excessive consumption of energy by installing sub-meters.
    (iii) Replacing obsolete systems does not have positive impact on energy conservation.
    (iv)   Training does not play a vital role in conserving energy.
    (v)   New designs should always take into account the advancing technology in the field of energy conservation.
    (vi)   Participation of every employee is a key factor of success to save energy.
    (vii) Water treatment helps to conserve water.
    (viii) Installation of a radiator system with thermostatic controls helps to reduce energy consumption.
    (ix)   Preheating of oven at higher than the desired temperature is a right practice to conserve energy.
    (x)   During hot or cold weather, keep the curtains, blinds, and shades closed so as to reduce heating, which helps to conserve energy.
    (xi)   Centralized kitchen consumes less energy.
    (xii) Thawing of food helps to reduce power demand of a refrigerator.

NUMERICAL PROBLEMS

1. The following information about the food and beverage department of a five star hotel is given. Conduct an energy audit on the basis of the available information and find out the results.

Details of covers sold in the month of August.
- Banquet 14,000 covers
- Coffee shop 9,000 covers
- à la carte restaurant 8,000 covers
- Employee meals 3,500
- Total covers 34,500

Consumption of energy for cooking, dishwashing, and cold storage = 1,35,000 kWh

Consumption of energy for lighting, ventilation and hot water = 32,000 kWh

Water (cold and hot) 2,500 cubic metres

Electricity charges Rs 6.00 per kWh

Water charges Rs 12.00 per cubic metres.

(a) Convert the annual fuel oil, gas, district steam or hot water energy into kWh. Take the lower net calorific value.
- Natural gas cooking: 18,050 cubic metres
- Light fuel oil: 2,15,000 litres
- District hot water: 4,500 GJ

If total floor area is 12,000 square metres, calculate consumption per square metre.

(b) If annual consumption of electricity is 2,50,000 kWh and total floor area is 20,000 square metres, calculate the electricity per square metre of floor area per year.

PROJECT ASSIGNMENTS

1. Visit a local food service unit/laundry unit and conduct an energy audit. Compare the result with your friends who have also done the similar assignments in other units.
2. Formulate an action plan for energy efficiency for your institute.
3. Interview a chief engineer, plant manager, or head maintenance manager of a five star hotel and attempt to determine the management functions he or she is actively involved in. Also try to determine the role of the engineer or manager in energy conservation efforts.
4. Check with a local three star hotel and make a list of all the major energy consuming devices. Indicate the energy resource required for each device and energy consumption of each unit.
   (*Note:* limit your list to 20 major items in the building, counting the dining room as one, lighting, kitchen lighting, as other items, and each oven as one unit)

- What type/types of energy reduction goals would you recommend for the unit?
- How can these goals be obtained?
- What type of energy control equipment could be used to meet these goals? Prepare a report of your findings and recommendations.

REFERENCES

Borsenik, Frank D. and Alan T. Stuffs (1987), *The Management of Maintenance and Engineering Systems in the Hospitality Industry,* John Wiley and Sons, Inc. New York.

Stepat-Dewan, Dorothy, Darlene M. Kness, Kathyrn Camp Logan, and Laura Szkely (1980), *Introduction to Interior Design,* Macmillan, New York.

Picon, Liz (1993), *Environmental Management for Hotels: The Industry Guide to Best Practice,* Heinemann; Butterworth, U.K.

ANNEXURE

FHRAI Environment Awards 2004–2005
Questionnaire for Hotels
Please give facts and figures for financial year 2004–2005, unless otherwise stated.

Membership No.: Star Category:
1. Name of Hotel ....
    Address:
    Phone:
    Fax:
    E-mail:
    Affiliation (chain):
    When did the hotel start operations? (for new hotels) ....
2. Description of Property:
    (i)   Total Area (in sq. m.) ....
    (ii) built up Area (in sq. m.) ....
    (iii) No. of storeys ....
    (iv) No. of rooms ....
    (v)   Stand alone plot or part of a building complex:
          □ Stand-alone □ Part of a building
    (vi) New areas/facilities introduced in 2004–2005 ....
3. Environment Policies and Management
    (a)   Does the hotel have an environment policy?
          Written policy: □ Yes □ No
          Prepared by: □ own staff □ chain head office experts □ outside consultant
          When was the policy approved?
          Since when was it implemented?
          Main components of the policy (Please attach a note if required)
          Who all get a copy of this policy?
    (b)   Has the property got an environment audit done?
          □ Yes □ No
          By which Company?
          Year of Audit:
          How is it being implemented?
          Significant results achieved..
    (c)   Status of ISO14000 certification: Planning on starting: □ Yes □ No
          Consultant appointed and under preparation: □ Yes □ No
          If the hotel is ISO 14000 certified, give details of the year of certification and date till the certification is valid.
    (d)   Do you have written policy for energy conservation?
          □ Yes □ No

(e) Do you have written policy for eco purchase?
□ Yes □ No

(f) Do you have written policy for water management?
□ Yes □ No

(g) Do you have a written policy for waste management and minimizations?
□ Yes □ No

(h) Do you have a policy of containing and dealing with leaks in chemical containers/tanks?
□ Yes □ No

(i) Do you have a policy for using non-CFC equipment?
□ Yes □ No

(j) Have you received any notice for any statutory violations or been fined/penalized? Give details.

4. Energy Management:

(a) Has the property got an energy audit done? □ Yes □ No
Annual Energy consumption 2002-03, 2003-04, 2004-05
Remarks:
- Total annual consumption of electricity (kWh). Comparison of three years
- Consumption per occupied guest room (kWh)
- Total LPG (kg.) consumed annually
- Total LDO/FO (kl) consumed annually
- HSD (kl)
- Natural gas (kg.)
- Any other fuel source of energy used

(Please explain in the remarks column, if there has been a significant change in the facilities accounting for higher or lower consumption. Otherwise, it is presumed that the variations are on account of efficiency/inefficiency of operations.)

(b) Measures adopted for energy conservation:
- Installed energy efficient lights (CFL):
□ Yes □ No
- Installed energy efficient lights (CFL) .... % of hotel guest rooms
- Installed energy efficient lights (CFL) .... % of the other areas
- Equipment for reducing HVAC (heating, ventilation, air-conditioning) consumption. Give details.
- Procedures for reducing HVAC (heating, ventilation, air-conditioning) consumption. Give details.
- Results achieved

(c) Has the hotel installed sub-meters in different functional areas like kitchen, rooms, laundry, etc.?

□ Yes □ No. If yes, give details along the following

- Area in which sub-meter installed: % of area covered
- Monitoring procedure:
- Results achieved:
- (Depending on the no. of (e.g. monthly/quarterly review rooms/ banquet halls/or any others) restaurants covered.
  - o Guest rooms/floors
  - o Banquet areas
- Restaurants and bars
- Kitchen
- Laundry
- Lobby and front office
- Administrative offices
- Recreation facilities
- Staff and service areas
- Compounds/gardens/other public areas
- Any others

(d) Single point room lights, AC/key card or switch being used:
□ Yes □ No

(e) Energy savings for windows by glazing, screens, filming, awning or other means. Please specify.

(f) Sensors or dimmers in corridors or other unused areas:
□ Yes □ No

(g) Sensors for AC control of rooms when not occupied:
□ Yes □ No

(h) Any other

(i) List out equipment, systems, procedures, training, monitoring, and results achieved for energy conservation in following areas:
- Housekeeping
- Laundry
- Kitchen
- Restaurants
- Common areas inside the hotel
- Outside areas if any
- Any other

(j) Have you taken steps for reducing consumption of following energy sources? Please list.
- Fuel Oil
- Diesel
- LPG
- Any other

(k) Are you using any of the following renewable energy source? Give details
- Solar water heater
- Photo voltaic cells for lighting
- Bio-gas/Bio-mass
- Any other

(l) Do you have a heat recovery system in the hotel? Give details
- Air conditioners
- Boilers
- Generators
- Laundry condensation, flash steam recovery
- Any other

(m) Do you have ceiling fans in guest areas and office areas to reduce the use of air-conditioning?
☐ Yes ☐ No

(n) Do you have sectional switches and/or dimmers in restaurants and other areas to switch off or dim lights in unused, low use areas?
☐ Yes ☐ No

Give details

5. Water Management

(Include all sources of water like municipal, under ground, purchase, etc.)

(a) Annual Water consumption (kilo litre) 2002–03, 2003–04, 2004–05 Remarks

(Please calculate and give final ratios wherever requested.)

$$\frac{\text{Total Sales turnover (Rs)}}{\text{Total Water consumed (kL)}}$$

$$\frac{\text{Total Covered Area (sq.m.)}}{\text{Total Water consumed (kL)}}$$

Consumption per seat of the restaurant (kL)
(Account of all restaurants in the hotels)

Water consumption per occupied room (kL)

(b) Have you installed water meters in different areas? ☐ Yes ☐ No
If yes, in what areas have these meters been installed?
What results have you achieved because of these meters?

(c) Water saving equipment, procedures, training, monitoring, put in place and results achieved in following areas. For example, list if you are using low flow shower heads, tap aerators, toilet dams, tank fill diverters, photo electric cell activated control systems.
- Guest rooms
- Public/staff toilets
- Laundry

- Kitchen
- Garden, lawns and plants
- Boilers
- Any others

(d) What system of rain water harvesting do you have?

(e) Do you have a policy of testing drinking water? ☐ Yes ☐ No

(f) How are you purifying drinking water?

(g) Do you have a policy of testing water for other uses?
e.g. swimming pools, laundry, kitchen, rooms, etc.: ☐ Yes ☐ No
If yes, how are you ensuring that quality as per standards is maintained?

(h) Do you have an effluent treatment plant? ☐ Yes ☐ No. If yes, give the following details?
- Type:
- Capacity:
- Date of Installation:
- Last fitness clearance (date):
Briefly describe its maintenance programme.
What are the COD/BOD levels in the final discharge?

(i) Do you have a system in place for secondary use of water (grey water - already used water to be reused)? Please describe.

6. Hazardous Chemicals and Eco-purchasing and Recycling:

(a) Do you have a policy of not using hazardous chemicals and cleaners?
☐ Yes ☐ No
If yes, list the products/ingredients that you are avoiding and name the alternatives you are using.

(b) Do you buy in bulk or concentrates? ☐ Yes ☐ No
If yes, specify products for bulk and concentrates.

(c) Are you successfully recycling, sending back to the supplier any items?
Please list them.

(d) Do you buy biodegradable products? ☐ Yes ☐ No
If yes, list as many cases as you can where you have changed the product in favour of alternate biodegradable product.

(e) In what areas do you use plastic and polythene bags/products?
In what areas are you using alternatives to plastic and polythene products?

(f) Do you have a policy of recycling paper and envelopes, restricting use of paper? ☐ Yes ☐ No
Describe the policy, examples and extent of success achieved.

(h) Have you shifted to bio-pesticides and bio-fertilizers as against chemical pesticides and fertilizers? ☐ Yes ☐ No
If yes, list the products and percentage of total quantity covered by these products

(i) Are you buying or growing organic food?

(j) Do you have special procedures for disposing off unused chemicals and their containers?

7. Waste disposal and solid waste management:

(a) How are you using/disposing off left over food? Please describe the measures and results.

(b) Are you separating plastic, metal, glass, and other solid waste?
☐ Yes ☐ No
At which point do you separate the solid waste?

(c) How are you recycling and disposing off such wasted (discarded) items?

(d) Do you separate wet and dry waste in kitchens/restaurants? ☐ Yes ☐ No

(e) How do you dispose wet garbage/waste from kitchen and restaurant?

(f) Is your wet garbage storage facility air-conditioned? ☐ Yes ☐ No

(g) How are you disposing dry organic waste like used flowers, etc.?

(h) Any other measures, e.g., using shredded paper for packaging, using 'rest of toilet paper rolls for staff toilets, short pencils collected and donated to schools, stained or worn linen/towels to be used for cloth bags/rags/laundry bags.

8. Air pollution control and air quality

(a) Have you had Indoor Air Quality testing done? ☐ Yes ☐ No

(b) Are you aware of the IAQ standards? ☐ Yes ☐ No

(c) Are you taking steps to maintain and monitor Indoor Air Quality? Describe them.

(d) Do you have both fresh air and exhaust systems in kitchen, laundry boiler room, plant room and service areas?
Describe the areas and results.

(e) Do you provide treated fresh air in guest rooms, restaurants and banquets? ☐ Yes ☐ No

(f) Do you use ozonators for rooms? ☐ Yes ☐ No

(g) Do you have separate no-smoking rooms and floors? ☐ Yes ☐ No

(h) Do you provide exhaust in guest room toilets? ☐ Yes ☐ No

(i) Do you have separate no-smoking areas in restaurants/bars? ☐ Yes ☐ No

(j) Do you use scrubbers for DG Exhaust and boiler exhaust? ☐ Yes ☐ No
Describe them and the results achieved.

(k) Describe areas/equipment where non-CFC equipment is used.

(l) Do you send discarded CFC using equipment to dealers who recycle CFCs Give details?

(m) Do you ask for certification from your equipment servicing company to ascertain how they dispose off the CFC?
☐ Yes ☐ No

(n) Do you use fresh air ionizers in Tempered Fresh Air (TFA) circuits?
☐ Yes ☐ No

9. Noise Pollution Control:
   (a) Do you inform your banquet clients about the noise pollution levels and timings as applicable in your area?
       ☐ Yes ☐ No
   (b) Is your banquet sales department aware of the noise pollution rules and standards? ☐ Yes ☐ No
   (c) What measures have you put in place to control noise pollution irritation to guests?
   (d) What measures have you put in place to control noise pollution effects on staff working in engineering/air-conditioning/laundry department?
   (e) What measures have you taken to insulate your hotel from external noise from street/ surrounding areas and activities?

10. Communications:
    (a) How do you communicate your environmental policies to your guests?
    (b) How do you involve your entire staff in implementing and monitoring your energy and environment policies?
    (c) How do you communicate your environmental policies to your suppliers with regard to eco-purchasing and disposal?
    (d) How do you communicate your environmental policies to outsiders like local community/media/shareholders/financial institutions, etc.?

11. Training:
    (a) Please describe your policies for training, motivation, rewarding staff at all levels for implementation of eco-friendly measures:
        • Training on the hotel's overall environmental policy.
        • Training to the hotel staff on specific energy conservation measures.
        • Training to the hotel staff on specific water conservation measures.
        • Training to the hotel staff on specific waste minimizations and waste management measures.
        • Any others.
    (b) What system is in place for rewards?

12. Please describe any other policies and measures not covered in the above headings and to give any reasons for your being given the Award. Please highlight steps taken recently, especially in the year 2004–2005, the period for which the data is being considered for the Award. However, the cumulative effect of earlier measures will add to the environment profile of your property.

Name of the Manager Answering the Questionnaire
Designation

Position/role in the Environment Team of Property
Signature

CHAPTER 9

Facilities for Physically Challenged

Chapter Outline:

The following topics are covered in this chapter
- Types of physically challenged guests
- Guidelines for facilities planning
- Government norms on the hotel facilities to be offered to the physically challenged guests

Learning Objectives:

This chapter will enable you to understand
- The definition of physically challenged guests
- The various kinds of facilities to be offered to physically challenged guests
- The new concepts and facilities available for physically challenged guests
- The norms outlined by the government for such guests

INTRODUCTION

Around 10 per cent of the world's population, or roughly 650 million people, live with a disability*. In India, more than 21 million people suffer from one kind of disability or the other, such as blindness, hearing or, immobility, etc. This, according to the 2001 Census, accounts for almost 2.1 per cent of the total population. According to a research paper, two out of every thousand guests received at hotels are either physically challenged or suffer from speech, mobility, or visual impairment. It thus, becomes imperative for the hospitality industry to cater to the needs of this special class of guests, by providing facilities that do not discriminate against them and are easily accessible to them.

The Union Ministry of Tourism, in 2009, made it mandatory for all star categories hotels to add facilities for the physically challenged people in various categories. The government has issued specific guidelines on the subject. In this chapter, we shall focus our discussion on the special guests, the various facilities that properties need to install to cater to their needs, and the government guidelines in this regard.

Types of Physically Challenged Guests

Depending on the various kinds of impairments either in body organs, such as limbs, hands, spinal cord, etc., or of sensory organs, such as eyes, ears, speech, etc., people may suffer from various disabilities. As a result, our physically challenged guests, hereafter referred to as special guests, are categorized into the following types.

- Special guests with mobility difficulties
  - o Special guests who are assisted on wheelchair
  - o Special guests unassisted on wheelchair
- Special guests with deafness or hearing impairment
- Special guests with speech impairment
- Special guests with visual impairment
- Special guests with learning disabilities/mental impairments

GUIDELINES FOR PLANNING FACILITIES

The physical needs of each of the above-mentioned kinds of guests are different. However, with slight modifications in various areas of the hotels, not only can these properties be *rendered easily accessible to them*, but by integrating

---

* *Source:* http://www.disabled-world.com

simple unobtrusive facilities in the design structures, the special guests can go about freely without hassling other guests. For instance, a ramp at the entrance, or wide space in corridors can enable a guest on wheelchair to go about independently in a hotel without *inconveniencing* co-travellers, or even the host property. The industry guidelines with respect to planning various facilities for differently-abled people are described as under.

Access for Guests with Mobility Difficulties

Most of the physical modifications to a hotel property are made to meet the needs of guests with mobility impairments, those who use wheelchairs, canes, or crutches. Remember, this includes not only people with disabilities, but also senior citizens—a growing segment of the travelling public. Guests with wheelchairs need access to parking lot, entrances, front desk, restrooms, guest rooms and other areas of your hotel, such as meeting rooms and restaurants. Many of the people in this class could move on their own, provided the following points are borne in mind and incorporated into the various areas of the property.

Public entrance   The industry guidelines for public entrance are as follows.

- A public entrance must be accessible to wheelchair use from a setting down or car parking point.
- Where a hotel has a car park, a reserved parking space should be available for a disabled guest, on request.
- The path from parking point or space to the entrance must be sound in construction, and free from obstacles. Deep gravel, cobbles, and pot-holed surfaces must be avoided.
- The entrance door must have a clear opening of not less than 67 cm.
- Where there is no ramp, there must be not more than 3 steps to the entrance at any one point.
- Within the reception area, there must be an unobstructed space of not less than 110 cm × 70 cm.
- Ramps, where present, should not have a gradient at any point of more than 1:12.
- Steps to be used by a special guest should have risers, not more than 19 cm, with treads not less than 25 cm deep and 75 cm wide.

Interior (general)

- Public pathways that lead to the restaurant/dining room, lounge, TV lounge, (unless TV is provided in the bedroom), bar, the special guest's bedroom and bathroom should be not less than 75 cm wide.

- Doors to the rooms referred to above should have a clear opening of not less than 67 cm.
- There must be no more than 3 steps, at any point, in the corridors that guests with difficulties in mobility would be required to use, or at the entrance of the rooms referred to above.
- Where the special guests may be required to use a lift, its door should have a clear opening of not less than 67 cm, and the interior of the lift should be not less than 110 cm deep by 70 cm wide.

Bathroom

- The bathroom must be *en suite* or on the same floor as the special guest's bedroom.
- Where a bath is provided, it should have a horizontal or angled support rail on the far side (25 cm above rim).
- Where only a shower is provided, it must have a seat (recommended 45–50 cm above floor) and a support rail on the far wall (recommended 25 cm above top of the seat and a maximum of 50 cm from centre of the seat).
- Where there is a step into the shower, it should have a riser of not more than 19 cm.
- There must be a washbasin within the bathroom/bedroom.

Water closet (WC)

- The WC must be *en suite* or on the same floor as the special guest's bedroom.
- Toilet paper must be within the reach of the guest.
- Where the WC is separate from the bathroom there must be a washbasin within the same room.

Guests who are assisted on wheelchair

Public entrance

- The entrance door must have a clear opening of not less than 75 cm.
- Where there is no ramp there must be not more than one step to the entrance at any one point.

Interior general

- The public passways that lead to the restaurant/dining room, lounge, TV lounge, (unless TV is provided in the bedroom), bar, the special guest's bedroom, and bathroom should not be less than 80 cm wide and not less than 120 cm on the opposite side of the doors to the rooms referred to above.

- Doors to the rooms referred to above should have a clear opening of not less than 75 cm.
- There must be no more than single steps, at any point, in the corridors that a guest on wheelchair will be required to use.
- Where the guest may be required to use a lift, the door should have a clear opening of not less than 75 cm and the interior of the lift should be not less than 110 cm deep by 80 cm wide.
- In the restaurant/dining room there must be at least one accessible table with a clear under space at least 65 cm high. Blocks, to lift a table when required, are acceptable. Where three or more bedrooms meet such requirements, at least two such accessible tables should be provided.
- There can be a succession of single steps, provided there is sufficient space after each step for a wheelchair to sit comfortably and safely, with all four wheels on the ground.
- Removable ramps, unless installed permanently, are not acceptable.
- Threshold to rooms to which the wheelchair user requires access must not be higher than 2 cm.

Bedroom

- There must be unobstructed space not less than 110 cm × 70 cm.
- There must be space alongside at least one side of the bed of not less than 80 cm to allow lateral transfer.
- At least one bedroom must be designed to such specifications for the mobility disadvantaged guests.

Bathroom

- There must be unobstructed space not less than 110 cm × 70 cm.
- Where a bath is provided, there must be a seat alongside of not less than 80 cm to allow lateral transfer.
- Where only a shower is provided, it must have a level entry, i.e., no rim; a lateral transfer space of not less than 80 cm and a seat.
- The washbasin, either within the bathroom or bedroom, must have sufficient clear under space and/or level taps to enable it to be used by someone in a wheelchair.
- Only one bathroom, separate or *en suite* with the bedroom(s) must meet these requirements.

Water closet

- There must be a lateral transfer space to the WC of not less than 80 cm.
- The rim of the WC seat must be between 45 and 50 cm above the floor.

- There must be a horizontal or angled support rail opposite the transfer space. It should be 20–30 cm above the seat.
- If separate from the bathroom, there must be unobstructed interior space of not less than 110×70 cm^2 and a washbasin with clear under space.

Unassisted guests on wheelchair

Public entrance

- If there is a car park, there must be a level reserved space with a minimum width of 3.6 m.
- The route from parking point or space to the entrance must be levelled or ramped.
- The threshold at entrance must be not higher than 2 cm.

Interior general

- All paths to be used by the special guests must be levelled or ramped.
- Where the guest is required to use a lift, it must have automatic doors and the controls must be 140 cm or less in height from the floor.
- Access to the restaurant/dining room, lounge, bar, bedroom, bathroom, and WC (where not *en suite*) must be levelled or ramped with threshold not higher than 2 cm.

Bedroom

- The surface of the bed must be between 45 and 54 cm from the floor.
- Door handles, light switches, TV controls, curtain pulls, wardrobe rails, etc. should be accessible and not more than 140 cm from the floor.
- Light switches and telephone (where provided) should not be more than 50 cm from the bed.
- At least one bedroom needs to meet these requirements.

Bathroom

- The door handle and light switch must be 140 cm or less from the floor.
- The horizontal or angled support rail at the far side of the bath must be no more than 30 cm above the rim.
- The rim of the bath must be from 45–50 cm from the floor.
- Where only a shower is available for the guest, the controls must be 140 cm or less from the floor.
- Only one bathroom, separate or *en suite* with the bedroom(s) must meet these requirements.

Water closet

- The horizontal support rail on the opposite side of the transfer space must not be more than 50 cm from the centre of the seat.
- Only one WC, separate or *en suite* with the bedrooms(s) above, should meet this requirement.

Kitchens (self-catering units only)

The following guidelines may be adhered to by self-catering units

- There must be a minimum clear floor space of 120 cm in front of units and work surfaces.
- At least one work surface or table should have a clear under space between 65 and 80 cm height.
- The hob (cooking appliance with burners) should not be more than 80 cm high. It should have clear under space below or alongside and accessible controls.
- The oven should have front controls and base between 65cm and 80cm above the floors.
- The sinks should have lever taps and a clear under space.
- The base of wall cupboards and shelves should not be more than 120 cm above the floor.
- Light switches and door handles should not be more than 140 cm above the floor level.
- Power sockets should not be more than 140 cm from the floor and unobstructed (extension sockets acceptable).
- A fire extinguisher or fire blanket not more than 140 cm from the floor should be placed between the hob and doorway, and should be accessible.

Creating Services for Guests with Other Disabilities

Some guests may have disabilities that are easily visible like a person using a wheelchair/crutches. Other disabilities such as impairments of various sensory organs may not be as obvious: deafness, blindness, speech impairment, mental retardation, or a learning disability. Following are some basic facilities and services that should be available in a property to enable it to serve such guests better.

Visually impaired guests   A sizeable number of travellers today are visually impaired. Certain areas of hotel property may be required by law to display instructions and signs in Braille for the convenience of the visually challenged persons. Buttons of elevators, directions to restrooms, other public areas such as restaurants, lobbies, bars, etc. are areas where such special guests would welcome Braille. Providing elevators with audible sounds indicating floors also help visually impaired guests.

Braille menus in restaurants, room service menus, and Braille guests service directories in rooms are appreciated a lot by guests who cannot see. However, not every visually impaired guest knows Braille. Front office employees and other guests-service staff must be adequately trained and prepared to read out written information to guests. Some useful tips in this regard are as follows.

- When talking to such guests, employees should introduce themselves and also identify any other person with them.
- Many visually impaired guests prefer to pay for hotel services with cash. When handing out change, lay the bills flat on the guest's palms and identify the denomination of each bill as you give it to them. Count out coins separately.
- If the guest requests a guide to their guest room, offer your arm or shoulder and provide verbal commentary as you proceed through the property. For example: 'The elevator is to your right. Your guest room is three doors past the elevator on the left. The key card slot is located two inches above the door handle.'
- Explain where emergency exits are located relative to the guest's room and note the numbers to dial on the telephone to reach the front desk and other services.
- If a guest has a guide dog, don't play with the animal. It is performing a job and should not be distracted.
- It would be advisable to give the guest a room with easy access to the grounds on the property for them to walk their dogs when needed.

Deafness or hearing impairment Just as not every blind guest can read Braille, not every deaf or hearing-impaired guest can read lips or communicate in sign language. Staff communication with the hearing impaired guests may keep the following points in mind.

- Let the guest determine the communication method with which he/she is comfortable: whether that is reading the lips, speaking in sign language, writing messages, or conversing through an interpreter.
- If there is an employee or staff member who knows sign language, they may be deputed for communication with such guests.
- When speaking to a person who is deaf, touch them lightly to get their attention, then speak normally—don't shout.
- Talk directly to the guest, even if he or she has an interpreter. Realize that people who read lips also rely on body language and facial expressions

to convey meaning; therefore, don't exaggerate or underplay your expressions.

Room facilities for the hearing impaired   A hotel should have one or more guest rooms specially equipped for the hearing impaired guests. These rooms should include the following.

- a telephone with a flashing light to indicate an incoming call
- a television decoder for reading closed captions or programmes.
- a smoke alarm with a flashing light.
- a knock light for the door; and a vibrating alarm clock.
- a TDD (telecommunication device for the deaf), also called a TYY (tele-typewriter), which attaches to a telephone to enable a hearing-impaired guest to write out phone conversations.

Guests who are mute or have speech impairment   Guests with a speech-impairment (who either do not speak at all or whose speech is difficult to understand) may not require special equipment, but they do need understanding and patience from all hotel staff. Employees should not try to complete another person's sentences or act impatient or rushed when dealing with such guests. If you cannot understand the person, ask him/her politely to repeat what he/she said. If you still cannot understand them, offer them a pen and paper to communicate in writing.

Learning disabilities or mental impairments   Some guests may have learning disabilities or mental impairment. While such guests may not require special infrastructural designing to cope with, they do require courteousness and patience on the part of their hosts to understand them. As it is, it would be a rare occasion for such guests to be unaccompanied. The staff can bear the following points in mind while communicating with them.

- Be patient and take your time explaining the information to them.
- Do not assume that the person is not listening if they do not give verbal or visual feedback to your part of the dialogue.
- Ask the guest if they understand or agree.
- Offer to read written material, if necessary.

Other afflictions   Other indiscernible or hidden impairments could include heart conditions, emphysema or asthma, cancer or other terminally ill conditions. The best rule to follow with such guests is to remember that a person is a guest first, and a guest with a disability afterwards. Let them tell you what they need from you, and then provide it to the best of your property's ability. A helpful, courteous attitude is one of the most-appreciated services, a physically challenged guest can receive from you.

INDIAN GOVERNMENT RULES FOR THE PHYSICALLY CHALLENGED GUESTS

In 2009, the Union Ministry of Tourism made it mandatory for all star category properties to incorporate the following infrastructure/services for all disabled guests by September 2010.

1. Easy access for the differently-abled guests.
2. At least one room for the differently-abled guest. Minimum door width should be one metre to allow wheelchair access with suitable low height furniture, low peep hole, etc. Cupboard to have sliding doors with low clothes hangers, etc.
3. Room to have audible and visible (blinking light) alarm system.
4. Ramps with anti-slip floors at the entrance. Minimum door width should be one metre to allow wheelchair access. To be provided in all public areas.
5. Free accessibility in all public areas and at least one restaurant in 5 Star and 5 Star Deluxe properties.
6. Minimum door width of a bathroom should be one metre. Bathroom to be wheelchair accessible with sliding doors, suitable fixtures like low washbasin, low height toilet, grab bars, etc. No bathtub required.
7. Public restrooms to be unisex. They must be wheelchair accessible with low height urinal (24" maximum) with grab bars. Minimum door width should be one metre and mandatory to all star hotels.

The Ministry also developed a new format of assessment of category of all star hotels in the month of August 2009 (refer to chapter one for marksheet of assessment). Five marks are allotted for facilities to be offered to physically challenged persons in the star category system. Distribution of marks for various facilities is as follows:

1. At least a room for physically challenged persons   1 mark.
2. Public toilet in lobby   1 mark.
3. Telephone in public places   1 mark.
4. Ramps, etc.   1 mark.
5. Facilities for aurally and visually handicapped   1 mark.

AMERICAN NORMS FOR SPECIAL GUESTS

The guidelines for the hospitality industry in the United States pertaining to physically challenged guests are laid in the Americans with Disabilities Act (ADA). It states that a hotel must take 'readily achievable steps' to accommodate people with disabilities by building or retrofitting their facilities to be more accessible. Other guidelines for the American hoteliers include the following.

- Properties should have at least one handicap-accessible parking space for every 25 spaces.
- These spaces should be located near each of the property's entrances, not just the main entrance.
- It is important to realize that it is not adequate simply to offer valet parking. Many people with disabilities have custom-made vehicles that would not be operable by someone who has not been specifically told to do so.
- Sidewalk curb cuts, wider sidewalks to fit wheelchairs, and ramp access are essential.
- Doors to the property should open automatically or have an easy pull force so that a person in a wheelchair can open the door with little difficulty.
- Inside the hotel, at least one section of the registration desk should have a counter height of 36 inches (91cm) so that a person in a wheelchair can comfortably carry out paperwork. If you are unable to have a counter like that, front desk employees must be trained to bring the paperwork out from behind the counter and meet the guest in the lobby.
- Do not grab a guest's wheelchair or try to push them without their permission. The wheelchair is considered a part of their personal space; grabbing it is like grabbing an able-bodied guest by the arm or shoulder.
- Let the guest take the lead as to how he or she wants to be treated.
- Accessible guest rooms should have wider doorways, wider space around furniture, and lower wall controls (light switches thermostats).
- They may have a roll-in shower or a bathtub with grab bars and special seat. Door locks and view ports need to be lower, as would clothes-rods in closets and drapery pulls.

SUMMARY

Personalized service is all about creating a sense of well-being in our customers—making them feel special and valued by ensuring that their slightest needs are looked after. Thanks to education and development, the frequency of physically challenged people taking to travel has increased considerably. Today, a considerable proportion of travellers worldwide are the ones who may be suffering from one kind of impairment or the other. As facility planners, we have to be sensitive and very careful to ensure facilities for such special guests.

The HRACC has set certain norms regarding the provision of facilities for the physically challenged in hospitality properties. There are also marks allocated for the same while classifying hotels. Besides that, being a good human being demands that one provides comfortable facilities to guests with special needs. The key to success in the hotel business is to provide a high standard of service—both material and personalized service. Every hotel provides its guest with food, accommodation, and drinks but if your hotel provides a high level of personalized services to this section of guests with a high level of warmth, then your property has a competitive edge.

CONCEPT REVIEW QUESTIONS

1. Explain the facilities offered by a five star hotel to the physically challenged guests.
2. Explain the recommendations and norms of HRACC regarding the facilities provided by a five star hotel to physically challenged guests.
3. Discuss the possible types of physically challenged guests that a hotel might receive.
4. Quote any instance from your own experience when you were unable to provide facilities to a physically challenged guest and why so.
5. Prepare a checklist of facilities that need to be provided to physically challenged guest with specifications.
6. State whether the following are true or false:
   (i)   The surface of the bed must be between 55 and 64 cm above the floor.
   (ii) Door handles, light switches, TV controls, curtain pulls, wardrobe rails, etc. should be accessible and not more than 175 cm from the floor.
   (iii) Light switch and telephone (where provided) should not be more than 50 cm from the bed.
   (iv) All paths to be used by the disabled guests must be levelled or ramped.
   (v)   Where a physically challenged guest is required to use a lift, it must have automatic doors and the controls must be 140 cm or less from the floor.

PROJECT ASSIGNMENTS

1. Visit a five star hotel in your city and list the facilities offered by them to the following guests:
   (i)   Special guests with mobility difficulties
   (ii) Special guests with deafness or hearing impairment
   (iii) Special guests with speech impairment
   (iv) Special guests with visual impairment
   (v)   Special guests with learning disabilities/mental impairments

2. Interview the duty managers on how they cope with physically-challenged guests.
3. What other facilities would you recommend for special guests as a student of facility planning?
4. Compare the facilities offered by the hotel with a super-specialty hospital of repute in your city.
5. Critically evaluate the Marriott concept, 'Touch service' and make a presentation of the same for your class.

REFERENCES

Worldtravelguide.net: accessed on 11 November, 2009

Hotel and Restaurants Network (2008), 'The agenda for the benefit of hotel industry with guidelines for serving disabled guests,' July–August.

CHAPTER 10
Masterpieces in Facility Planning

Chapter Outline:

The following topics are covered in this chapter

- Selected examples of masterpieces in hotel facility planning

Learning Objectives:

This chapter will enable you to understand

- The applications of principles of hotel facility planning
- How hotel properties make the most of available resources, including ambience, to set them a class apart

INTRODUCTION

We have so far literally covered all dimensions of planning a hotel facility right from the drawing board to making it a successful operational reality. The nitty-gritty of planning and designing various facilities of a property, as also the probable hindrances and useful tips have been discussed in detail throughout the book. The theory, however, would be incomplete unless we studied the translation of the principles into reality.

This chapter describes briefly some renowned hospitality and restaurant properties in the country, with an explanation of the planning, designing and other aspects of those facilities. These provide valuable examples of putting the theory to test in real life. It may be clarified here that the list of properties taken up is selected at random and is in no way an exhaustive list of master-pieces in the country. While the first section focuses on some hotel properties, the second section describes the design of some famous eating joints in the world.

HOTELS

Grand Hyatt, Mumbai

The complex is set on 10.5 acres of prime land in Mumbai, India's financial capital and its most cosmopolitan city. The hotel features significant works of art specially created by some upcoming as well as established national artists and is curated by Rajeev Sethi. It is luxuriously decorated with inner courtyards, unique water features, natural wood, and granite.

It is a multi-dimensional lifestyle complex comprising 547 rooms and 147 serviced residences, stretching over 1 million sq ft. Contemporary art is an inescapable element at Grand Hyatt.

It has been designed by an international team of designers and consultants. The complex was conceived by the internationally renowned architecture firm, Lohan Associates, Chicago. The interiors have been designed by Chhadha, Seimbieda and Remedios of Long Beach, California.

Entrance   The hotel building is eight storeyed and has a series of rectangular glass windows (Figure 10.1). A polished brick wall surrounds the building. Right at the entrance, there is a gigantic deconstructed jigsaw puzzle of the Sadashiva icon. Envisioned by curator Rajeev Sethi, it stands sentinel and hints at what lies within. Occupying centre-stage in the courtyard is a contemporary marble statue of Nandi facing a lingam of crystals within a cascading 40 ft waterfall.

Figure 10.1   Exterior of the Grand Hyatt, Mumbai

Lobby The lobby of the hotel showcases themed art installations: the windows are based on the premise of Shiva as a divine Yogi, the resilience of Mumbai's slums with their roadside shrines and close-knit communities, paper pillars lit from within, and among others, a three dimensional mural that pays tribute to the perennial ritual of the immersion of Ganapati against the backdrop of the city.

Restaurants The four food and beverage outlets in the hotel have an open-plan design with materials like steel, lightwood moulded glass, and stone. Each restaurant expresses its individuality through its cuisine. These include the *M restaurant and bar* (Figure 10.2) with a seating capacity of 60 people. It

Figure 10.2   The M Restaurant

has a wooden flooring with glass partitions between the tables. Another restaurant is the *Celini*; its interiors are contemporary and simple, using interesting textures of natural wood, stone, matte finished steel, and sand blasted glass. The restaurant has a tastefully-designed show kitchen with an inbuilt wood-fired pizza oven, rotisserie, and charcoal grill. The Indian restaurant *Soma* with granite flooring has contemporary artworks on display. The *Grand Café* is a spacious restaurant with wooden flooring and a stylishly designed bar, set in the centre of the restaurant.

Figure 10.3   A Guest Room at Grand Hyatt, Mumbai

Rooms   The hotel accommodation includes 12 grand executive suites, 12 veranda suites, four diplomatic suites, seven grand suites, and three presidential suites. Exclusive Grand Club accommodation, exclusive grand club lounge, and meeting rooms are available on two floors of the hotel.

Amongst the most spacious in the city—approximately 40 square metres—all rooms are designed in a contemporary, open-plan layout with spacious bathrooms. All the rooms are centrally air-conditioned, with individual temperature control and electronically controlled window shades (Refer Figure 10.3).

All guest rooms are seamless and contemporary in design with luxurious bathrooms featuring separate bath and shower areas. The rectangular shaped granite bathtub and vanity counter is separated by a glass partition that adds to its elegant look. The rooms have Sycamore wood paneling and golden Jaisalmer stone combined with understated artwork that induces a sense of serenity. Natural materials such as wood, granite, and marble create a feeling of warmth and luxury.

The floors of the rooms are carpeted and the colours used for the walls are light with mostly shades of brown and yellow that make them look wider. Use of wood can be seen in abundance.

Marriott Hotel, Goa

Set in a scenic locale along the Mandovi River, the Goa Marriott Resort is surrounded by mystical hills and lush green trees. It is situated in central

Panjim and runs parallel to the beach, affording stunning views of the Arabian sea on one hand and the verdant Western Ghats on the other to its guests.

It is built in a predominantly heavy old-world style, which was suitably redesigned by Rajive Saini with a maroon and dark green to conform to the global image of the Mariott chain.

Restaurants The three restaurants at the resort are *Palmeria, Wan Hao*, and *The Waterfront*. Palmeria is a casual restaurant serving Indian, Asian, and Western cuisine. Wan Hao specializes in Schezwan and Cantonese cuisine, while The Waterfront comprises a pool bar and restaurant for a relaxing evening with snacks. It also houses a lobby bar and a cake shop.

The total area covered by the restaurant is 6,000 sq. ft. The restaurant has natural stone floors and there is an in situ *terrazzo* wall, with a floral pattern, at the far end of the restaurant. Two private dining spaces with elevated wooden floors are kept cozy to allow a view. There is a square island bar with the frontage of the bar studded with fibre-optic lighting, mirrors, and frosted glass to add glamour to the space.

Rooms The rooms are made in a linear compact space and to make them look bigger, the furniture is cantilevered or on delicate legs. The new wing that involved a major renovation and extension houses 25 rooms, 5 suites, an executive lounge, and a main restaurant. A huge glass window is provided in the rooms between the bedroom and the bathroom which not only allows the natural light into the bathroom but also makes a dramatic statement.

In the suites, the basic elements of the old-style have been retained. The openness of space is evident and spaces flow easily into one another. Large panes of glass separate the living area from the bedroom. In an extension of the idea of the see-through bathroom, the tub has been brought into the bedroom though it can be screened off if desired. The suites are given patterned terrazzo flooring that runs through the wings as a common feature with bathroom walls in matching terrazzo.

Amarvilas, Agra

Only 600 metres from the Taj Mahal stands the Oberoi Group's luxury resort, the Amarvilas. The manicured Mughal gardens, terraced lawns, fountains, reflection pools, and pavilions complement the classical architecture of the hotel. The hotel has been designed to give guests uninterrupted views of the architectural marble marvel from all its rooms and suites (Figure 10.4). The lobby, restaurants, bars, and tea lounge also offer spectacular views of the 17th century monument, which is arguably the prime tourist attraction in the country.

Figure 10.4   A View of the Taj Mahal from a Guest Room

Figure 10.5   The Entrance of Amarvilas, Agra

The attention to detail is evident in every aspect of architecture, décor, and landscaping, with all spaces being imbued with distinctive character.

Entrance   The grand entrance of the hotel comprises arches facing exquisite Mughal gardens, dipping and rising quadrants of lawns and fountains, providing an incredible ambience amidst flaming gas lamps, and cleverly lit floral murals—a conflagration of blues, greens, and golds—on the farther wall. Refer Figure 10.5.

Reception area   The reception area is dominated by a large chandelier under a cobalt and gold-leaf dome. The reception is lavishly furnished with camel bone inlay tables and the laptops on the tables are discretely embedded in aquamarine cases.

Restaurants   The hotel has two restaurants and a bar. *Isphahan*, the Indian restaurant, has been made using deep red and wooden latticework. There is a glass-fronted kitchen where chefs can be seen at work. *Bellevue*, the all-day multi-cuisine restaurant, has used ample glass for its modern décor.

The hotel has an austere masculine bar with wood panelling and bronze relief, and a tearoom with deep armchairs reminiscent of a French *boudoir*. Discretely tucked away are stately ballrooms, plush conference rooms, a branch of Jaipur's Gem Palace, and a shopping arcade with a standard bookshop.

Guest rooms   The hotel has 112 rooms, each of which is constructed in such a way that it provides a view of the Taj Mahal. Each bedroom has an

Figure 10.6 A Guest Room in Amarvilas

area of approximately 42 square metres. The Deluxe rooms have richly detailed interiors. A striking feature of these elegantly appointed bedrooms is the large hand-embroidered headboard and the arched window framing a beautiful view of the Taj. Refer Figure 10.6.

Each suite room has an area of approximately 85 sq.m. with a private terrace overlooking the Taj Mahal. The executive suites are large one-bedroom suites about 75 sq.m. in area. Each suite has a living room, bedroom, and a separate powder room. The interiors are richly detailed with fine fabrics and furnishings, hand-crafted furniture, and exquisite accessories.

The luxury suite is about 175 sq.m. in area and has a private open-air terrace. These splendid suites have an entrance foyer, a separate living-cum-dining room, and a spacious bedroom, furnished in Burma teak, Greek marble, and with sandstone flooring.

The Kohinoor suite is an expansive 280 sq.m. with a large living room, dining room, study, spacious bedroom, bath and shower that run in a full glass-fronted line overlooking the Taj, adjoining a large terrace that runs around this lengthy flat.

Some rooms also have floors made of teak wood. The rooms have spacious marble and granite bathrooms with separate shower stalls, while luxury suites are provided with twin vanity counters.

The Bangla

The Bangla is an early 20th century residence built in the style of an English planter's bungalow on the outskirts of Karaikudi, a town in the Ramnad district of Tamil Nadu. It has been restored and converted into an exquisite boutique hotel. The hotel's architecture is a mix of Italianate palace, with Mughal-style arched openings, towers, turrets, balconies, open terraces, and closed inner courtyards, while the porches are in Hindu temple style, full of carved pillars. It is a magnificent example of the Baroque architecture.

The special features of the hotel are its massive pillars, some of them built with the finest tropical Burma teak; the extraordinary carvings on the doors, lintels and sides of the entrances to the main rooms, and the decorative tiles, originally from Japan, inset along the walls and in the flooring.

Entrance The building of the hotel is painted white. Small turret-like projections accentuate the walls at the top surrounding the flat roof. The dark green of the wooden leaves, supplemented by simple bamboo chiks, form a

Figure 10.7 The Bangla

dramatic contrast to the white of the pillars holding up the sloping roof, the white of the walls and the dark mosaic terracotta red of the floors.

Another completely unexpected touch is the use of silver paint to highlight and enhance some parts of the structure. The wooden frames and shutters of the windows have been painted silver because it lasts long. Square shaped wooden bars are provided to protect the opening of the windows and top of the square pillars. These give the place a neo-classical elegance.

The closed and covered verandahs (Figure 10.7) in front of the rooms allow the air to circulate through pierced *jaalis* and wire mesh covered expanses. All along the main frontage there is a charming tiled and sloping roof verandah, fringed with a hanging wooden canopy that imitates the pattern of hanging mango leaves.

Guest rooms The Bangla offers eight large double rooms (two with double beds, six with twin beds). The living and dining rooms are common. The right side of the main entrance is where the guest rooms are located. These are long high-ceilinged rooms that have wooden shutters and colourful mosaic floors.

The master bedroom on the first floor facing the village pond has rare pieces of furniture. The rooms have been carved and decorated with ceramic tiles. At the other end of the room, there is a very elegant modern bathroom. The tiles in the bathrooms have been chosen in black and white.

Some of the other bedrooms are larger, having spacious bathrooms renovated in modern style. Long courtyards surrounded by pillared verandahs succeed the more formal rooms.

Figure 10.8 The Lobby

The Park, Bengaluru

Located on MG Road, in the heart of the city's business district, The Park is a unique 109-room experience, designed by Conran and Partners, UK. The design philosophy is a fusion of the vibrant colours and landscapes of India with international style. Each area is specially designed to provide a distinctive flavour. The pristine white four-storeyed structure belies the luxury and flamboyance of the interiors. The façade is broken by flashes of brilliant colours from the balcony windows. A cobbled driveway highlights the simple exteriors.

Lobby The lobby of the hotel is kept simple with the walls draped with red silk curtains. The reception is not protruding out but is made in a cut portion of the wall. There is a huge black pillar in the middle of the lobby that provides a stark contrast to the interiors. The pillar is made in ancient Indian style with lot of carving. Refer Figure 10.8.

Restaurants The hotel has three restaurants *Monsoon*, *Italia*, and *I-Bar*. I-Bar is the lounge bar that encapsulates the energy and dynamism of the wireless era. The unique techno-electric feel of the space, transports the guests to a high-energy field. Hot neon colours, gleaming in the dark, create a funky mood. The wall is decorated with a rich carpet, woven in a pattern that is suggestive of a circuit board. Refer Figure 10.9.

Figure 10.9 A Restaurant at The Park

Italia has a masculine dark timber floor that complements the charcoal black upholstery. The main bar counter has huge pillars on both the sides. The entire wall on one side is covered with glass. The design is kept simple with plain roof and walls.

Banquets   A ceremonial entrance from the lobby leads to a space of contemporary calm, *The Oak Room*. Rich and elegant panels clad in oyster coloured 'bamboo fabric' with discreet shuttering along the window wall contribute to the plush décor. The doors open out on to a specially landscaped terrace.

All the sides of the *Blue Box*, as the 'screening' room is christened, are cobalt blue. It is an intense abstract space, which can be dimmed down to a night setting or be illuminated for a Board Room situation. It can be laid out as a table for 14; two tables of 10 each, a formal cinema for 24 or a chill-out space for up to 20 people. The back wall is built out as a projection facility and there is a retractable screen opposite.

Rooms   Move on to the residential floors by lifts that luxuriate in rich black leather. The doors open onto a splash of colourful carpet that picks up the landscape of each floor. Each floor is seen as a panorama, containing an oasis indicated by intense spots of colour in a large landscape and suggestive of the variety of experiences and cultures throughout India. The first floor depicts a cool expanse of water signified by the base colour of 'aqua' with a burst of the sun signified by dashes of 'orange'. The next suggests a mountain landscape with the use of 'iris' with 'pale lime' trees providing the relief.

The 'bright lime' of the jungle on the third floor, is offset with regal 'emperor red' flowers. The fourth floor—The Residence—reflects elegance with 'saffron' denoting the desert and the oasis being reflected in splashes of 'ultramarine blue'.

The luxury of the rooms using silk, leather, pure oak wooden floors, and glass—a blend of materials, modern and traditional, create a unique in-room experience.

The Taj Mahal Palace and Towers, Mumbai

Built in 1903, the hotel is an architectural marvel and brings together Moorish, Oriental, and Florentine styles. Offering panoramic views of the Arabian Sea and the Gateway of India, the hotel is a gracious landmark of the city, showcasing contemporary Indian influences along with beautiful vaulted alabaster ceilings, onyx columns, graceful archways, hand-woven silk carpets, crystal chandeliers, a magnificent art collection, an eclectic collection of furniture, and a dramatic cantilever stairway.

Over the past century, The Taj Mahal Palace and Towers, Mumbai has amassed a diverse collection of paintings and works of art and is a veritable treasure trove of artefacts from the modern and bygone eras. From Belgian chandeliers to Goan Christian artifacts, the hotel incorporates a myriad of artistic styles and tastes.

Entrance   At the very entrance of the hotel, there is a glass slab with water flowing over it that not only enhances the entrance but also acts as a contrast to rest of the building, giving it a new innovative designing idea. The staircases inside the hotel are constructed in a circular way going upwards supported by brackets.

Restaurants   Taj has nine restaurants. *Souk* is an award winning, rooftop restaurant that offers spectacular views of Mumbai. One side of the restaurant wall consists of a series of windows that look out into the Arabian sea, the roof of the restaurant is supported by beams and pillars, while the side stations are positioned systematically between these pillars. *Masala craft* is designed in typical Indian style with netted black windows as in Mughal architecture, with huge black sculptured pillars supporting the roof, while the flooring is in off-white marble.

Banquet   The conference space spreads through eight rooms. It is 20,000 sq ft., with a capacity of holding 500 to 2,000 people.

Guest rooms   The presidential suites feature a grand living room, a private patio with port, harbour, and city views, a master bedroom, and a private balcony overlooking The Gateway of India. The roof of the presidential suite is in the form of a dome, supported by wooden beams. The huge windows have wooden pelmets; marble has been used for the flooring; and the colour used for the walls is pale yellow.

The Rajput suite is elegantly designed combining contemporary and classic styles; the richly hued interiors of the suites epitomize luxurious living. The walls and pillars of some of the suites are made up of huge blocks of stone that were used in olden times to build castles and forts. The windows are arched and the railings in some of the rooms have a network design that was widely used in Mughal architecture. In some suites, the walls are covered with polished wood.

The flooring used is different for different rooms with some having black and white chequered flooring, while others with white marble flooring. Some rooms are carpeted. The grand luxury suites are designed around a central theme such as the Sunrise Suite, the Moonlight Suite, and the Bell Tower Suite. The luxury grand rooms are kept plain and simple with arched openings having rectangular windows facing the sea.

Taj Residency, Lucknow

Hotel Taj Residency, Lucknow is set amidst 33 acres of landscaped gardens. With architecture that is reminiscent of the glories of the *Nawabi* era, the hotel brims with design details that reflect the grandeur of the past. Graceful pillars, rich tapestries, and intricate decoration evoke fairytale luxury.

Entrance The exterior of the building is based on Roman architecture with spherical and cylindrical spaces supported by pillars and a huge dome on top. A swimming pool is provided on the backside of the building. At the very entrance, there are stairs and a ramp which leads to a huge glass door that opens into the lobby. The flooring of the lobby has been artistically made in marble and granite. Huge pillars support the lobby. At its far end, is a semi-circular sitting place that provides a good view of the swimming pool through huge arched windows. This place is separated from the main lobby by a wooden railing that joins the two pillars. In the centre of the lobby is placed a metal artefact on a wooden table. The reception is on the left hand side of the lobby with a circular bell desk adjacent to it.

Restaurant On the right hand side of the lobby is the *Sahib Café*, a square-shaped restaurant that is surrounded by wooden railings on all the four sides. In the middle of the restaurant an elevated area with a dome shaped roof supported by pillars that provide space for a larger group.

Next to the Sahib Café is an elegant bar called *Mehfil,* and leading off the corridor flooded with natural light through the arched windows, is the specialty Indian restaurant, *Oudhyana*. The décor is typically of the region, with a fine blend of occidental and oriental culture.

Banquet On the right hand side of the Sahib Café leading off the lobby is the 760 sq ft. hall called *Mulaquat*. Straight left from Mulaquat is the *Crystal hall* built in an area of 5,300 sq ft. It can be separated into three halls by huge wooden partitions. In front of the hall is a bow shaped curved pre-function area with an attached terrace. The walls and supporting pillars of the entire area including the lobby are covered with polished wood with narrow arched glass windows. The floor is covered with granite. On both sides of this function area, is a driveway leading to the *Gulistan* lawns spread over 7,500 sq ft.

Guest rooms On the right hand side of the reception is a lobby provided with elevators and staircase leading to the upper and lower floors. The floor of the lobby is covered with white marble and the walls have spaces spared for mirrors with beautifully carved wooden frames. The lobby leads to the guest rooms. The hotel has 110 guest rooms including 4 suites. The executive rooms are rich in Indian design cues like traditional *Awadhi chikan* embroidery, colourful palace rugs, and artefacts. All rooms offer the pool view. The deluxe room offers a separate sitting area. The executive suite unit offers plenty of space with a bedroom and well-planned living area. Some rooms offer balconies as well as interconnecting rooms. The rooms are given pale colours in shades of yellow and brown. The floors of all the rooms are covered with red carpets.

ITC Grand Maratha, Mumbai

ITC Grand Maratha Hotel and Towers is one of the latest mega hotels that have come up close to the international airport. It has created a dazzling array of architectural markers to anchor the building within a distinctive cultural context (Figure 10.10). It is designed in Classical Colonial style with an incredible blend of local cultures to create richness, depth, and quality.

Entrance   At the entrance stands a pink water fountain, facing the cavernous car porch with two lion heads seemingly on guard. The striking feature is the massive use of Jodhpur pink sandstone that has been handcrafted to create the façade.

The focal point of the hotel outside is a cupola, and there are several circular domes and cupolas inside also. The one at the far end of the atrium, which is carved in pink and white stone—as a homage to the Gateway of India—stands like an airy pergola over a bandstand.

The other cupola hovers like a stone umbrella at the end of the swimming pool. As a tribute to the Bollywood city, the swimming pool is lined with a series of stone lions, arranged like performers in a circus ring, all spewing water into the pool.

The modernist design element of the hotel is clearly articulated in the straight lines that link the different parts of the interiors.

Figure 10.10   The Grand Exterior of ITC Grand Maratha

Lobby The ceiling of the lobby is designed so remarkably that the concealed lighting gets reflected on the floor. On the opposite side of the entrance is a glass curtain on which is an emblematic Tree of Life in white, against a pattern of symbols in what looks like hand written script. The lift lobby is located between two sheets of etched glass.

The reception is divided into half by a modernistic flower arrangement that has as its backdrop, a raised outline of Mumbai's Fort area in white relief work. All the pillars and wall surfaces here have been executed in rough-finished, off-white Gangapur sandstone. Small lights are set into the square corners at the base of the pillars.

Towards the left, is the passage leading to a more public area, the convention halls, reception rooms, the business and conference centre that has a separate entrance altogether with circular domes at the small foyer. The colours are warmer, with formal portraits of the Peshwas decorating the walls. The foyer leads into the atrium through an arched opening. The overriding theme of the atrium seems to be the Buddhist caves of India.

Restaurants To one side of the atrium is the vista that stretches right in to the formal gardens. Beyond is a bar named Bombay High and a charming glass conservatory that doubles as a restaurant, named Catherine's.

There are three different tires of architectural styles, from the Victorian on the ground floor, to the carved, latticed windows on the first three floors, to etched glass at the very top. Steel supports, like giant brackets, curve up towards the roof. Each segment has an airy grid of black squares. Behind it is the very exclusive upper crust lounge, a library, and a dining room. The roof is glassed and in regular squares.

A strong visual language is provided by the use of squares, rectangles, and in some cases circles as part of the design element, which is ingrained in the texture of the surfaces.

The arched colonnade not only links all the public areas, such as the multi-cuisine restaurant around the atrium, but has also been designed to stand out from the rest of the building.

Just below this, is the spacious buffet area of the *al-fresco* restaurant at the atrium. Art nouveau touches are seen creeping in along the sides of the railings that demarcate the pavilion.

The next three floors have a Maratha touch. They consist of a series of square modules inset between the long vertical lines of the structure.

Conference centre The Grand Maratha business and conference centre has a separate entrance. The colours here are warmer with portraits of the Peshwas looking down from the walls. The flooring is carpeted and stretched through the entire room.

Figure 10.11 A Guest Room

Guest rooms The bedrooms have been designed with comfort in mind. The walls are kept plain with some rooms having a part of one wall covered with wood, which acts as a base for framed photographs and pictures (refer Figure 10.11).

The flooring in some rooms is carpeted whereas in some rooms wooden flooring has been provided. The bathroom and luggage areas are tucked away very neatly behind sliding wooden screens, which can be accessed from the interior of the bedroom.

Flooring The mosaic style of flooring that used to be a feature of the older establishment in the city has been adapted in different ways. On the ground floor, a dramatic chequer board pattern of squares in polished teak and green marble is used instead of a carpet. Creamy white marble is inlaid with metallic squares, or has been combined with bands of grey, green, black, and yellow marble.

At the Peshwa pavilion, the floor is a swirl of mosaic design. The sideboards and counters have also been inlaid with round circles of coloured stone.

Red marble squares in regular patterns, or rectangular pieces, set against a white background also accentuate the different areas of some of the bedrooms.

The paving stones at the entrance of the hotel have also been designed with chunky pieces of flamed granite in five different colours that have been laid in a continuous wave pattern.

RESTAURANTS

Dining at some of the world's finest restaurants is a very pleasant experience. This section seeks to highlight the main characteristics of some of the best restaurants in the world and find out what is it that sets them a class above others. It may be borne in mind that the list of restaurants discussed here is only selective and not exhaustive.

Bayamo, New York

In New York there are young professionals called 'yuppies' who like to visit East Village and Lower Broadway in the south of Manhattan. 'Bayamo' is an ethnic food restaurant situated in Lower Broadway. 'Bayamo' is the name of a town in Cuba, and the cuisine served here is a unique mix of Latin and Chinese dishes accentuated with a spicy taste. In the restaurant, which is situated in a remodelled warehouse, finely designed columns and large wall art by the entrance highlight the feeling of spaciousness (Refer Figure 10.12). The corrugated bar counter is eye-catching.

Number of seats: 300

Number of employees: 65

Design features

- The interior features decorated columns and avant-garde wall art.
- The second floor dining area introducing decorative flows to exhibit a smooth or graceful continuity and the corrugated bar counter on the first floor.
- The wall art painted fully in the high space.

Figure 10.12   Bayamo

Café Iguana, New York

Situated in the South of midtown Manhattan, 'Café Iguana' derives its name from *The Night of Iguana*, a movie that most charmed its owner Joyce Steins, and the interior reproduces its scenes (Figure 10.13). The wide dining area has a tropical ambience, and the floor is composed like a stage accented with multi-coloured lighting and an eye-catching brass-made iguana which is as long as 10 feet. The restaurant mainly serves casual Tex-Mex (Texas-Mexican) cuisine and grill dishes.

Number of seats: 300 (dining area only)

Figure 10.13   Café Iguana

Design features

- The scenes from the movie are reproduced on the spacious floor that is 900 square feet (about 836.1 m²). Climbing the central staircase, one reaches the tropical bar, restaurants, Cancun rooms, etc.
- In the first floor bar corner, crystal iguana eyes (lighting) stand out very impressively.

Rebecca's, Venice, CA

With the presentation of strange aquatic images, 'Rebecca's' is a Mexican restaurant designed by Frank Gehry. Its owner–chef Bruce Marder offers new style Mexican cuisine. Two huge crocodiles about 19 feet (5.7m) and a giant octopus props are suspended from the ceiling, while light is so cast that the wall surface stands out, thereby expressing aquatic fantasy. Situated in Venice in the South of Santa Monica, the restaurant is frequented by artists, yuppies, etc. (refer Figure 10.14)

Number of seats: 160

Number of employees: 70

Figure 10.14   Rebecca's

Design features

- The guest seating area with a giant octopus and huge crocodiles (5.7m long) provides a strange impression.
- The entrance features onyx and a uniquely designed door.

Casa Gallardo, Orlando, Florida

A Mexican restaurant chain headquartered in St. Louis, 'Casa Gallardo' means the house of Mr Gallardo, the owner (refer Figure 10.15). The interior uses the terrace of a Mexican building as its theme, and the pieces of furniture, fresco design and colours may be said to be the very essence of Mexico. The main customer profile comprises adult couples aged 18–45.

Number of seats: 400 (dining 300, bar 100)

Number of employees: 140

Figure 10.15   Casa Gallardo

Design features

- The dining area's interior reminds one of a Mexican residence.
- The dining area imaging a patio.
- The colourfully presented bar corner.

China Grill, New York

An 'international food' restaurant opened by Japanese chef, Mako Tanaka. 'China Grill' serves cuisine by blending Californian dishes with Japanese, Chinese, Indonesian, Vietnamese and French foods. The interior décor is impressive with an oval lampshade under a high ceiling reminiscent of the Japanese '*shoji*' (sliding paper screen), agreeing well with the moderate wall colours. The floor space is composed of a guests' seating area in several partitions, an open kitchen in the centre, slender bar counters on both sides, etc. (refer Figure 10.16).

Figure 10.16 China Grill

Number of seats: 225 (dining 185, bar 40)

Number of employees: 125

Design features

- Using different floor levels and ceiling height effectively, the dining area is accented with a lampshade which images Japanese 'shoji'.
- The dining area by the entrance viewed from the bar counter.
- The bar counter and open kitchen; on the straight line drawn across the floor leading into the inner dining area, sentences from Marco Polo's 'Book of Macro Polo' (Record of experiences in the East are written).

El Teddy's, New York

A Mexican restaurant opened in Tribeca by Andrew Young and Christopher Chestnut, 'El Teddy's' mainly serves traditional Mexican food, plus a menu which changes from day to day, vegetarian foods, etc. (refer Figure 10.17). Since 1925 when the building was used by Teddy, who opened a cafeteria, it has been used for various types of eateries, such as steak and *tapas* (a Spanish dish). The façade is unique with a huge crown of the Statue of Liberty placed on the roof, which has been taken over from the 'El International' restaurant which opened in the mid-1980s and was very much talked about in those days.

Figure 10.17 El Teddy's

The interior retains the tiled frescos and mosaic wall from the cafeteria days which, together with modern artistic pieces, produces a unique atmosphere.

Numbers of seats: 100

Numbers of employees: 30

Design features

- The façade retaining some vestiges of 'El International' features a symbol designed by replicating the crown of the Statue of Liberty.
- The dining room.
- The staircase handrails of scrap iron, and two barbecue skewers are hung on the wall.
- Pieces of modern art are displayed.

REFERENCES

www.hyatt.com, accessed on 27/2/2008

www.marriott.com, accessed on 12/4/2008

www.theoberoiamarvilas.com, accessed on 25/4/2009

www.indianheritagehospitality.com, accessed on 25/4/2009

www.thepark.com

www.tajhotels.com, accessed on 25/12/2009

www.tajhotels.com, accessed on 25/3/2008

www.itcgrandmarathasheraton.com, accessed on 21/12/2008

Model Test Papers

Model Question Paper 1

Max. Marks: 100   Time: 3 hrs

Note: Attempt all questions. All questions carry equal marks.

1. State the basic considerations in the design of a hotel. Explain any two in detail.

OR

With the help of a neat diagram, explain the sequential procedures of systematic layout planning (SLP). List the four phases of SLP.

2. What are the general features, facilities, and services essential for being classified as a four star hotel?

OR

With respect to any four of the following criteria, state whether the criteria are classified as essential, necessary, or desirable. Also, mention the maximum points allotted to each criterion for a four star hotel.

Construction	Cuisine
Housekeeping	Hygiene
Bathrooms	Parking
Lobby	Conference facilities

3. List the basic guidelines for network construction. Draw the network for the activities given below.

Activity	Duration (in weeks)
A-B	5
B-C	4
B-D	6
B-E	7
C-D	3
D-E	4

4. Explain and compare Critical Path Method (CPM) and Program Evaluation Review Technique (PERT).

5. Prepare a write-up on the energy conservation programme of a five star hotel.

6. What is network crashing? Explain the term critical path with the help of a neat network diagram.

7. Give the standard purchase specification for the following equipment:
   (a) Dessert trolley
   (b) Tilting brat pan—100 litres capacity
   (c) 4 burner cooking range
   (d) Deep fat fryer

8. Write short notes on any four of the following:
   (a) Kitchen stewarding
   (b) Role of colour scheme in restaurant design

(c) Facilities for physically challenged guests

(d) Structural features of store

(e) Bar counter

(f) Energy audit

9. Explain with the help of diagrams possible kitchen configuration of a star category hotel.

10. (A) State true or false:

(a) A five star hotel should have a minimum of 25 rooms.

(b) Hotel classification is done by FHRAI.

(c) Fine dining requires 14–16 square feet per person.

(d) Anchors are the most prominent props for a nautical theme.

(e) Pellet ovens are used in airline catering.

(B) Fill in the blanks:

(a) .... may be defined as a block of clay or other ceramic used for construction and decorative facing.

(b) One litre of LPG produces .... Kcal.

(c) EOQ stands for ....

(d) Operational research is a bunch of .... techniques to break industrial problems.

(e) Size of a bathroom in a five star hotel is .... square feet.

Model Question Paper 2

Max. Marks: 100   Time: 3 hrs

Note: Attempt all questions. All questions carry equal marks.

1. Explain the different architectural styles of a hotel design.

OR

Discuss the different phases of layout planning of a hotel building. Explain briefly.

2. Give the criteria for classifying a five star hotel as per guidelines set by the Government of India for the classification of the hotel industry.

3. Draw the layout plan of a 100 covers coffee shop (Assume necessary information).

4. As a facility planner, give the standard specification while placing the order for the following equipment:
   (a) Room service trolley
   (b) Stainless steel hot food counter with six-in-one (bain-marie)
   (c) Water boiler 100 litre capacity
   (d) Potato peeler
   (e) Chamber's maid trolley

5. Explain systematic layout planning (SLP) with the help of a neat diagram.

6. Differentiate between any four of the following:
   (a) Carpet area and plinth area
   (b) Safety and security
   (c) City hotel and resort hotel
   (d) Financial and marketing feasibility
   (e) Design and layout

7. Explain the characteristics of critical path method (CPM) and programme evaluation and review technique (PERT).

OR

What are the factors that influence the choice of location for opening a restaurant?

8. Draw a network diagram for the given project and find out the critical path.

Activity	Predecessor Activity	Time Estimate (Weeks)
A	------------	4
B	------------	3
C	A	2
D	A	7
E	B	6
F	C	4
G	D, E	2

9. Enumerate the features, facilities, and services for being classified as an apartment hotel?

10. Draw a detailed layout of an Indian kitchen for a three star hotel (to scale) and propose a list of heavy-duty equipment.

OR

What do you mean by total float, free float, and independent float? Explain briefly.

Model Question Paper 3

Max. Marks: 100   Time: 3 hrs

Note: Attempt all questions. All questions carry equal marks.

1. What are the general features, facilities, and services required for being classified as a three star hotel?

   OR

   Discuss the criteria for a hotel to be deemed in a heritage hotel category as per the guidelines set by Department of Tourism, Government of India.

2. Draw the layout plan of a kitchen of 100 covers specialty restaurant. (Assume necessary information).

   OR

   Discuss the utility of work flow diagram in kitchen planning and design.

3. In hotel project management, critical path method (CPM) and programme evaluation and review technique (PERT) play an important role. How do you make a comparative analysis of these two?

   OR

   Make a neat sketch of the layout of a kitchen of a 50-room hotel property and the also indicate the major equipment.

4. Differentiate between any four of the following:
   (a) Beer cabinet and display cabinet
   (b) Fish sinks and drop-in sinks
   (c) Greek architecture and Roman architecture
   (d) Concrete and polymer concrete
   (e) Low pressure burner and heavy pressure burner

5. Discuss the facilities provided by a five star hotel to deal with physically challenged guests.

6. Enlist the points to be considered while designing a theme restaurant. Propose a list of artefacts and props for creating a nautical theme.

7. Discuss the role of décor, colour, and ambience in designing a restaurant. Determine the space and furniture requirement of 120 covers Chinese specialty restaurant.

OR

Activity	Predecessor Activity	Time Estimate (weeks)
A	Nil	10
B	Nil	6
C	A	3
D	A	4
E	C, D	3
F	B, D	8
G	F	6
H	E	2
I	E	3
J	G, H, I	7

Using the information as furnished, develop a network diagram, identify the critical path, and determine the project duration.

8. Write short notes on any four of the following:
   (a) Crashing
   (b) Energy conservation
   (c) Limitations of CPM/PERT
   (d) Safety education
   (e) Storage facilities
   (f) Facilities for special guests

9. Define a feasibility report. Explain its importance as a facility planner.

10. Kitchen stewarding plays a vital role in success of food and beverage operations of a hotel. Comment.

OR

Discuss the rules of network construction. Explain briefly.

Model Question Paper 4

Max. Marks: 100   Time: 3 hrs

Note: Attempt all questions. All questions carry equal marks.

1. What is PERT and CPM? Explain its application in hotel project management.

OR

   Explain why layout planning is essential for smooth functioning of a hotel.

2. Explain four configurations of the layout of a commercial kitchen.

3. Write short notes on any two of the following:
   (a) Car parking
   (b) Blue print
   (c) Plinth area
   (d) Space allocation in kitchen planning

4. Draw a network diagram and find out the critical path for the given project:

Activity	Time Estimates (in weeks)
A – B	4
A – C	6
B – C	6
B – D	8
B – E	12
C – E	10
D – 3	6
D – F	10
E – F	6

5. Explain in 1–2 lines any ten of the following:
   (a) Blender   (b) Tenderizer   (c) Microwave oven   (d) Potato peeler
   (e) Cellar   (f) Pasta machine   (g) Ventilation hood   (h) Water boiler
   (i) Floor plan   (j) Chef's table   (k) Blast freezer   (l) Benchmarks

6. Recommend the structural features of a good store and propose documents used in store control.

7. What are the factors that influence choice of location for opening a hotel.

8. State the requirement of space for a 1000-room five star hotel property for various areas:
   (a) GM's office   (b) Banquet office   (c) Coffee shop   (d) Chef's cabin
   (e) Storage area   (f) Main kitchen   (g) Barber's shop   (h) Pump room
   (i) Linen room   (j) Parking area   (k) Chest room   (l) Account's office

9. Propose a checklist of equipment required for 100 covers bar or a medium-sized bakery shop.

10. Differentiate between any four of the following:
    (a) Slip forming and tri-arch building
    (b) Below grade and above grade parking
    (c) Energy conservation and energy audit
    (d) Capsule hotel and boutique hotel
    (e) Pot wash and dish wash
    (f) Modern architecture and innovative architecture

Index